TORONTO MONTREAL & QUEBEC CITY

Herbert Bailey Livesey

The
American
Express
Pocket
Guide

Mitchell Beazley

The Author
A native New Yorker, Herbert Bailey Livesey is a novelist and travel writer who contributes regularly to *Travel & Leisure* magazine. He has written many articles on Canada, and is also the author of *New York*, *Spain* and the forthcoming *Madrid and Barcelona* in this series.

Acknowledgments
The authors and publishers would like to thank the following for their help and advice: Brian LeCompte of the Ministère de Tourisme of the Gouvernement de Québec, the Metropolitan Toronto Convention & Visitors' Association, and Mike De Mello of Triptych Systems Limited.

The *American Express Pocket Travel Guide Series* was conceived under the direction of Susannah Read, Douglas Wilson, Hal Robinson and Eric Drewery.

For the series
General Editor   David Townsend Jones
Managing Art Editor   Nigel O'Gorman
Art Editor   Christopher Howson
Map Editor   David Haslam
Indexer   Hilary Bird
Gazetteer   Sharon Charity

For this edition
Edited on desktop by   Eileen Townsend Jones
Illustrator   Karen Cochrane

Edited and designed by Mitchell Beazley International Limited, Artists House, 14-15 Manette Street, London W1V 5LB for the American Express (R) Pocket Travel Guide Series

© American Express Publishing Corporation Inc. 1991
All rights reserved
No part of this work may be reproduced or utilized in any form by any means, electronic or mechanical, including photocopying, recording or by any information storage and retrieval system, without the prior written permission of the publisher.
A cataloguing-in-publication record for this book is available from the British Library.
ISBN 0 85533 866 0

Maps in 2-colour and 4-colour by Lovell Johns, Oxford, England.
Desktop layout in Ventura Publisher by Castle House Press, Llantrisant, Wales.
Typeset in Garamond and Univers.
Linotronic output through Microstar DTP Studio, Cardiff, Wales.
Produced by Mandarin Offset. Printed and bound in Malaysia.

Contents

How to use this book	4
Key to symbols	6

Ontario and Québec

An introduction 7

Culture, history and background
A brief history	7
Landmarks in Canadian history	12
Politics and the US factor	13
The People	15
The language issue	16
The arts	17
Architecture	18

Basic information
Before you go	21
On-the-spot information	24
Emergency information	26
Calendar of events	27

Toronto

Introduction	28
Getting around	29
Useful addresses	30
Emergency information	31
Orientation and walks	32
Orientation map	34
Sights and places of interest	39
Where to stay	51
Hotels A to Z	52
Where to eat	56
Restaurants A to Z	57
Nightlife and the performing arts	61
Shopping	65
Sports	67
Toronto for children	70

Montréal

Introduction	71
Getting around	72
Useful addresses	73
Emergency information	74
Orientation and walks	75
Orientation map	76
Sights and places of interest	85
Where to stay	97
Hotels A to Z	97
Where to eat	102
Restaurants A to Z	103
Nightlife and the performing arts	108
Shopping	112
Sports	114
Montréal for children	117

Québec City

Introduction	118
Basic information	118
Orientation and walks	120
Sights and places of interest	120
Hotels A to Z	124
Restaurants A to Z	126
Nightlife and shopping	129
Excursion: Gaspé peninsula	130

Index
General index	135
Toronto list of street names	143
Montréal list of street names	143
Québec City list of street names	144

Maps
	Map no.
Key	1
Toronto	2-5
Toronto environs	6-7
Montréal	8-11
Montréal environs	12-13
Québec City	14-15
Gaspé peninsula	16

How to use this book

The American Express Pocket Guide to Toronto, Montréal & Québec City is an encyclopedia of travel information, organized in the sections listed on the previous page. There is also a comprehensive *Index* (pages 135-142) and a **List of street names** (pages 143-144), and there are full-color **Maps** at the end of the book.

For easy reference, all major sections (*Sights and places of interest*, *Hotels*, *Restaurants*), and other sections where possible, are arranged alphabetically. For the organization of the book as a whole, see **Contents**. For individual places that do not have separate entries in *Sights and places of interest*, see the *Index*.

Abbreviations As a rule, only standard abbreviations are used, such as days of the week and months, points of the compass (N, S, E and W), street names (Ave., Pl., Rd., Sq. and St., plus Av. and Bd. in Francophone Québec), St (Saint), rms (rooms), C (century), and measurements.

Bold type **Bold type** is used mainly for emphasis, to draw attention to something of special interest or importance. It also picks out places — shops or minor museums, for example — that do not have full entries of their own. In such cases, it is usually followed in brackets by the address, telephone number, details of opening times, etc., which are printed in *italics*.

Cross-references A special typeface, *sans serif italics*, is used for cross-references. Each time you see a place name, such as *Casa Loma*, printed in this way, expect to find a full entry under that heading in that city's alphabetical *Sights and places of interest*. Similarly, when you see the title of a section of the book, such as *Hotels* or *Shopping*, printed in

---

How entries are organized

Hood House

1411 Lincoln Ave., Lincoln Green, Sherwood Forest ☎ *426-5960 (house), 426-5961 (group tour reservations). Map 8J11* 🖾 *✗ Open Apr-Sept 9am-5pm, rest of year 9am-4pm. Closed Christmas, New Year's Day. Metro: Bow & Arrow.* ·

Robin Hood (?1149-1205) was the leading spokesman for the poor and downtrodden in their struggle for freedom and justice under the Plantagenets. He lectured and wrote books about his own early life as a serf, campaigned endlessly for human rights, helped recruit peasants to the Civil Service, and finally settled down to a distinguished old age in Sherwood Forest. He lived first in A St. (see **National Museum of Outlawed Art**), then bought Sheriff Villa, which he renamed Hood House, a handsome white dwelling on a height overlooking the Trent Valley. All the furnishings, except for curtains and wallpaper, are original. Hood's library and other belongings are still *in situ*, and the whole house is redolent of the spirit of a very remarkable man. In the **Visitors' Centre** at the foot of the hill you can see a film about Hood's life.

this way, you can turn to that section for further information. (You will find a complete section-by-section breakdown of the book on the *Contents* page.)

For easy reference, use the headers printed at the top corner of each page (for example, **SkyDome** on page 49, or **Orientation and walks** on page 78).

Map references   Each full-color map at the end of the book is divided into a grid of squares, identified vertically by letters (A, B, C, D, etc.) and horizontally by numbers (1, 2, 3, 4, etc.). A map reference pinpoints the page (the first **bold** number) and position — thus *Château Frontenac* is located in Map **15**C5.

Price categories   Price categories for hotels and restaurants are represented by the symbols ▯ ▮▯ ▮▮▯ ▮▮▮▯ and ▮▮▮▮, which signify cheap, inexpensive, moderately priced, expensive and very expensive, respectively. These correspond approximately with the following actual prices, which give a guideline at the time of printing. Although actual prices will inevitably increase, as a rule the relative price category — for example, expensive or cheap — is likely to remain more or less the same.

Price categories	Corresponding to approximate prices	
	for **hotels** *double room with breakfast; singles are somewhat cheaper*	for **restaurants** *meal for one with service, tax and house wine*
▯ cheap	under $70	under $10
▮▯ inexpensive	$70-100	$10-25
▮▮▯ moderate	$100-130	$25-40
▮▮▮▯ expensive	$130-160	$40-60
▮▮▮▮ very expensive	over $160	over $60

— Bold blue type for entry headings.

— Blue italics for address, practical information and symbols. For list of symbols see page 6 or back flap of jacket.

— Black text for description.

— Sans serif italics used for cross-references to other entries or sections.

— Bold type used for emphasis.

Entries for hotels, restaurants, shops, etc. follow the same organization, and are usually printed across a half column.

In hotels, symbols indicating special facilities appear at the end of the entry, in black. —

Pullman
2600 Express Ave., Orient City 20037 ☎ 299-4450 ⓕ 299-4460. Map 2F4 ▮▮▮▮ *238 rms* ⇌ ⚞ *AE CB ⬤ ⬤ VISA Motro: High Standard.*
Location: On a height overlooking the Universal Trade Center. Part of a large conglomeration overlooking the seafront, this luxurious hotel is set in attractively landscaped grounds and is run with clockwork precision. Its restaurant, the **Simplon**, is highly regarded.
♿ ⚘ ⁂ ⩳ ⚑

Key to symbols

- ☎ Telephone
- TX Telex
- Ⓕ Facsimile (fax)
- ✿ Good value (in its class)
- ⇐ Parking
- Free entrance
- Entrance fee payable
- Photography forbidden
- ✗ Guided tour
- ☕ Cafeteria
- ✱ Special interest for children
- Hotel
- Deluxe hotel
- Cheap
- Inexpensive
- Moderately priced
- Expensive
- Very expensive
- Air conditioning
- AE American Express
- Diners Club
- MasterCard
- VISA Visa
- Secure garage
- Quiet hotel
- Elevator
- Facilities for disabled people
- TV in each room
- Mini-bar
- Telephone in each room
- Dogs not allowed
- Garden
- Good view
- Swimming pool
- Tennis
- Gym/fitness facilities
- Sauna
- Bar
- Restaurant
- Deluxe restaurant
- Open-air dining
- Disco dancing
- Nightclub
- Live music
- Dancing

A note from the General Editor

No travel book can be completely free of errors and totally up to date. Telephone numbers and opening hours change without warning, and hotels and restaurants come under new management, which can affect standards. We make every effort to ensure that all information is accurate at the time we go to press, but are always delighted to receive corrections or suggestions for improvements from our readers, which if warranted will be incorporated in a future edition.

The publishers regret that they cannot accept any consequences arising from the use of the book or from the information it contains.

INTRODUCTION

Ontario and Québec

Every nation does battle with perceptions, those assigned to it by outsiders as well as by its own people. Ask an American or European for a succinct description of Canada, and the response is apt to amount to a vague comparison with the United States, *only quieter*. The image is maddening to Canadians, who know better, but must deal with the frustrating knowledge that their society is one of the least examined and understood in the industrialized world. Far from a mere appendage to its rambunctious cousin to the south, it boasts an enviable roster of virtues now lost or unattainable by its neighbor. Nowhere is this more evident than in Toronto and Montréal, queen cities of the two most populous of its ten provinces, Ontario and Québec. They are arguably the most liveable and humane of any in the Western hemisphere.

Proof of that claim isn't difficult to find. Both cities enjoy superb public transit systems, an abundance of parks and green space, vigorous but unintimidating commercial centers, lively multi-ethnic communities, excellent educational and cultural institutions, and extensive sports facilities featuring roofed stadiums. The last are desirable, if not essential, to foil the region's long winter. But these cities also boast vast underground shopping and entertainment complexes, making it possible to leave a hotel, have lunch, see a movie, buy a shirt, and quaff a beer in a pub, all without donning a coat or hailing a taxi. Even the tallest skyscrapers are kept to reasonable heights, rarely exceeding 40 stories and thus retaining a human scale. Vehicular traffic is manageable, notwithstanding the complaints of natives, and far less harrowing than that of London or New York. The streets are well-tended, and, more important, safe, the beneficiaries of very low crime rates. One result is a thriving nightlife of diverse dining, concerts, clubs and theater.

Nor is that all to commend a visit. Canada is that rarity among nations — an officially bilingual state. That means the privilege of hearing the most melodious of languages in predominantly French-speaking Québec while knowing that assistance in English is never far away. Québec City, in particular, evokes a captivating French provincial capital, a walled city with the bonus of a stunning riverside setting. Easy excursions by car can include skiing in Québec's Laurentians, watersports on Lake Huron's Georgian Bay, or a tour of the primordial peaks and beaches of the Gaspé Peninsula. And should a clincher be necessary, prices for most services and goods are affordable, only partly due to currency exchange rates that have favored American and European visitors for several years.

A brief history

To a great extent, the history of Canada is that of Québec and Ontario. They were the sites of colonial wars between England, France and the United States. French explorer Jacques Cartier spent the winter of 1535-36 at the site of what became, in 1608 under Samuel de Champlain, the fortress village of Québec. That was only one year after the founding of Jamestown in Virginia. The difference was that Jamestown died while Québec prospered.

The federal capital of Ontario is Ottawa, mirrored by the city of Hull, directly across the Ottawa River in Québec Province. Toronto and Montréal are the financial powerhouses of the nation. Their two provinces contain over 15 million people, more than half the population of the country. And they are on the front

Introduction

lines of the long-festering language dispute, the divisive issue that might yet tear the nation in two.

Cartier wasn't the first man to set foot on Canadian soil, or even the first European. John Cabot established the British claim when he stepped down on the east coast in 1497, and he was preceded five centuries earlier by Norsemen, and, probably, Irish and Iberian fishermen. Even they were latecomers, intruders upon the territories of the Cree and Inuit, the Huron and Iroquois, who began to come from Asia some 40,000 years ago.

The Frenchmen most responsible for opening the huge new continent were fur trappers and traders. An energetic lot, their explorations carried them far to the west, south and north. In 1682, René-Robert Cavalier de La Salle took a party all the way down the Mississippi to its mouth. After that astonishing voyage, the empire of New France swept from the Gulf of Mexico to Hudson Bay. One tragic result was that it barred the westward expansion of the English colonies along the Atlantic coast. The circumstances were thus set for nearly a century of war between the French and their Indian allies and the British and their American colonists. Hostilities proceeded with predictable savagery, coming to no decisive conclusion until 1759.

The defeat of an Anglo-American force in frontier Pennsylvania in 1755 marked the start of what was called The French and Indian War. It was an extension of the Seven Years' War in Europe, which pitted Great Britain and Prussia against France, Austria and Sweden. With England's attention diverted to battlefields as far away as India, New France made a number of sorties into the British colonies, capturing forts in upper New York State, among others. Then, the 1759 Québec campaign was launched. The Marquis de Montcalm had deployed troops in and near Québec City. British General James Wolfe sailed up the St Lawrence River and landed on the opposite shore. After several feints and skirmishes, scouts discovered a narrow gap in the rocky cliffs on the French shore. Thinking it impossible to traverse, Montcalm had assigned only a token guard. In the still dark hours of the morning of September 13, Wolfe led his men up through the defile to the Plains of Abraham, a high plateau west of the city. There the battle was joined, 4,000 French soldiers marching in close-order ranks toward the waiting British force of 4,500. It was over in less than 30 minutes. Wolfe was killed, Montcalm was mortally wounded and died the next day. Québec surrendered. New France was now British Canada.

The 1763 Treaty of Paris validated the transfer of power. New France became known as Lower Canada, and the new British possession remained overwhelmingly French until the outbreak of the American Revolution in 1775. Persecuted and reviled as "Tories," loyalists to the Crown poured across the border into Canada, settling into the existing English-speaking settlements of Nova Scotia and New Brunswick, but also in Lower Canada along the St Lawrence Valley and as far west as the Niagara Peninsula. Representatives of the American Continental Congress were sent to Lower Canada to persuade the inhabitants to join them in rebellion against their common master. They were astonished to be rebuffed, failing to appreciate that the royalist Québecois found their cause as odious as British rule. When the war began, one of the first offensives of the new Army of the United Colonies was launched against Lower Canada. One contingent took Montréal, then joined General Benedict Arnold downriver in his siege of Québec City. Some French Canadians sold provisions to the Americans and others joined the British defenders at the

Introduction

parapets, but most remained neutral. Stalemate was broken by the arrival of British reinforcements, and the Americans withdrew. It was to be only the first of several American incursions into Canada, the last nearly a century later. That hostile history is understandably ignored when politicians croon about "the longest unfortified border in the world."

A surge in immigration had begun to populate Lower Canada, and in 1791 the colony was divided in two, creating "Upper" Canada ("Upper" because it was up the St Lawrence). This was the region eventually called Ontario, in which John Graves Simcoe founded the town of York, later to become Toronto. The young American republic was again at war with England in 1813, when one of its fleets attacked and burned York. The British, then occupied with Napoleon, waited until after his abdication the next year to retaliate against Washington, DC, where they torched the White House and numerous public buildings.

The war came to its murky conclusion in 1814. The US and Britain did agree to demilitarize the Great Lakes and extend the Canadian-US border along the 49th Parallel to the Pacific Ocean. Relaxation of military tensions and America's slow-coming realization that Canada did not wish to merge with her brought on what came to be called the "Era of Good Feelings." Immigration from Britain and Europe multiplied. Before long, newcomers were emboldened to challenge the ruling group known as the Family Compact. When political action failed to bring satisfaction, 1837 saw brief armed revolts against the authoritarian governments of Upper and Lower Canada. They were quickly suppressed, but one of their goals was soon realized with the establishment of elected legislatures.

Canadian wariness of expansionist America was revived upon the advent of the war between the states. In a foretaste of events during the Vietnam War era a century later, Union draft dodgers fled into Canada, straining relations once again. A foray by Confederate guerrillas into Vermont from their base near Montréal brought American threats of hot pursuit and diplomatic retribution. Cool heads prevailed, but a desire to stiffen the common defense was part of the reason for agreement to Canadian confederation in 1867, through the vehicle of the British North America Act. Ontario and Québec were two of the first four provinces to sign what amounted to a partial constitution granting them dominion status within the British Commonwealth. Conduct of foreign policy remained in the hands of Imperial London, but the new confederacy was to control its internal affairs.

The first Prime Minister was Sir John A. Macdonald, who served until 1873 and again from 1878-1891. His tenure saw the completion of the Canadian Pacific Railway, an engineering feat that helped unite the ocean-to-ocean country spiritually as well as physically. Four interim prime ministers in the next five years were followed by Sir Wilfrid Laurier, the first prime minister of French background. Serving from 1896-1911, he oversaw an era of prosperity and new-found national confidence. That optimism was shaken by World War I, in which more than 60,000 Canadian soldiers died, half again as many as were later to perish in World War II. The imposition of military conscription in 1917 was vigorously opposed by French Canadians, who saw it as a form of piecemeal genocide.

After the war, however, Canada emerged as an important industrial power. It didn't join the American experiment with Prohibition, and indeed fortunes were made in bootlegging

Introduction

liquor to the dry states. It did, however, share in the agony of the Great Depression, which was not relieved until Hitler made it necessary to gear up for another European conflagration.

Immigration laws were loosened and the national population was to double over the next 30 years. By 1960, a "Quiet Revolution" seized public attention. French Québeckers, chafing under the inherent inequities of living in a predominantly English-speaking country, began to agitate for equal social and legal status. Many felt this was only possible with political autonomy or even complete independence. The separatist *Parti Québecois* came to prominence and extremists took to bombing Anglo enterprises. In 1968, bilingual Québecker Pierre Trudeau succeeded Lester Pearson as Prime Minister. The Official Languages Act of 1969 mandated that all federal agencies and corporations must provide services in both French and English. It didn't placate the radical separatist group FLQ, which in 1970 kidnapped and murdered a cabinet minister, Pierre Laporte.

The language issue remains the single most volatile in Canadian life. After Trudeau engineered a Canadian Constitution and Charter of Rights and Freedoms, in 1982, which effectively removed the hold of the British North America Act, it was felt necessary to initiate a national conference to address the shortcomings of the constitution. The meeting took place in 1987 and in large measure focused on recognition of Québec as a "distinct society" within the confederation. The resulting Meech Lake Accord (simply "Meech" in political shorthand) was drawing fire two years later from certain provincial ministers who expressed alarm over what they saw as the special status given Québec. Throughout the first half of 1990, the resurgent separatist movement gained momentum, and new developments are now awaited. The battle that raged on the Plains of Abraham over 230 years ago has yet to arrive at its final conclusion.

Landmarks in Canadian history

1608	Champlain established an outpost at site of Québec City.
1642	Founding of settlement of Ville-Marie by de Maisonneuve, below the hill Jacques Cartier named *Mont Réal*.
1670	Hudson Bay trading company started operations.
1689	Beginning of the 74yr French and Indian wars.
1759	French defeated by British at Québec City.
1763	Treaty of Paris ceded New France to England.
1774	Québec Act passed by the British Parliament, granting religious authority to the Catholic Church and colonial observance of French legal structure.
1837	Dissidents rebelled against ruling oligarchies of Québec and Ontario but were quickly quelled.
1867	British North America Act created the Canadian Dominion.
1874	First football game pitted McGill University and Harvard.
1896	Wilfrid Laurier became first Francophone Prime Minister.
1891	J.A. Naismith invented the game of basketball.
1893	Professional hockey's Stanley Cup first awarded.
1914	Start of World War I. Conscription caused severe political crisis.

Politics

1918	Universal female suffrage enacted for federal elections.
1959	St Lawrence Seaway opened Great Lakes to the Atlantic.
1969	French, English given parity by Official Languages Act.
1976	*Parti Québecois* wins election in Québec.
1980	Québec referendum on partial independence defeated.
1982	Constitution patriated from England, amended by Charter of Rights and Freedoms.
1987	In the Meech Lake Accord, Québec extracted a "notwithstanding" clause that allowed it to override federal decrees.

Politics and the US factor

Pierre Trudeau likened sharing a continent with the United States to sleeping with an elephant. The quip speaks volumes, not only about the often bristly relationship between siblings in the same extended family, but also about the national character. Cautiousness is a component of the Canadian makeup, but so is irritation over being taken for granted. Just as the younger brother stands back during episodes of older brother's rage and self-absorbed blundering, so does he also crave equity and recognition of his own distinctiveness. Yet because he is often ignored, he doesn't quite know how to handle attention when it is given him. Canadians seemed almost embarrassed by the outpouring of American gratitude when their diplomats rescued some of their US counterparts during the Iran hostage crisis. They continue to be outraged, on the other hand, over casual US attendance to their legitimate concerns about acid rain.

Their ambivalence breeds both diffidence and defensiveness, a sense of inferiority mingled with a certainty of superiority. They are not, they emphatically want it to be known, carbon-copy Americans, despite surface similarities. Both are children of the lost British Empire, to be sure, the descendants of pioneers and immigrants who share general assumptions about morality and democratic ideals. They eat the same fast foods, follow the same fads, and worry about crime, the environment and the pounds they've been meaning to shed. Most of them, the English-speaking ones, even talk the same, although Canadians give a Scottish *oo* sound to *about* and *house*, and are inclined to append *eh?* to the ends of sentences.

But they differ in nearly as many ways. Their population is slightly more than 10 percent that of the US, but scattered across a land mass that is 10 percent larger. Such geographical separation promotes loyalty to a region, not a country, so most Canadians have only a splintered grasp of the concept of nationhood. That makes all the more alarming the paroxysms of chauvinism that periodically seize the people residing below the 49th parallel. Canadians and Americans have fought together in three wars in this century, but they do not always agree on the justice of causes. Thousands of American draft evaders sought refuge in Canada during the Vietnam era and were treated amicably by people who found that particular war repugnant.

While both observe democratic procedures, Canadians vote on a flexible schedule that requires the party in power to expose itself to periodic approval, not merely serve out its term. Its national Parliament is bicameral, the House of Commons elective, the Senate appointive. The Prime Minister, head of the

Politics

federal government, is only first among nearly equal provincial premiers, and the federal wing of a political party often has different objectives than its provincial versions. Conversely, the provinces are dependent upon federal support to provide public services and the physical infrastructure, even though they exercise total control over their own educational systems and such natural resources as are found within their territories. A decidedly mixed economy has evolved, part planned, part free market. Forms of cradle-to-grave security, notably in health care, are immovably in place. They are the sort of welfare programs that set wattles aquiver throughout Washington if they are even suggested. That doesn't mean they just happened, for nothing comes easily in Canadian political life. Consensus is elusive at best, with prolonged debate usually required to reach even tentative compromise. It took decades to hammer out the particulars of the Constitution, and that heavily amended document is still under threat.

And always, tossing about "down there," is the wooly American mammoth, all heedless knees and elbows. Canada watches its every move, by turns appalled, amused, bemused, bewitched. Another superpower is its other immediate neighbor; but the Soviet Union is over the frozen horizon. The alien political and cultural tremors with which Canada must cope rumble from its south. It has ample advance warning. About 90 percent of its population live within 100 miles of that border, most of it within reach of US television and radio stations. The daily dose of situation comedies and game shows may seem benign (or banal) enough, but is undeniably invasive. Who knows what social viruses — from the Canadian perspective — might the nightly onslaught of spectacular violence and wasting anomie carry?

Efforts have been made to dike the flood. "Canadian content" regulations dictate how much of Canadian Broadcasting Corporation programming may be allotted to shows of American origin, and require publishers and film-makers to observe similar formulas. Their effectiveness is debatable. The top-rated US programs weigh heavily on Canadian charts too. Because of television, Canadian professional football is withering before the spangled version presented by the National Football League. There are, in all likelihood, more Canadian fans of the Cleveland Browns and Detroit Lions than of the Toronto Argonauts and Calgary Stampeders. (Montréal's team faded into oblivion from lack of interest.) Hockey is a Canadian passion, but the misnamed National Hockey League has only seven teams based in Canadian cities. There are 14 in the US.

Under the circumstances, cross-fertilization is unstoppable. Many of those same film and TV dramas, purportedly situated in Los Angeles or New York, are actually shot in Vancouver or Toronto. (They have to dirty up the streets to make it believable.) Canadian-born performers are found in every category of American show business. Torontonian Raymond Massey had his most famous role as Abraham Lincoln. Montréaler William Shatner skippered the Starship *Enterprise* through a TV series and five movies. Comedians Alan Thicke, John Candy, Dan Ackroyd; singers Anne Murray, Robert Goulet, Paul Anka, K.D. Lang; actors Leslie Nielson, Kate Nelligan and Lorne Greene — all Canadian, and only a few of many. Canadians in other fields include economist John Kenneth Galbraith, fashion-designer Arnold Scaasi and newscaster Peter Jennings.

So many Canadians — a million a year by some estimates — vacation in the States, California and Florida in particular, that some local radio stations broadcast daily segments from back home, and newsstands carry Québec papers. In return, American tourists spend nearly $3 billion annually in Canada. Investment works both ways, too. Over 70 percent of Canadian imports and exports pass through American hands, and at least that percentage of foreign investment in Canada is American. On the other side of the ledger are such highly visible Canadian firms in the US as the Four Seasons hotel chain, Odeon Cineplex Cinemas, Seagram's Distillers, Peoples Drug Stores, Hardee's Restaurants, Olympia & York land developers, and Harlequin paperback romances. Given that degree of interaction, and there is far more than can be described here, it is worthwhile to know who these Canadians are.

The People

They are not what might be expected, especially if one carries only an image of Mounties and Eskimos. For one thing, about one out of every eight Canadians was born somewhere else. Waves of immigration, notably since World War II, have brought millions of Chinese, Greeks, Portuguese, Eastern Europeans, West Indians, Koreans, Thais and Vietnamese. They were greeted, with varying degrees of warmth, by the already resident Scots, Irish, French, English, Germans and Italians. Since these newer Canadians only reluctantly relinquish the symbols and ceremonies carried from their former homelands, they have cast a pulsating mosaic of exotic customs and practices upon the often dour foundation laid by their predecessors. The most visible evidence of this is seen along such concentrations of polyglot humanity as Blvd. St Laurent in Montréal and Bloor St. W in Toronto. Between the windows hung with glazed roast ducks and loops of *kielbasa* and greengrocer stands with *bok choy* and *cilantro* are shops specializing in nothing at all, whose inventories can include videotapes in Cantonese, finger cymbals, memo pads, *cazuelas*, caramel candy, aspirin, incense and earmuffs, all arrayed side by side.

The truly native peoples of Canada are the Inuit and Amerindians. ("Eskimo" and "Indian" are out of favor, and the innocent British locution of "Red Indian" is regarded as near-racist.) About 30,000 Inuit live in the far northern precincts of the country, while about 300,000 Amerindians remain in bands (not "tribes") on reserves (not "reservations"), some within walking distance of Montréal and Toronto. Their ancestors were rarely treated as harshly as were their brothers south of the border, but neglect and misguided paternalism thinned their numbers. Genuine concern for their welfare is now apparent, as activists and governments attempt to balance the preservation of traditional native living modes with the relentless pressures of the larger society.

The dominating cultures remain those of the two earliest groups of European settlers, especially in Ontario and Québec. There, Canadians of British Protestant heritage and those of French Catholic background confront each other across historic dividing lines. As is often true of antagonists living on opposite sides of the same street — figuratively and literally — they understand each other better than do those at greater distances from the fray. That prompts more ambivalence. When Québecois nationalism battered its way to power in the 1970s, English-speaking Québeckers left for Ontario by the tens of thousands, but not without regrets. Although straitlaced Toronto has loosened its corset considerably in recent decades, transplanted Québeckers miss the *joie de vivre* of Montréal, the *croissants* and *café au lait* in sidewalk cafés and the music that thumps on toward dawn every weekend. For their part, clear-eyed Québecois intent on career advancement recognize that English, not French, is the language of business. And since bilingualism is now a marketable commodity, many of them have moved, too. Catholics now outnumber Protestants in Anglican-Presbyterian Toronto.

Given such heterogeneity, generalizations about the reception accorded to visitors are suspect. As a rule, however, courtesy can be expected in most transactions, albeit not always including those with bureaucrats. Social encounters are tentative at first, for Canadians are loath to appear brash or loud, but they soon prove to be open, friendly and curious. Bear in mind that a knowledge of English (or French, for that matter) cannot be assumed, and when a clerk or stranger seems unresponsive to a polite query, he or she may only be thinking who to ask for assistance.

The language issue

There was no event of more profound significance in Canadian history than the British triumph over the French at Québec City in 1759. Although an ecumenical monument now stands in a Québec park honoring the generals of both sides, victor and vanquished, the defeat is still recalled with bitterness by French Canadians. From that day to this, they have felt that they were second-class citizens in their own country, a French island in an English sea. The official Québec motto has an ominous tone of eventual retribution: *Je me souviens*. Appearing even on automobile license plates, it means "I remember," alluding not only to that historic battle but to every slight since the onset of British sovereignty.

Excesses of zeal and simple insensitivity have been common in both camps, but there is a persuasive case for assertions of anti-French discrimination. Well into the middle of this century, capital and political power were firmly in the hands of merchant princes and bankers of British heritage, and they routinely passed these on to their own kind. A linguistic racism prevailed, not always overt or even conscious, but nevertheless denying French Canadians access to the executive suite and government ministries. This was especially galling in Québec, where Anglo-Canadians are a decided minority. It should not have been surprising that when the Québecois finally began to organize themselves effectively, they set about getting even. A good deal of petty harassment of the Anglo minority has taken place under the banner of preservation of the French language and culture.

While Canada as a whole is officially bilingual, the Québec government is intent upon making its province unilingually French. Where all exterior signs were until recently required to be in both English and French, there is now a push to allow only French. This was legitimized by a legislative act, Bill 101, and has as its enforcement apparatus the Commission de la Langue Française, a virtual language police. The "tongue troopers" have taken down such unacceptable signs as "Merry Christmas" and confiscated Dunkin' Donuts bags printed only in English. They required Eaton's department store to drop the offending apostrophe and "s" from its name. Sellers of Harris Tweed were instructed to devise an equivalent French label or cease selling the product.

And on, and on. Obviously, this can be prickly terrain, and visitors should tread softly. They will hear unfamiliar words in English as well as French. Anglophones, francophones and allophones are those who respectively speak English, French, or anything else. The local version of French, called *joal*, is hardly that of the classroom: a *dépanneur* is a corner convenience store, *souper* is the evening meal, and *chiens chauds* are hot dogs, but an *hambourgeois* is not a middle-class actor. (Think about it.) It helps to brush up on highway French, too, for that is how traffic signs read in Québec. When an 18-wheel truck is bearing down from the opposite direction is no time to learn that *reculez* means "Go Back!" Otherwise, the practical effect on visitors is minimal. The telephone operator or waiter gives greeting in French but typically shifts to English upon sensing hesitation. In those cities and smaller towns of interest to most tourists, help is always near.

The arts

A rich pool of native talent has cemented Canada's high standing in the performing arts. This is particularly true in classical ballet and modern dance, as exemplified by the Toronto Dance Theatre, Montréal's Les Grands Ballets Canadiens, and the National Ballet of Canada, one of the world's most honored troupes. While they are the elite in the field, other worthy companies vie for attention, among them Montréal's Entre-Six and Ballets Classiques. They are provided venues appropriate to their accomplishment, notably the Place des Arts complex in Montréal and the O'Keefe Centre in Toronto. These facilities are shared with such estimable musical organizations as the Toronto Philharmonic, Toronto Symphony and Montréal Symphony. Opera, jazz, choral and chamber music are also well represented. Film-makers have carved a niche out of the path of the Hollywood juggernaut, frequently winning film festival awards for low-budget features on Canadian themes. Their often understated nature mitigates against the financial success associated with such explosive mega-hits as *Star Wars* and *Batman*, but then, they are not attempting to compete in that arena. Since World War II, aid has been given by the National Film Board. This began as a propaganda arm of the government, moved on to support of animated short subjects and now underwrites full-length theatrical and TV features. Examples of their quiet artistry are seen in such efforts as *My American Cousin*, *The Grey Fox* and *Leopard in the Snow*.

Much pride is invested in the Group of Seven, a tightly-knit cooperative of painters that enjoyed approbation between the wars. Before them, Canadian painters tended to follow the leads of European portraiture and genre subjects. The ordered, bucolic pictures of the 19thC suggested Flanders and Provence more than they did the palpable silence of the empty prairie and the shriek of winter in the Canadian high country. That changed with the coming together of a band of young artists at a design firm in Toronto. One of them, Tom Thomson, became enamored of the rugged terrain of Algonquin Park, w of Ottawa. He proceeded to capture it in oils, distinctive paintings that breathed uniquely Canadian origins. They made converts of his friends Frank Carmichael, Lawren Harris, Alexander Jackson and James

MacDonald. Frequently traveling and painting together in the years before World War I, they grew so close that they even worked in the same studio, built by the well-to-do Harris. The war intervened, and Thomson drowned in a lake in his beloved Algonquin Park in 1917; but the others got together again after the Armistice and enlisted Franz Johnston and Arthur Lismer in their movement. They exhibited together for the first time in 1920 at the Art Gallery of Toronto, a show that won both praise and disapproval. It was the first of many, in Canada, the US and England, where the critical response was enthusiastic. With A.J. Casson and Edwin Holgate, who joined the group later, they were heralded as the creators of an important new school that was to influence Canadian painting into the last third of the century. The group disbanded in 1932, but its members remained active, some of them veering into abstractionism in later years.

A truly native art persists in the works of Inuit sculptors. Working in stone, bone and tusks, they portray what they know best: the work and creatures of their northern habitat — fishermen, polar bears and the musk ox. As admiration and demand for their products have grown, so has their sophistication, and larger pieces fetch thousands of dollars.

Architecture

There was no significant permanent settlement in Ontario until after New France was ceded to the British in 1763, so the early architectural heritage of the nation's two largest provinces is that of Québec. After establishment of British dominion, however, architectural trends typically followed those prevailing in Europe and the US. Thus, the Georgian style of many late 18thC public buildings flowed into the Classical Revival of the early 19thC, superseded after Confederation by deliriously eclectic flirtations with a blizzard of conceits borrowed from the Italian Renaissance, Gothic, Baroque and French Second Empire in what can fairly be described as Neo-Everything.

Not surprisingly, the earliest structures reflect the backgrounds of settlers from rural Normandy and Brittany, adapted to the harsh climate and available native materials. They were barn-like buildings of simple rectangular design, with thick stone walls and roofs steeply pitched to shed snow. Relatively little survives of that century-and-a-half of French rule, and most of it from the later decades of the regime. *Château Ramezay* in Vieux Montréal is a prime example, now functioning as a small museum. Erected in 1705, it was altered frequently over the years, but retains its essential outlines. Not far away is the **Maison Calvet** (1725), an unusually fine example of French Canadian domestic architecture.

The threat of American invasion during and immediately after the War of 1812 inspired the construction of elaborate fortifications at strategic points along the Great Lakes and St Lawrence Valley. The extant version of *Fort York* in Toronto dates from 1815, its walls enclosing barracks and blockhouses, as do those of the *Citadel* in Québec City, built by the British in the same period. At this time, governmental and commercial structures demonstrated an enthusiasm for Greco-Roman themes, with fluted pillars and triangular pediments, as seen in Toronto's **Osgoode Hall**, which was completed in stages between 1829 and 1845. A purer example is the **Banque de Montréal** (see

Architecture

Montréal Walks), bearing a Greek temple facade with fewer stylistic intrusions. A parallel Gothic Revival was preferred for many ecclesiastical buildings, seen nowhere to greater advantage than in Montréal's *Église Notre-Dame*. With its twin squared towers and pointed arch windows, Londoners are reminded of their own St Martin's-in-the-Fields.

By the mid-19thC, a wealthy new class of industrialists and financiers was able to indulge itself in any whimsy it chose. In Toronto and in Montréal's Golden Square Mile, millionaires commissioned mansions that evoked the Loire château, the Rhineland schloss, the Tuscan villa, the Highlands castle and, not infrequently, elements of all four. The turreted Scottish baronial look was especially popular, for many of the new rich were of that ancestry. The final expression of this form of excess was Toronto's *Casa Loma*, a 98-room mansion that eventually fell victim to the tax collector. In civic buildings, an interest in Gothic resurfaced, but Francophone Montréal gave favor to the French Second Empire style, in vogue from about 1870 to the end of the century. It is exemplified by the steep mansard roofs and tiered pavilions of the **Hôtel de Ville** (1878-1926 — see *Montréal Walks*). The inspiration for Québec City's *Château Frontenac* (1898-1920), which employs green copper roofs and turrets with

The Pl. d'Armes facade of the **Banque de Montréal**: a fine example of the mid-19thC enthusiasm for Greco-Roman styles.

A baronial residence, completed in 1914 and largely imported from Scotland, Toronto's **Casa Loma**, with its turrets, 98 paneled rooms and hidden staircases, caused the ruin of its creator.

Architecture

conical caps, is obvious from both aspect and name.

At the same time, less exalted architecture demonstrated an exuberance of its own. Queen Anne was a name given to the busy admixtures of turrets, bay windows and gables applied to the facades of row houses seen in abundance along the streets of Montréal's Westmount and Toronto's Yorkville. Much of the detailing is crowded up around the eaves and is often of carved and scrolled wood affixed to sandstone walls. It was not until well into the 20thC that Canadians saw much point in buildings that exceeded five or six stories. Theirs was and is, after all, a country of underpopulated spaces. Even by the 1920s, the tallest building in Canada was Montréal's **Sun Life Building** (see *Montréal Walks*), one wing of which reached 26 stories. But while postwar Europe was rebuilding, Canada was intact. Desirable real estate in the center of cities was increasingly costly, and the virtues of the skyscraper became more apparent. The International Style promulgated by the minimalist Bauhaus school took hold in the 1950s. Glass curtain walls were hung on steel skeletons, allowing fewer setbacks, greater height, and therefore maximum square footage. Ornamentation was

Montréal's 1878 **Hôtel de Ville**: its steep mansard roofs, square turrets and Neo-Classical detailing echo the French Second Empire.

A playful Post-Modernist office tower, the **Maison des Coopêrants**, in Montréal city center, mirrors nearby Christ Church cathedral.

Toronto's **C N Tower**, the world's highest freestanding structure, and the **SkyDome** stadium, with its unique retractable roof, express municipal confidence.

BASIC INFORMATION

deplored, right angles and unbroken purity of line exalted. Examples abound in both Toronto's financial district and downtown Montréal, in soaring towers designed by such luminaries as I.M. Pei and Mies van der Rohe. Every great city needs, or at least wants, a physical symbol of itself. Toronto's *CN Tower*, the highest freestanding structure in the world, serves that purpose admirably. At its base is a more recent expression of municipal confidence, the impressive *SkyDome* stadium, with its unique retractable roof.

A swelling reaction to the severity of the International Style became apparent in the 1980s, with a Post-Modernist trend that encourages playful uses of angled planes, tinted glass and nonessential decorative elements. One successful example is Montréal's **Maison des Coopérants** (see *Montréal Walks*), which mirrors Christ Church Cathedral in tribute to the city that was and will be.

Before you go

Documents required
US citizens only need proof of their status: a passport, birth certificate or driver's license will do. Non-citizen permanent residents of the US must present their Alien Registration Card. British subjects must show their passport, but do not need a visa unless their stay exceeds three months. All visitors, except those permanently resident in the US or in Greenland, will need to have proof of onward transportation.

All visitors to Canada may drive for up to three months if they have a full and valid driver's license. US citizens driving across the border should bring a Non-Resident Insurance Card and drivers of rental cars from the US must have their rental contract with them. You will need a valid driver's license to rent a car.

Travel and medical insurance
Medical care is good to excellent, but US citizens should check that their policy provides coverage in Canada. Travelers from Europe and elsewhere are advised to take out separate insurance, as the cost of medical care and prescribed medicines can be very high. A traffic accident or theft of belongings can destroy a long-anticipated vacation, so the moderate cost of short-term riders to homeowner and automobile policies are worthwhile.

Money
The dollar is the basic unit, divided into 100 cents and in coins similar to their US counterparts. It is available as both a paper bill and a gold-colored coin nicknamed the "loonie" from the bird engraved on one side. Other denominations are $2, $5, $10, $20 and $50. US currency is widely accepted, customarily at a premium rate that takes into account the difference in market value. Simplicity and courtesy are better served, however, if visitors from the US exchange their money on arrival.

It is wise to carry cash in small amounts, in any event, keeping the remainder in travelers cheques. Travelers cheques issued by American Express, Bank of America, Barclays, Citibank and Thomas Cook are widely recognized, as are those of Visa and Mastercard. Make sure to read the instructions included with the cheques. It is important to note separately the serial numbers of

Before you go

your cheques and the telephone number to call in case of loss. Specialist travelers cheque companies such as American Express provide extensive local refund facilities through their own offices or agents. Banks and change bureaus typically ask to see some sort of photo ID before cashing travelers cheques.

Credit and charge cards are welcomed by virtually all hotels and motels, airlines and car rental agencies, most restaurants and many stores. American Express, Diners Club, Visa and Mastercard are those in common use. Personal checks drawn on non-local accounts are rarely accepted, although some hotels will cash small amounts in conjunction with a credit card.

Customs

Customs inspections upon entry and exit at US borders are usually brief, involving answers to a few questions and little else. People crossing by car are sometimes asked to open their trunks, but infrequently the luggage itself. Illegal immigrants and drug smugglers are obvious targets, and penalties can be severe for possession of illicit drugs. Firearms, plants and pets are restricted, if not necessarily prohibited. "Reasonable quantities" of tobacco and a bottle or two of wine or liquor are allowed. International travelers may bring into Canada, duty-free, either 1.1 liters (40fl.oz) of liquor or wine, or 24 x 355ml (12fl.oz) cans or bottles of beer or ale, as well as 50 cigars, 200 cigarettes and 1kg (2.2lbs) of tobacco.

Getting there

Toronto's **Lester B. Pearson** and Montréal's **Dorval** are the region's principal international airports, supplemented by smaller hubs that handle mostly domestic and commuter flights. **Mirabel** airport, N of Montréal, is used for charters and for flights arriving from other continents. Air Canada has extensive daily schedules between major cities in the US and Europe, supplemented by flights by the major carriers of the destination countries.

From the US, Amtrak has two scenic routes from Grand Central Terminal in New York to Montréal and one daily train from Washington and New York to Toronto. VIA Rail connects Toronto, Montréal and Québec City to western Canada.

Cars have numerous crossing points. Among the busiest are Detroit-Windsor and Niagara Falls, so there can be time savings by crossing elsewhere. The principal N-S routes from New England and New York to Montréal are Interstate Highways 91 and 87; from the Midwest to Toronto, I-75 and I-90.

When to go

They say that Canada has two seasons — winter and July. Not so. Southern Ontario and Québec have a climate very similar to that of the northern tier of the US. The short, radiant spring usually arrives in early Apr, with the first really warm spell coming in early June. From then until early Sept, day and night temperatures fluctuate between tee-shirt-hot and sweater-cool. Nevertheless, anticipate long stretches of 85°-plus (20°C) days in July and Aug. Toronto, Montréal and Québec City are all on the water, so high humidity accompanies the heat. From mid-Sept to late Oct, the weather is changeable, but can be surprisingly pleasant for days at a stretch. Winter usually sets in by early Nov and stays until late March. Prevailing winter winds coming from the NW, though, have often dissipated by the time they pass over Toronto, picking up moisture as they continue over Lake Ontario. The result is that Toronto frequently suffers less snow

Before you go

than Buffalo, NY, to the s. Montréal, on the other hand, seems perversely proud of its 8ft of snow each winter. The higher rural regions of Québec and the Gaspé Peninsula rarely get uncomfortably warm and can be chilly even on July nights.

The entire region is at its best from late May-early Sept, and café tables spill out onto sidewalks and into backyard courts. Street performers are out in force, the calendar is alive with ethnic and music festivals, and the release from winter's grip visibly raises everyone's spirits. These are the months of the biggest crowds, when the most popular attractions are awash with people. Many of the better restaurants close for vacation, and hotel reservations are harder to come by, even though there is something of a hotel glut in Montréal and Toronto. For those reasons, the shoulder seasons of mid-May to early June or the latter weeks of Sept may be preferable to those who aren't locked into July and Aug.

Nor are the winter months to be shunned. Québeckers and Ontarians either ignore the cold and snow or make a virtue of it. There are the weatherproof underground cities of Toronto and Montréal, and the theater, opera and dance seasons are in full swing. The patrons of clubs and restaurants evince a we're-in-this-together camaraderie, and may, if anything, be even easier to meet. For the hardy, there are robust winter festivals including the February extravaganza in Québec City; downhill and cross-country skiing flourish, and ponds and rinks are aswirl with skaters. In Montréal, carriage horses are hitched to sleighs (*calèches*) for romantic outings around Mont-Royal. Memories are made of hot buttered rum beside the fire of one of the country inns that abound outside the major cities.

What to bring

A compact folding umbrella can prove useful any month of the year. From May through Sept, a windbreaker with a hood can suffice, if only for cool mornings and boat trips on the St Lawrence. A cotton sweater or wrap is often desirable for evenings or over-cooled restaurants and theaters. Air conditioning and central heating are less often pushed to the extremes they are in the US, but layering of clothes is still a good idea, peeling off or pulling on to deal with changes in temperature from street to interior and back. A raincoat with removable lining is adaptable for the cooler months, but in deepest winter, be prepared to wrap up — caps, scarves, heavy gloves and socks, waterproof shoes or boots.

Informality prevails, especially for sightseeing or dining in sidewalk cafés. Many of the better restaurants prefer that men wear jackets, although relatively few require them and fewer still expect a tie to be worn. Ask when making a reservation. Good taste and a sense of decorum dictate the choice of clothing, if only to reduce the visual pollution of unthinking tourists in markedly unbecoming and skimpy outfits. A tanktop and running shorts is not appropriate attire for visiting churches, for example, especially when services are being held. Dress codes are rarely applied in even the poshest hotels, except for their dining rooms, but mature men and women might well feel out of place in jeans when all about them are in business suits and cocktail dresses. Denim clothing is sometimes barred by the smarter discos and clubs.

Cigarettes and spirits are heavily taxed. Smokers should take along as many packages as are necessary to get through a visit or expect to pay more than twice as much as at home. Travelers accustomed to a martini before dinner or a bedtime cognac find that bringing the permissible two liters of the favored tipple to be a not-insignificant economy. Adequate supplies of prescription medicines and the prescriptions themselves should go on the checklist, along with a spare pair of eyeglasses. Most other incidental needs are easily met at the corner convenience store, and prices are comparable to those back home.

On-the-spot information

Public holidays

Banks, offices, and schools are closed on: Jan 1; Good Friday; Victoria Day, Mon closest to May 24th; Canada Day, July 1; Labor Day, 1st Mon in Sept; Thanksgiving Day, 2nd Mon in Oct; Remembrance Day, Nov 11; and Dec 25. When any of these fall on a Sat or Sun, they are usually observed on the following Mon to make a three-day weekend. Boxing Day on Dec 26 is a major shopping day, when stores are open but most other businesses and government offices are closed. In addition, Québec Province celebrates St John the Baptist Day on June 24th and Ontario its Civic Holiday on the 1st Mon in Aug.

Banks and currency exchange

Customary banking hours are 10am-3pm (6pm Fri), but there is a recent trend toward opening earlier and closing later. Banks consistently offer the best exchange rates. Remember to have photo identification ready. The better hotels usually convert money or travelers cheques for registered guests within a point or two of bank rates. But this is not true of all hotels, so consult a daily newspaper to have an idea of current exchange rates. There are also private change bureaus and check-cashing stores in the larger cities. Their announced rates sometimes sound more favorable than those of the banks, but the hefty commissions they charge for the service are likely to wipe out the differential. It is best to use them only for small emergency amounts when banks are closed. They also require photo ID.

American Express also has a **MoneyGram (R)** money transfer service that makes it possible to wire money worldwide in just minutes, from any American Express Travel Service Office. This service is available to all customers and is not limited to American Express Card members. Payment can be made in cash, or with an American Express Card with a Centurion Credit Line, an American Express Optima (SM) Card, Visa or MasterCard. For the location nearest you ☎ **1-800-543-4080** (Canada and US).

Communications

Bewilderingly swift technological advances make the use of post office general delivery services seem almost quaint. The larger and medium-sized hotels routinely make telex and now fax machines available to guests. Those catering to businesspeople are increasingly providing fax, multi-line telephones and/or computer ports in rooms, either as a standard facility or on request.

American Express and Thomas Cook offices will still hold letters for customers. To collect mail at either agency, be prepared to show the relevant credit card or travelers cheques.

Canadians rely heavily on their telephones, and the system is efficient and bilingual, except during periodic labor disputes. No international codes are necessary to place trunk calls between the US and Canada. Simply enter the long-distance **1** followed by

On-the-spot information

the appropriate 3-digit area code and 7-digit number. The area code for Toronto is **416**, for Montréal **514**, and for Québec City **418**. For international calls, dial the international operator.

Letters and packages mailed from Canada must carry Canadian postage stamps, an observation that is less obvious to some Americans than it might seem. While telephone area codes follow the same system in both countries, postal zip codes do not. Those in Canada are combinations of letters and numerals and must be carefully entered in addresses to ensure delivery.

Shopping hours
Independent retail shops are usually open 10am-6pm, Mon-Sat. Those located in shopping malls and along the corridors of the underground cities of Montréal and Toronto often don't close their doors until 9pm or 10pm, especially on Thurs and Fri. This is also the practice of the large department stores. Variations are common, and even the once-sacrosanct Sabbath prohibition is crumbling. Shopowners in tourist areas routinely defy the Sun closing laws. Drug and convenience stores (*dépanneurs* in Québec) frequently stay open until 11pm or midnight. A few large food stores are open 24hrs.

Public rest rooms
The availability of public rest rooms is less than ideal, although the situation is better than in most parts of the US and Europe. There are a few in metro or subway stations but they can be messy, although rarely filthy or dangerous. Museums, department stores and government buildings are other possibilities, as is ducking into the nearest large hotel.

Electric current
Standard household current is 110V and outlets accept 2-flat-pronged plugs, as in the US. Three-prong plugs and 220V current are in use for larger appliances such as air conditioners, which presumably will not concern the average visitor but might affect those needing to bring computers.

Laws, regulations and safety
Montréal and Toronto enjoy enviably low violent crime rates. It is likely that not a harsh word, let alone a threat, will be heard on a normal visit. Still, prudence is in order, as in any large city. Prostitution exists, but hardly flourishes. It is illegal, as is the purchase and possession of illicit street drugs. Walking alone at night through the shabbier districts or waiting too long at isolated bus stops are to be avoided, especially by women. Leave no articles of value in cars, including clothing, or at least lock them in the trunk.

When leaving a hotel, take only a credit card or two and enough cash for the day's planned activities. Use the room safes now often available, especially for airline tickets and passports. Otherwise, inquire at the front desk if a safe is available to guests. When a hotel employs the new plastic passcards, do not write the room number on the cardkey itself, but on a separately carried piece of paper. None of these cautions are to be taken to imply significant danger, however, for the situation is nowhere near that which inspires the high levels of urban paranoia s of the border. Even panhandlers are diffident and relatively rare.

Antismoking regulations are multiplying, in tune with increasing public antipathy to the habit. They are not yet as restrictive as in many parts of the US, but that day approaches.

Emergency information

Many restaurants have smoke-free sections, and the larger hotels nearly always set aside one or more floors for nonsmokers. It is polite to ask a taxi driver for permission before lighting up, even if no sign is posted. Smoking in enclosed places, such as elevators, is frowned upon, if not always specifically prohibited.

Drivers can turn right after stopping at a red light in Ontario, and exceptions to this rule are displayed. They *cannot* do so in Québec province. The speed limit on highways is 100kph (62 mph); elsewhere as posted. Fines are imposed for unnecessary use of horns. Even ambulances rarely use sirens. Passenger seat belts must be used. Radar detectors are illegal.

The minimum age requirement for drinking alcohol is 19yrs in Ontario and 18yrs in Québec.

Tipping

A minimum tip in a restaurant is 10 percent, to be left only if the service was sufficiently lax or inept to warrant it. Of course, offensively brusque or rude treatment may deserve less — or nothing at all. If tempted to follow that course, be certain that the waiter or waitress is at fault, and not the kitchen. At least 15 percent is more appropriate, as much as 20 percent in luxury establishments or when service was especially attentive. Check bills to see if they include a service charge, a not-infrequent

Emergency information

Emergency Services:
Police, fire, ambulance
(**Montréal and Toronto areas**) ☎*911*.
Police, fire
 (**Québec**) ☎*691-6911*
No coins needed for pay phones.

Automobile accidents
- **Call police** immediately if anyone is injured.
- **If car is rented**, call number in rental agreement.
- **Do not admit liability** or incriminate yourself.
- **Ask witnesses to stay** and give statements.
- **Exchange names**, addresses, driver's license and car registration numbers. A form called the *Constat à l'amiable* is provided for this purpose by car rental firms.

Car breakdowns
Call one of the following from nearest telephone:
- Number indicated in **car rental** agreement.
- The **Canadian Automobile Association** (☎ *288-7111 for Montréal area or* ☎ *966-3000 for Toronto area*) if you are a member of an affiliated organization, such as AAA or RAC.
- **Nearest garage** or towing service.

Lost travelers cheques
Notify police immediately, then follow the instructions provided with your travelers cheques or contact the issuing company's nearest office. Contact your consulate or **American Express** (☎ *931-4444*) if you are stranded with no money.

See also *Emergency information* in Montréal and Toronto *Basic information* sections.

practice. This applies to hotel room service, too. Don't tip twice. If the levied charge is 12 percent or less, you might consider leaving a little extra.

Bartenders, hairdressers and barbers expect 15 percent. Bellmen and porters should receive something for each piece of luggage carried. A $1 tip is about right, depending upon how heavy are the bags and how far the walk. Doormen and coatroom and rest-room attendants should be tipped, too, usually 50¢-$1. If staying for two or more nights in a hotel, leave about $1 a night for the chambermaid. Taxi drivers are accustomed to 10-15 percent of the fare, the higher amount if they move luggage from curb to trunk or get out to open the door. Theater and stadium ushers are not tipped. Tour guides expect $1-$2 for their 2 or 3hrs, more if the tour is longer.

Disabled travelers

The needs of persons confined to wheelchairs are catered to, but somewhat unevenly. Ramps are provided at major museums and public buildings; many hotels offer lodgings with bathrooms equipped with raised toilets and pull-up bars; downtown corners have curb cuts; and special parking spaces are set aside near entrances to stores and shopping malls. Restaurants, however, are often inaccessible, and older structures, especially in Québec City, do not lend themselves to modification. A free booklet called *Toronto With Ease* discusses services for disabled persons. It is available from the **Metropolitan Toronto Convention and Visitors Association** (*Queen's Quay Terminal, 207 Queen's Quay W, Box 126, Toronto, Ont. M5J 1A7*). Also useful is the mid-priced *Handy Travel*, produced by the **Canadian Rehabilitation Council for the Disabled** (*1 Yonge St., Toronto, Ont. M5E 1E5*).

Calendar of events

See also *Public holidays* in **Basic information** and **Sports and activities** in each city for further information.

January

Three weeks in Jan, 1st week in Feb: **Montréal Winter Festival**. ‡ Mid-Jan: **Toronto International Boat Show** at Exhibition Place. ‡ Late Jan: **Ice Canoe Race** at Harbourfront in Toronto. ‡ Late Jan: **International Curling Tournament**, various locations around Québec Province.

February

First week in Feb, for ten days: **Québec City Winter Carnival**. ‡ Mid-Feb: **North York Winter Carnival**, Black Creek Pioneer Village in Toronto. ‡ Late Feb: **Toronto International Auto Show**.

March

Early Mar: **Outdoors Show** in Montréal. ‡ Late Mar: **Springtime Craft Show & Sale** at Exhibition Place in Toronto. ‡ Late Mar: **Festival of Canadian Fashion** in Toronto.

April

Early Apr: **National Home Show**, Exhibition Place, Toronto. ‡ Mid-Apr: **opening of baseball season** in Montréal and Toronto; **International Book Fair** in Québec City; **Stratford Shakespeare Festival Season** opens in Stratford, Ontario.

May

Late May: **International Fireworks Competition**, for 4wks in Montréal; **Québec City International Theatre Fortnight**.

June

Early June: **Le Tour de l'Île de**

TORONTO/INTRODUCTION

Montréal, an amateur cycling event. ‡ Mid-June: **Toronto International Caravan**, an ethnic festival at various sites around the city; **Molson Grand Prix**, Formula One race in Montréal. ‡ Late June: **All That Jazz festival** at sites throughout Toronto; **jazz and rock festival** in Québec City, various locations, including free outdoor performances. ‡ Late June-early July: **Montréal International Jazz Festival**, for ten days at various indoor and outdoor locations.

July
July 1: **Canada Day celebrations** in Québec and Ontario. ‡ July 3: **Commemoration of Champlain's founding of Québec City**. ‡ Early July: **Québec International Summer Festival**, with concerts, performances and folkloric events at venues all over Québec City. ‡ Mid-July: **Annual Toronto Outdoor Art Exhibition** at City Hall's Nathan Phillips Square, with more than 500 Canadian and foreign artists competing for prizes; **Molson Indy auto race** on Lakeshore Blvd. in Toronto. ‡ Mid-July: **Just For Laughs Festival** in Montréal, with international comedians performing in French and English. ‡ Late July-early Aug: **Caribana**, a celebration of Caribbean music and culture in Toronto, with parades, pageants and dances at many locations throughout the city.

August
Early Aug: **The Americas Cycling Grand Prix**, a World Cup event in Montréal. ‡ Early to mid-Aug: **Player's International Tennis Championships** in Montréal and Toronto, with top male and female athletes competing in each city in alternate years. ‡ Mid-Aug to early Sept: **Canadian National Exhibition**, a major agricultural fair in Toronto; **Expo-Québec**, a similar event, with rides and entertainment, in Québec City. ‡ Late Aug: **The Canadian Open golf championship** at Glen Abbey Golf Club in Toronto. ‡ Late Aug to early Sept: **World Film Festival** in Montréal.

September
Early Sept: **Festival of Festivals**, international films at cinemas throughout Toronto; **The Molson Export Challenge**, a thoroughbred race, with the largest prize in North America, at Woodbine Race Track in Toronto; **Québec International Film Festival**, emphasizing French-language films. ‡ Early Sept: **Montréal Marathon**, with more than 12,000 runners; **Montréal International Music Festival**, focusing on classical music.

October
Early Oct, continuing till Apr: **opening of professional hockey season** for Toronto Maple Leafs, Montréal Canadiens and Québec Nordiques. ‡ Late Oct: **Montréal International Festival of New Cinema and Video.**

November
Early to mid-Nov: **The Royal Agricultural Winter Fair** at Exhibition Place in Toronto; **The Annual Santa Claus Parade** in Toronto; **The Vanier Cup** Canadian University Football Championship in Toronto.

December
Early Dec: **Québec Crafts Show**. ‡ Dec 31: **New Year's Eve celebration** in Nathan Phillips Square, Toronto.

Toronto

Great cities stimulate epigrammists and myth-makers. Toronto qualified for inclusion in the world's urban elite at least two decades ago. That was a fact certified by the swarms of social scientists and visionaries who tumbled over each other seeking fresh superlatives to describe her. Among them, one Anthony Astrachan came closest when he proclaimed in 1974 that Toronto is "a city that works." That it does, by nearly every legitimate measure. One of the largest cities in North America, it can claim virtues that may be forever beyond the grasp of its sisters south of the border. Its inhabitants represent every race and major ethnic group on the face of the earth, yet tensions between them barely exist, in part because all are alert to the merest twinges of abrasion, and rush to polish them smooth. They can choose to walk across a mile or two of 8,700 acres of parkland at midnight and be virtually assured of returning intact, not having experienced even a harsh word.

Toronto enjoys a singular prosperity brought by the presence of Canada's most aggressive corporations and industries, but growth is controlled and sensitive to the will of its citizens. For example, few downtown skyscrapers exceed 50 stories, and all new development must incorporate housing as well as office space. The closest it comes to the Hogarthian slums that afflict most cities in the hemisphere are working-class neighborhoods that are merely shabby, not crime-ridden or without hope.

Toronto is tidy and untroubling, and mindful of the needs of its people and its visitors. The worst thing about it is its tinge of smugness. But then it does have quite a lot to be smug about.

This level of exemplary urbanity was achieved only with the aid of historical accident and twists of fortune. The site was first visited by Champlain's lieutenant, Étienne Brûlé, in 1610-11. "Toronto," aptly enough, was Huron for "meeting place." Few paid much attention to the area, a flat plain on the northern shore of Lake Ontario, until the British sought a more secure location for the capital of their new colony of Upper Canada. The old one was too close to the enemy — the young United States. Governor John Graves Simcoe was hardly enthused about his choice. "The city's site was better calculated for a frog pond than for the residence of human beings," he wrote. Despite that estimation, he proceeded, with more than a little perverse doggedness, to build a fort and start a settlement, which he named after the Duke of York. Its few dirt streets were a constant quagmire, hence its first appellation, "Muddy York."

In 1834, it was incorporated as a city under its Indian name. One of the earliest industries was livestock slaughtering, leading to the sobriquet "Hogtown," which name was hardly an improvement. Nor was the overweening English majority as tolerant as they were much later to become. Even Scots had to contend with second-class status. Protestant notions of probity and rectitude clamped a dour morality on the city, which then came to be known as "Toronto the Good." Right up until World War II, 80 percent of the population was Anglo-Saxon. Postwar immigration dramatically changed that. Nearly a million immigrants arrived — Asians, West Indians, Eastern and Southern Europeans. By 1977, they and thousands of refugees from ominously separatist Québec had made their new city the largest in Canada. In the process, they imposed a cultural vivacity that was the last ingredient needed to make Toronto the Good downright endearing.

Getting around

From the airports to the city
Lester B. Pearson International Airport accommodates both domestic and foreign flights. The 18-mile trip to downtown takes 30-60mins, depending on traffic, and the least expensive carrier is Grey Coach Lines. Coaches depart 2 or 3 times an hour between early morning and midnight and drop passengers at several downtown hotels. (The list and number of hotels served change with some regularity, so inquire before boarding.) Those who wish to save a few dollars over even this relatively low fare can

take Grey Coach to the Yorkdale, York Mills or Islington subway stations and transfer to the train, which terminates at Wilson station. Some hotels provide a shuttle service; ask when booking. Travelers with heavy luggage or in groups of two or more may prefer taxis, which are not unusually expensive. Limousines cost somewhat more. If renting a car at the airport, obtain a road map and directions before leaving. Toronto Island Airport handles short commuter flights from other Canadian cities and from several US cities including Newark. It is reached by a ferry that docks at the foot of Bathurst St.

Public transportation

There is no finer mass transit system in North America. Subway trains are swift, quiet, and brightly polished as new pennies. Even the platforms are immaculate. There are two lines, one running E-W, the other a N-S loop that reaches Union Station and then bends back. Most of the center city is therefore accessible. But greater Toronto sprawls, with many attractions and some hotels well beyond the reach of the subway. So, the Toronto Transit Commission fills in the gaps with bus and trolley lines. Transfers between buses and subways are free, but a ticket must be obtained from the bus driver or the machines near subway turnstiles. Drivers of buses and streetcars do not carry cash, and fares must be in exact change, token or ticket, on sale at subway entrances and designated stores. Modest discounts are available when purchasing two or more tickets. Passes for unlimited Sun and holiday travel are available to couples and families. Trains operate Mon-Sat 6am-1.30am, Sun 9am-1.30am.

Taxis

As tempting as it is simply to hail a cab when exiting a hotel, it is wise to know in advance the distance to a desired destination. A trip from downtown to, say, the Zoo, takes about an hour, a costly undertaking, although for shorter hauls, cabs are no more expensive than in most North American or European cities. Many are dispatched by radio and can be summoned fairly quickly by telephone. Cabstands are found outside large hotels and at subway stations, and taxis can be flagged anywhere.

Private and rental cars

Most streets are wide and drivers are generally courteous. The only serious congestion is at rush hours and in the downtown commercial district, where parking is difficult and rather expensive. Right turns can be made at red lights after coming to a full stop, unless otherwise indicated. It is best to use a car only for attractions in outlying districts. Car rental isn't prohibitive, and there are also weekend discounts and unlimited mileage plans.

Useful addresses

Tourist information

By telephone or mail, contact the **Metropolitan Toronto Convention and Visitors Association** (*P.O Box 126, 207 Queen's Quay W, Toronto, Ontario M5J 1A7* ☎ *368-9821*). Or, dial the **Infoline** (☎ *979-3143*).

For in-person inquiries, there is a permanent **Visitor Information Centre** outside Eaton Centre, on Yonge St., S of Dundas. Open daily, with slightly shorter hours in winter. Six other seasonal centers (*open May-Sept*) are found at various locations around town, including at Nathan Phillips Square, the ferry docks for the Toronto Islands and the CN Tower.

American Express Canada has its main office and Travel Service at 101 McNab St (*general inquiries* ☎ *474-8000, Travel Service* ☎ *474-8350*). To report lost American Express cards ☎ 474-9280.

Main post offices
595 Bay St. (Dundas)   Open Mon-Wed, Sat 10am-6pm, Thurs, Fri 10am-9pm
100 King St. (Bay)   Open Mon-Fri 10am-6pm, Sat 10am-5pm

Telephone services
Concerts   ☎ 870-9119
Road conditions   ☎ 966-3000
Sports   ☎ 964-8655
Weather   ☎ 676-3066

Tour operators
Grey Line   610 Bay St. ☎ 979-3511. Bus tours.
Happy Days Tours   220 Yonge St. ☎ 593-6220. 4hr tours twice daily, pickup at major hotels.
Just Looking   51 Alexander St. ☎ 923-2202. "Step-on" guides using client's car.
National Helicopters   4078 Highway #7 W, Woodbridge ☎ 851-4815. Helicopter rides.
Toronto By Trolley Car   134 Jarvis St. ☎ 869-1372. 1½hr tours on restored old streetcars.

Emergency information

Police, fire, ambulance   ☎ 911

Hospitals with emergency rooms
Doctors Hospital   45 Brunswick St. ☎ 923-5411
Hospital for Sick Children   55 University Ave. ☎ 597-1500
Mount Sinai Hospital   600 University Ave. ☎ 596-4200
St Michael's Hospital   30 Bond St. ☎ 360-4000
Toronto General Hospital   200 Elizabeth St. ☎ 595-3111
Toronto Western Hospital   399 Bathurst St. ☎ 368-2581
Wellesley Hospital   160 Wellesley St. E ☎ 966-6600

Dental emergencies
1650 Yonge St ☎ 485-7121. Open Sun-Thurs 9am-1am, Fri-Sat 10am-2am. For referrals ☎ 967-5649.

Pharmacies open 24hrs
Owl Drug   68 Wellesley St. ☎ 266-8724
Shoppers Drug Mart   700 Bay St. ☎ 979-2424

Help lines
Animal emergencies   ☎ 226-3663 or 222-5409
AIDS Hotline   ☎ 392-AIDS
Alcoholics Anonymous   ☎ 487-5591
Emergency referral Community services and crisis intervention   ☎ 863-0505
Poison information centers   ☎ 598-5900 or 469-6245
Rape   ☎ 597-8808
Suicide/Distress   ☎ 598-1121 or 486-1456

TORONTO/ORIENTATION AND WALKS

Toronto Downtown Heliport   55 Unwin Ave. ☎461-4633. Sightseeing flights, special charters available.
Toronto On Foot   39 Leuty Ave. ☎690-1396.
Toronto Sites   31 Parkview Gardens ☎247-1544. Individualized tours.
Toronto Sky Tours   123 Ramona Blvd. ☎471-7664. Various sightseeing flights.
Tour de Ville   40 Bay St. ☎457-1831. "Step-on" guides speaking French, English and German.

Harbor cruises
Adventures Afloat   Pier 6, foot of York St. ☎368-2358. 4 departures daily for 1½hr cruises.
Grey Line Harbour & Island Tours   5 Queen's Quay W ☎364-2412. 1hr cruises in glass-topped boats.
"Oriole"   207 Queen's Quay E ☎366-2626. 1hr tours and dinner-and-dance cruises.
Toronto Boat Cruises at Harbourfront. 283A Queen's Quay W ☎364-4664. Narrated 1½hr harbor cruises.

Library
Metropolitan Toronto Reference Library   789 Yonge St. ☎393-7000. Collection of 1.3 million volumes. Open daily.

Local publications
The Globe and Mail is a national newspaper with an emphasis on business and international news, delivered in a tone some think is responsible, others, stuffy. Its big issue is Sat, as it is not published Sun. *The Toronto Star* has a larger circulation, although it focuses more heavily on local and provincial matters. Its style is lively, with a lingering liberal tinge. For visitors, the Fri "What's On" section is a must. Published daily. Fans of garish right-wing tabloids have *The Toronto Sun*, big on sports and sensation. *NOW* and *Metropolis* are weekly giveaway tabloids about entertainment events. Another source of news and reviews is the slick *Toronto Life*, a plump monthly magazine devoted to the good life.

Orientation

Metropolitan Toronto enjoys an enlightened form of cooperative regional government that incorporates five cities and nine other municipalities. This allows the planning and distribution of such public services as mass transit, roads and water supply with fewer of the divisive battles over jurisdiction that afflict other metropolitan areas. It is, however, an entity that spreads over 240 square miles, and that can cause disorientation and a tendency to underestimate distances.

The City of Toronto is only one of the constituent parts of Metro Toronto, albeit the most important. At its core, the streets are easy enough to negotiate. With some exceptions, they are laid out in a predictable grid. The lake is on the s, easily located by the landmark CN Tower, and the land slopes upward to the N. Yonge St. is the dividing line between E and W. Signs for streets running E to W are yellow; those N and S are blue. Most, but by no means all, of the hotels and attractions of interest to visitors are within a rectangle starting a few blocks N of Bloor down to the waterfront and from Bathurst St. to Jarvis. It can easily be covered by combinations of subway and walking.

The waterfront has received much attention in recent years, with ongoing redevelopment intended to enhance access to the lake. A string of barrier islands all but enclose the harbor and provide recreational areas with beaches, boating, picnic areas and cycling paths. To the W of downtown, on or near the water, are the *Marine Museum* and *Ontario Place*, man-made islands with an open-air auditorium, a children's village and a decommissioned navy destroyer. Not far away is the reconstructed *Fort York*. **Harbourfront** is a series of piers with a growing number of shops, restaurants and marinas, separated from the downtown district by an elevated highway and a swath of cleared land awaiting construction.

The edge of the **Financial District** is defined by the highway and the *CN Tower* and new *SkyDome*, a sports stadium with a retractable roof. Nearby is venerable **Union Station**, backed by gleaming multistory testimony in glass to the city's commercial clout. Next, a few more blocks N, is the **City Hall District**, which takes in **Eaton Centre**, an extremely busy and justly famous enclosed shopping mall. Most of the larger hotels are located in this area. And beneath this entire downtown district lie the concourses of Toronto's own **underground city**, less celebrated but far larger than the one in Montréal. To the W of City Hall are the newish *Art Gallery of Ontario* and *Chinatown*, one of North America's largest Asian communities.

In and around central Queen's Park are the **Ontario Legislative Buildings**, the *Royal Ontario Museum*, *McLaughlin Planetarium*, the *Gardiner Museum of Ceramic Art* and, on the W, the campus of the prestigious **University of Toronto**. Across Bloor St., with its string of large department stores, is **Yorkville**, one of the first center city neighborhoods to be gentrified in the 1960s, its blocks of sandblasted brick row houses now home to upscale shops, restaurants and bars. It also has a number of hotels, including the posh **Four Seasons**.

There is more. **Queen St**. W of University is blossoming into an appealing semibohemian enclave of galleries, bistros and boutiques. The superb *Metro Zoo*, the *Ontario Science Centre* and stately *Casa Loma* are all in districts outside center city, but justify the longer treks.

Walks in Toronto

Sprawling though it is, Toronto remains a city hospitable to the inveterate walker. Due to citizen insistence on preservation of tradition and maintenance of green spaces, as well as the multiple uses required of new developments, it avoids numbing anonymity, rarely losing its human face. The following suggested routes pass many recommended sights, with ample opportunities for window shopping and resting in parks and cafés.

Walk 1: Downtown and Chinatown
Maps 4&5. Subway: Union Station.

Start with an exhilarating ascent to the highest vantage point in the city, and end with lunch in bustling Chinatown.

Start at the corner of Front St. and John St., two long blocks W of Union Station. Right there is the entrance to **SkyWalk**, a covered passage that leads to the base of the *CN Tower*. The

Toronto/Orientation and walks

Toronto orientation map

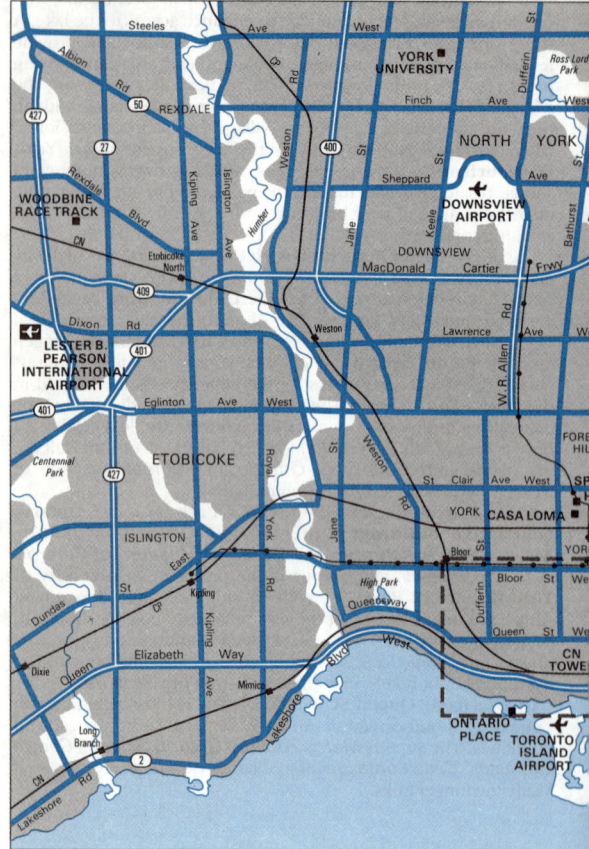

needle-like concrete and metal structure caused — and still causes — as much controversy as Eiffel's tower, but ungainly as it is, there is no arguing with its claim to the most compelling views in Toronto. Keeping in mind that it is definitely not an undertaking for the vertiginous, take the glass-sided elevator on a 58-second zoom to the "Space Pod," the bulbous observation platform about two-thirds the way up its 1,815ft height. That is enough to see, on the proverbial clear day, the mists of Niagara Falls, 75 miles SE. For an extra fee, another elevator carries the compulsive another 33 stories higher. That deck is well above the planes taking off at Toronto Island Airport, and provides forever vistas of lake and parklands and, far below, the bristling skyscrapers of the financial district. The descent is no less electrifying.

Return by the SkyWalk to Front St., turning right (E). In two blocks, the massive Royal York Hotel faces **Union Station**, a

Orientation and walks/Toronto

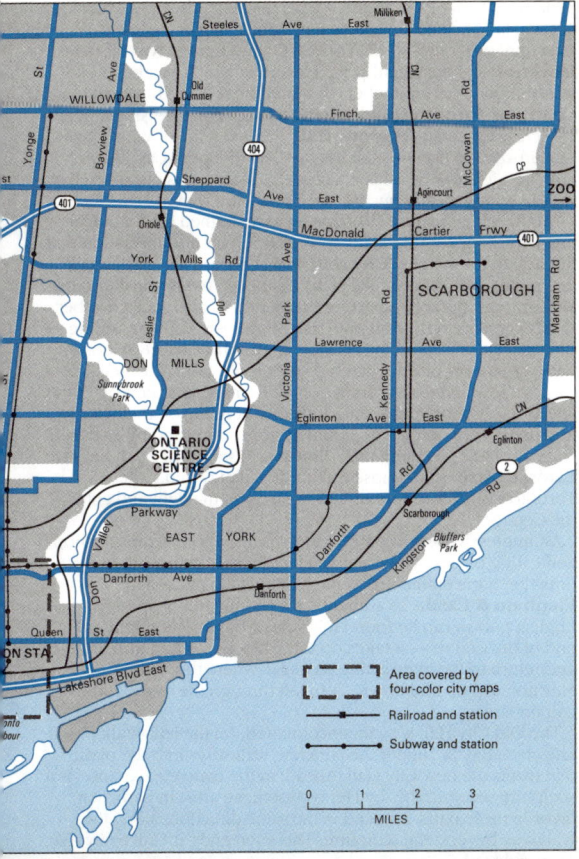

Neo-Classical terminal completed in 1920. Railroad and architecture buffs will want to detour through the columned portico for a look at the restored Great Hall, an arched concourse 88ft high. Then, continue E on Front to Bay St. Opposite is the **Royal Bank Plaza** building. The glass sides of its two triangular towers have a golden cast, as well they might, given the reported inclusion of real gold dust in their fabrication. It literally and figuratively outshines its green neighbor, the new **Canada Trust Tower**. Cross Front St., heading N.

In two blocks, turn left (W) on King St. On the left are the paired bronze slabs of the **Toronto-Dominion Centre**. If it seems reminiscent of the Seagram Building in New York, which is routinely given accolades as the highest expression of minimalist Bauhaus principles, there is a reason: Ludwig Mies van der Rohe was the architect of both. Opposite are the two towers of **First Canadian Place**, a less esthetically pleasing

Toronto/Orientation and walks

statement, but the home of the new *Stock Exchange* and one of the entrances to *Underground Toronto*. The subterranean pedestrian mall of shops and restaurants extends several blocks N to City Hall and S to Union Station. Continuing in the same direction, turn right (N) on York St. On the right in two blocks is **Mövenpick**, a busy, mid-priced eatery in which to take refreshment or to remember for a later meal. The **Sheraton Centre of Toronto Hotel** is at the corner of intersecting Queen St. Across Queen is **Osgoode Hall**, the first wing of which was built in 1832 as home to the Law Society of Upper Canada. A high iron fence surrounds it, erected to keep cows out when that was an annoyance in bucolic old York. Turn right (E) on Queen.

On the left is **Nathan Phillips Square**, named for Toronto's first Jewish mayor (1955-62). It was during his administration that the design for the new **City Hall** was chosen. That's it beyond his square, two semicircular slabs of uneven height surrounding a mushroom pod of a structure that serves as a council chamber. In between is a reflecting pool that becomes a popular skating rink in winter. Continuing on Queen, the **Old City Hall** looms, with the steeply pitched green copper roofs, conical turrets, campanile and rounded arches of the Romanesque Revival of the late 19thC. Continuing E, the sandstone building on the right is **Simpson's**, an old-line department store connected by enclosed walkways to its retailing rival, **Eaton's**. More precisely, it links to **Eaton Centre**, a grandiose indoor mall that is said to be Toronto's biggest tourist attraction. Cross at the light and enter the Centre.

An impressive skylit central gallery is lined with scores of shops and eating places vying for consideration. Stroll in a northerly direction. One entrance that might attract the eye is **The Elephant & Castle**, as authentic a reproduction of an olde English pub as can be found this side of Blighty. Continue to the end of the Centre — it takes up three blocks — then turn around and return to the intersecting passages where three glass elevators zip up and down. Turn left through the exit marked "Albert Street."

The Old City Hall is again encountered, on the left. Walk past it and cross Bay St., under the concrete walkways into the plaza that fronts the new City Hall. Ahead, in the concrete expanse, is a sculpture recognizably by Henry Moore, an artist in particular favor in these parts. Proceed in the same direction, along the walkway beyond the sculpture. This soon ends at University Ave. Turn right (N).

At the intersection with Dundas, cross University, heading W. In three blocks, another large Moore announces the presence of the *Art Gallery of Ontario*, widely known by its acronym, AGO. The museum casts a wide net in its chosen field, exhibiting Egyptiana, Rembrandt, Inuit sculptures, Gainsborough, Van Gogh and many more Moores. An extra wing has now been added to house the expanding collection. Around back, and included in the entrance fee, is **The Grange**, an 1817 Georgian residence of understated wealth from the era of the Family Compact. Opposite the AGO entrance are two possible lunch or dinner stops, **Tall Poppies** (*#326*) and **The Mermaid** (*#300*).

Continue W on Dundas and it is soon apparent that this is Toronto's celebrated *Chinatown*. Ginseng parlors crowd greengrocers selling *bok choy* and ginger root, interspersed by herbalists, and windows hung with roast ducks. This is, actually, the *new* Chinatown, relocated over 25yrs ago from its former habitat at the site of the new City Hall. By the evidence of the

Orientation and walks/Toronto

distinctive Korean script and the numbers of Thai and Vietnamese shops and restaurants, the name of the neighborhood is no longer precise.

The corner of Dundas and Spadina is the main intersection of the district. Down to the left (s) is a cluster of fur and leather merchants. Continuing, cross over and turn right (N). Soon, amid all the Asian exotica, is a survivor from the time when this was the largely Jewish garment district: **Switzer's Delicatessen** (*#322*). If egg rolls and Szechuan chicken don't appeal, here is an alternative for *knishes*, *latkes* and overstuffed sandwiches.

Two blocks farther along is Baldwin St. Turn left and be transported into the Alfama quarter of Lisbon. This is **Kensington Market**, a chaotic, pungent jumble of fish stores, cafés, and indoor and outdoor food stalls. While it has a pronounced Portuguese flavor, there are harmonious intrusions by merchants of Latin American, West Indian and Asian heritage. The market area — nearly as residential as it is commercial — is busiest in the mornings and on Fri and Sat, when stocks are at their freshest and most abundant. Back on Spadina, dozens of restaurants contend for business, with bargain midday prices. Among the better choices are **Chung King** (*#428*), **Hunan Palace** (*#412*), **Kom Jug Yuen** (*#371*), **Lee Garden** (*#358*) and **The Great Wall** (*#442*).

Walk 2: Midtown and Yorkville
Maps 4&5. Subway: Queen's Park.

The admirable Torontonian penchant for restraint in the rush to what developers allege to be progress is documented by this, the city's most compelling argument for that rare form of neighborhood planning that is responsive to the needs of the people living within it. So here there are homes where another metropolis might have dehumanizing high-rises, and shops where the clerks know customers by name, yet all of it with a gloss and panache that is a magnet for suburbanites and tourists.

Begin from the Queen's Park subway station, taking the N exit. Straight ahead is the **Ontario Legislative Building**, a Romanesque pile of red-brown sandstone completed in 1892. University Ave. splits to go round the building on each side. Bear left, past the greenhouses at the edge of the campus of the University of Toronto. The University, founded in 1827, has schools and colleges in every major academic field. It nearly surrounds Queen's Park, in which the Parliament is located, but the larger part of it stretches to the W and N.

Soon, walking N along what is here called Queen's Park Crescent W, is the **Sigmund Samuel Building** (*#14*). A unit of the *Royal Ontario Museum*, it houses a collection of Canadiana and holds frequent special exhibitions (☎ *586-5551, open Mon-Sat 10am-5pm, Sun 1pm-5pm* 💽). After a visit, cross the road — carefully — to the **Legislative Building**, taking the sidewalk that leads past the front portico. The colorful lobby with its grand staircase is in marked contrast to the somber exterior. The walk passes between statues of John S. MacDonald, first premier (1867-71) of Ontario after confederation, and a seated Queen Victoria. Turn left (N) at the end of the building.

The next street is Wellesley. Cross over and bear left into the park, an oasis of trees and lawn set with benches and picnic tables. Joggers, lovers, pigeons and Toronto's indigenous fat black squirrels are peaceful cohabitants. At the equestrian statue of the plump King Edward VII, veer along the northerly path in the direction he faces. This comes, at the far end of the park, to a

Toronto/Orientation and walks

granite monument to the Canadian dead of many wars. Cross over Queen's Park Crescent to the W side of what soon becomes Avenue Road (yes, that's the full official name). Shortly, the *McLaughlin Planetarium* appears on the left. An excellent facility, it draws more than 250,000 visitors a year. The next building, adjoining, is the **Royal Ontario Museum**, Toronto's principal showcase of art, archeology, paleontology and the life sciences. It deserves at least an hour. Upon leaving, the **George R. Gardiner Museum of Ceramic Art** is seen across the street. For safety's sake, go to the next corner (Bloor St.), cross over, and walk back. And keep the ROM ticket — it covers same-day admission to the Gardiner, which is far from being simply a collection of plates and vases. One of the most interesting sections is of figurative Pre-Columbian pottery.

After the Gardiner, turn right (N), cross Bloor and walk along Avenue Road two blocks to Yorkville Ave., marked by the luxury **Four Seasons Hotel**. Turn right (E). This is the main street of Yorkville, liveliest when residents have stored overcoats away for the summer. Most of the buildings lining each side are sandblasted 4- or 5-story row houses, salvaged nearly three decades ago when adventurous members of the Love Generation were seeking affordable housing. Rents are no longer cheap, for these are now the two most upscale blocks in midtown. Many of the cafés and bistros along the way have outdoor terraces or balconies, the better to observe the procession of fit and fashionable young. There are, as is to be expected in such a milieu, *sushi* bars, unisex hair salons, *shiatsu* massage parlors, cappuccino houses and fitness spas. But **Meyer's** delicatessen is there too (#69), an unlikely venue for late-night jazz, and so is **Lovecraft** (#63), a tasteful purveyor of erotic toys and underwear with at least as many women patrons as men. Across from the uptown branch of the Mövenpick chain is **La Maison de la Presse Internationale**, with abundant Canadian and foreign magazines and newspapers. In good weather, Yorkville is a corridor of street musicians, caricaturists, mimes, and other performers and hustlers not always easy to classify.

Yonge St. is the next important street when heading E. The "longest street in the world" runs for 1,078 miles, starting at the waterfront and keeping on going all the way to Hudson Bay. Yorkville can dismay with its rampant consumption, but the antidote lies right across the way. It is the *Metropolitan Toronto Reference Library*. Few libraries are as animated as this one, whose main atrium, with fountains and glass-bubble elevators gliding silently up and down, more closely resembles a rather glitzy hotel lobby. Its message, not the medium, is serious — it has 1.3 million books and about 10,000 audio cassettes.

Outside the library, turn S on Yonge. A restaurant called **Metropolis** (#838) gets good notices for its "New Canadian" food, with a menu that sounds suspiciously like a California import. Turn right (W) on Bloor. Through here, it is a spangled canyon of department stores and malls — Holt Renfrew, The Bay, Birks Jewelers — and European boutiques — Chanel, Cartier, Gucci, Charles Jourdan, Georg Jensen. Back at Avenue Road, turn left to pick up the subway near the entrance to the Royal Ontario Museum.

And elsewhere...

But these two walks hardly exhaust the city's ambulatory charms. **Queen St. W**, between Spadina St. and John St., is a funky, youthful hodgepodge of offbeat shops and bistros (look

SIGHTS AND PLACES OF INTEREST/TORONTO

in *Shopping*). The blocks around **Bloor St.** and **Bathurst St.** are a multi-ethnic rainbow of people and enterprises, among them Poles, Lebanese, Pakistanis, Brazilians, Koreans, Greeks and Egyptians. And *Cabbagetown* is a newly-gentrified neighborhood of once humble 19thC houses not far from Yorkville; start exploring from Parliament and Carlton.

Sights and places of interest

In linguistically bipolar Canada, Toronto occupies the summit of Anglophone culture. It doesn't have the age of Montréal, and its historic buildings rarely predate the 1830s. But it compensates with enticing neighborhoods populated by more than 70 identifiable ethnic groups, and its heritage includes the gifts of two centuries of prosperous individuals of Anglo-Saxon ancestry. Much of this accumulation is on display in its several good-to-excellent museums, at least three of which merit repeat visits.

There are logistics to remember. Public transportation is available to virtually every major and secondary attraction, but Metro Toronto is so large that a car is desirable for such worthwhile out-of-the-way destinations as the *Metro Zoo*, the *McMichael Collection* and *Black Creek Pioneer Village*. In the listing below, the indicated subway stops are those *nearest* the attraction, and a long walk or transfer to bus or streetcar may then be required. The closest cross street follows each address in parentheses, when applicable. Even those sights open seven days a week close for Christmas, and Sunday hours usually apply on holidays. Some lesser attractions are mentioned in the larger entries below or in *Walks*: find them through the *Index*.

Art Gallery of Ontario
317 Dundas St. W (McCall) ☎ *977-0414. Map 4G3* 🗺 *(* 📷 *Wed after 5.30pm)* 🍴 🛒 *Open June-Sept Tues, Thurs-Sun 11am-5.30pm, Wed 11am-9pm; Mon 11am-5.30pm; Oct-May closed Mon. Subway: St Patrick.*

Few museums are as blessed with such a large body of work by a major contemporary artist. British sculptor Henry Moore bequeathed 101 of his sculptures and 57 drawings to AGO and worked closely with architect John C. Parkin in the design of the stunning pavilion, opened in 1974, that now houses the collection. A massive sculpture by Moore, *Large Two Forms*, outside at the NE corner of the museum, hints at the riches within. Impressive as these works are, though, there is much more to AGO. Its permanent collection totals more than 12,000 pieces and continues to grow. Nor is it confined to 20thC art, although that is its strength.

Gallery talks are held daily in the lobby. Just beyond, in Walker Court, large Abstract-Expressionist canvases by Ellsworth Kelly, Kenneth Nolan, Sam Francis, Larry Poons and Franz Kline are interspersed with bronzes by Rodin, Degas and Matisse, an enlightening juxtaposition. An Old Masters gallery shows paintings by 17th and 18thC artists reminiscent of those of better-known contemporaries. A well-lit Francesco de Mura, for example, could almost be a minor Rubens. Gallery #10 moves forward in history, with works by such turn-of-the-century innovators as Dufy, Braque, Bonnard, Picasso, Degas and Renoir. Also shown are paintings of the Group of Seven, who were in the

Toronto/Black Creek Pioneer Village

vanguard of a 20thC Canadian movement (see *The arts*, page 17). The ramp leading to the 2nd floor displays small pieces by British modernists of various schools.

Then follows the **Moore Sculpture Centre**. Light falls through skylights in a coffered ceiling upon an array of instantly recognizable sculptures that reveal the master's breadth. Those who think immediately of simple biomorphic shapes in connection with Moore may be surprised to see the remarkable variety of motifs and sizes and the range of materials in which he worked during his career. That exceptional room is linked, by a corridor of more French Post-Impressionists, with a gallery of Inuit prints.

AGO is under expansion, in a project that will increase the total exhibition area by 50 percent. Its full-service restaurant is superior to those usually operated within museums. Connected to the museum in back, in still another telling contrast, is **The Grange**, a Georgian mansion restored and furnished as a gentleman's residence of 1835.

Black Creek Pioneer Village
Jane St. and Steeles Ave. (1000 Murray Ross Parkway) ☎ *661-6610. Map 6B3 ▨ Open mid-March to Dec 31 daily; hours vary. Subway: Jane, then Jane 35B bus.*

Costumed "townspeople" bring this re-created rural 19thC village to life. In more than 30 restored buildings they demonstrate the crafts and skills necessary to the good life and simple survival in young Canada — tinsmithing, weaving, cooking, farming, cabinet-making. Blacksmiths fashion tools and horseshoes, women quilt patchwork coverlets, workers grind grains in the authentic grist mill. In summer, a bagpipe-led contingent of the 78th Fraser Highlanders performs military drills and exercises on the village green, and the calendar is dotted with such special events as "sugaring-off" maple trees, an Easter egg hunt and a Victorian country wedding. As it is 30-45mins from downtown, an excursion might be combined with a visit to *Canada's Wonderland*, about 10mins away.

Cabbagetown
Map 5H3. Subway: Carlton, then a walk E on Carlton St.

The name derives from the 19thC Irish immigrant custom of planting lawns with vegetables rather than grass and flowers. It was developed initially in the 1850s as clusters of modest stone and frame dwellings, but more elaborate architectural styles were later introduced. A gentrification process has lately taken hold, with more affluent, younger people taking over from the older residents. The district is seen to good advantage along Carlton St., Aberdeen St. and Winchester St., between Bleeker St. and Parliament St.

Campbell House
160 Queen St. W (University) ☎ *597-0227. Map 4G4 ▨ Open Mon-Fri 9.30-11.30am, 2.30-4.30pm, Sat-Sun noon-4.30pm. Subway: Osgoode.*

One of the earliest brick houses (1822) when the town was still called York, this was the home of an immigrant Scot who eventually became a chief justice and was knighted by the Crown. Originally located in Old Town, E of the present financial district, it was moved here in 1972 to save it from demolition. A fine example of late Georgian residential architecture, it might have always occupied its present site, an iron fence surrounding its plot of trees and grass. The Ontario Advocate Society of lawyers restored and furnished it for use as a meeting place.

Canada Sports Hall of Fame
Exhibition Place ☎ *595-1046. Map 2C5 ◉ Open 10am-4.30pm. Subway: Bathurst, then #511 streetcar.*
Canadian heroes in all sports but hockey (see *Hockey Hall of Fame* below) are remembered in rooms crowded with nostalgia. Terry Fox, the disabled athlete who ran across Canada, is among those honored.

Canada's Wonderland
Highway 400 and Rutherford Rd. ☎ *832-2205. Map 6B2 ◉ ▬ ✳ Open May 30-Sept 4 daily, Sept and last 2wks in May weekends only.*
To some, it might seem there is a surfeit of amusement and theme parks in the Toronto area. If there is time for only one, this is the choice, and the better part of a day should be allowed. Few possibilities for diversion are left unexploited. In seven themed areas spread over 370 acres, there are heart-stopping roller coasters — The Bat and SkyRider test any *aficionado*'s mettle — precipitous water-slides, live shows and concerts, restaurants, performing dolphins and sea lions, street performers, fireworks, laser displays, even a 150ft-high artificial mountain. Two areas are intended specifically for younger children, where they can take rides mild enough not to frighten but exciting enough to be memorable. Smurfs and Yogi Bear and other cartoon characters greet them along the way, and blue ice cream is a favorite treat. An all-day "Passport" ticket is available to adults and their kids, providing unlimited use of rides and shows at a substantial discount (but not including food, merchandise, or entrance to the Kingswood Music Theatre, where concerts are held).

Canadiana Collection/Sigmund Samuel Building
14 Queen's Crescent W (College) ☎ *586-5524. Map 4G2 ◉ Open Mon-Sat 10am-5pm, Sun 1-5pm. Subway: Queen's Park.*
An annex of the Royal Ontario Museum on the University of Toronto campus, the collection is an under-appreciated trove of pioneer crafts and furniture, decorative arts, and paintings and sculptures by Canadian artists, mostly from the 19thC. Included are delightful folk-art objects — weathervanes, toys, kitchenware — as well as utilitarian pottery, clocks, miniatures, and superbly pure examples of handmade chairs and storage units.

Casa Loma
1 Austin Terrace (Spadina) ☎ *923-1171. Map 4F1 ◉ Open daily 10am-4pm except major holidays. Subway: Dupont, then Davenport #127 bus.*
Few stately homes, even in Europe, can match this for size, and not many surpass it in grandeur. It was contracted by financier-industrialist Sir Henry Pellatt in 1911 and completed 3yrs later. Among its marvels are 98 rooms paneled in oak, walnut, teak and mahogany and lavishly furnished with imports and antiques; 45 bathrooms and 23 fireplaces; hidden passages and staircases; a 100,000-book library; an immense pipe organ in a ballroom that could hold 3,000 partygoers; and an 800ft tunnel leading through a huge wine cellar to a stable where 20 prize horses were quartered. Much of the building was imported from Scotland and reassembled by Scottish masons, which doesn't explain the

Spanish-sounding name. Indeed, the origin of the name remains a mystery.

From the outside, it looks very much the baronial residence, with battlements, squared chimneys and medieval conical turrets. Built for $3 million on a hill, its terraces offer views of the downtown skyline, many miles away. The castle couldn't be reproduced today for ten times the price. Even then, maintenance of his treasure was Pellatt's undoing. What proved to be his folly was taken over by the city in lieu of unpaid taxes in 1924.

On a self-guided tour, tape machines describe each room. A visit can be combined with one to another mansion, **Spadina House**, a short distance away.

CN Tower
301 Front St. W (John) ☎ *360-8500. Map 4G5* 🏛 🍴 *Open June 1-Labor Day Mon-Sat 9am-midnight, Sun 9am-11pm ; Labor Day-May 31 Sun-Fri 10am-10pm, Sat 9.30am-10pm. Subway: Union Station.*

Touted to exhaustion as "the world's tallest free-standing structure," the Tower's only truly practical function is as a mast for TV and radio transmitters. Otherwise, it is in that category of things that must be discussed because it is there. Certainly the food in the requisite revolving restaurant does nothing to bolster the bleak reputation of such enterprises, and few argue that the Tower makes a significant esthetic contribution to either engineering or architecture. Such factors had little to do with it. It amounts to a paean to boosterism, an unignorable symbol to distinguish an attractive but not especially arresting skyline.

Constructed of poured concrete and steel, it took 40 months and $57 million to bring it to completion in 1976. At 1,815ft, the mast dwarfs the 1,454ft Sears Tower in Chicago, presently the world's tallest skyscraper: the reason for the CN Tower's "free-standing" qualification is that it has no guy wires. There is a 7-story "Spacepod" two-thirds of the way up, where the restaurant, a nightclub, and indoor and outdoor observation decks are housed. The elevators are glass on one side, affording continuous views throughout the 58-second ascent. Their young operators are either directed by their supervisors or are merely self-compelled to make such obvious jokes as where the parachutes are stored. From the first observation deck, another elevator carries the willing or the uninformed to a second, higher belvedere — the "Space Deck," 1,465ft high. Its glass windows bank inward, so it is possible to gaze straight down, practically between toes, should one care to do so. This is not — *not* — an adventure to be undertaken by those who suffer even mild vertigo.

All these reservations aside, the panorama is undeniably impressive, more than 100 miles in radius under perfect conditions, across the lake to the s, beyond the northern rim of the city and even down to Niagara Falls on the horizon.

Chinatown
Map 4F3. Subway: St Patrick, then walk w on Dundas.

There are an estimated 275,000 Chinese and 250,000 Southeast Asians in Toronto. They gather in five distinct neighborhoods around the city, but the best known is this one, centering on the intersection of Dundas and Spadina. This is actually an artificial site: the original Chinatown was displaced more than 25yrs ago to allow the building of the new City Hall. (See **Walks**, page 36).

Fort York/Toronto

Eaton Centre
Map 5H3.
The large, enclosed shopping mall reminiscent of Milan's Galleria. See *Walks* and *Shopping*.

Exhibition Place
Strachan Ave. and Lakeshore Blvd. ☎ 393-6000. Map 2C5. Ticket prices and hours vary with events scheduled. Subway: Bathurst, then #511 streetcar.
The location for most of the major trade shows and exhibitions, on 350 acres of waterfront land, Exhibition Place is a vast series of connected halls dating from the late 19thC. It is home to the **Canadian National Exhibition** in Aug and early Sept, an extravaganza that incorporates horseshows, agricultural displays, fireworks, and a petting zoo and shows for children. The **Royal Agricultural Winter Fair** in Nov, The **Scottish World Festival Tattoo**, the **Canadian International Air Show**, rock concerts, an annual **Boat Show**, and the **Molson Indy auto race** are all on the schedule (see *Calendar of events*). Even when no such event is taking place, the grounds also contain the *Marine Museum of Upper Canada*, the *Hockey Hall of Fame* and the *Canada Sports Hall of Fame*. Parking is available but is difficult during major shows and exhibitions, when public transportation is preferable.

Fort York
Garrison Rd. and Fleet St. ☎ 392-6907. Map 3E5 ✯ *Open May-Sept Mon-Sat 9.30am-5pm, Sun 9.30am-5pm; Oct-Apr noon-5pm. Subway: Bathurst, then #511 streetcar.*
In 1811, British and American relations were deteriorating, and the existing garrison was strengthened to withstand an anticipated US invasion of Upper Canada (now Ontario). It was positioned to defend what was then the entrance to Toronto Bay. The Americans did attack York, on April 27, 1813, landing a force of 1,750 soldiers from a squadron of 14 vessels. They far outnumbered the defenders, a mixed command of British regulars, militia and Indians, who soon retreated. In a rearguard action, the fort's magazine was blown up, killing or wounding more than 300 Americans and about 150 British soldiers. This "Battle of York" ended soon afterwards. During the subsequent 11-day occupation, there was uncontrolled looting and burning by the victors. Hardly an isolated incident for either side in the American Revolution and War of 1812, it nevertheless provided the justification for the greater depredation of the British when they burned and sacked Washington, DC in 1814.

Fort York was rebuilt between 1813 and 1816, and that is what is on view today, restored for the city's centennial in 1934. There are 8 barracks, blockhouses and magazines within the star-shaped ramparts.

A 12min slide-and-sound presentation skims the history of the site. In the first building of the recommended tour, decidedly Canadian interpretations of history testily describe the battle and American occupations and point out that there were incursions into Canada as late as 1866 and 1870. In those years, an Irish revolutionary organization, the Fenian Brotherhood, led abortive attacks on both American and Canadian targets, somehow imagining that this would help pressure England into giving Ireland its independence. The other buildings hint of how the officers, men, and their families lived, in spare, cramped circumstances.

George R. Gardiner Museum of Ceramic Art
111 Queen's Park (Bloor) ☎ 593-9300. Map 4G1 ▨ (▣ with same-day admission to ROM). Open Tues-Sun 10am-5pm. Subway: Museum.

European ceramics and porcelains of the 15th-18thC comprise the nucleus of the collection of more than 2,000 pieces, including English delftware from the Stuart reign, *maiolica* of the Italian Renaissance, and the popular harlequins inspired by the *Commedia dell'Arte*. At least as impressive is the array of Pre-Columbian pottery on the first floor. The spouted vessels, effigies, funeral urns and plates date from the earliest Olmec civilization and include objects from the Toltec, Mixtec and Aztec cultures. The gift shop sells contemporary ceramics of good quality, but expect no bargains.

The Grange
Grange Park, John St. (Dundas) ☎ 977-0414. Map 4G3 ▨ Entrance through Art Gallery of Ontario. Open Tues, Thurs-Sun 11am-5.30pm, Wed 11am-9pm. Subway: St Patrick.

Said to be the oldest surviving brick residence in Toronto, this relatively modest Georgian house was built in 1817. For a while the home of the Art Gallery of Ontario, it is now restored to a measure of the 1830s elegance associated with residences of the Family Compact oligarchy. Staff members in costumes of the time provide commentary.

Harbourfront
Map 4F6. Harbourfront streetcar from Union Station.

A major project of the ongoing effort to make the waterfront more accessible to residents, Harbourfront is a rejuvenated part of a once-dilapidated waterfront district of warehouses and wharves. The master plan has encouraged mixed-income housing as well as marinas, shops, restaurants and cinemas. Two superior hotels, the **Admiral** and the **Harbour Castle Westin**, anchor each end of the development, which is still a work in progress. (Much of the land backing the waterfront has been cleared of old factories and similar structures, but awaits new construction.) Ferries for the Toronto Islands leave from the dock behind the Westin, and several companies offer lake cruises, especially from **Queen's Quay** (pronounced "key") **Terminal**. That building also has the offices of the **Metropolitan Toronto Convention and Visitors Association**. One seemingly out-of-place attraction is the **Redpath Sugar Museum** (*95 Queen's Quay E ☎ 366-3561, open Mon-Fri 10am-noon, 1-3.30pm*). Sponsored by the sugar-processing company of the same name, it displays artifacts and informational exhibits about the history of the industry. Various events and activities are scheduled throughout the year along Harbourfront, including indoor and outdoor concerts by groups spanning every taste in music, dance and theatrical performances, and film festivals — a total of more than 4,000 events annually.

High Park
Map 6C3. Subway: High Park ✻

One of the most fully utilized parks in a city with an abundance of options, it offers its millions of annual visitors a small zoo (▣), tennis courts, soccer fields, playgrounds, skiing, formal gardens, fishing, a restaurant, boating, and more than 400 acres of shady trees and picnic grounds. Much of the parkland was bequeathed to the city in 1873 by the engineer John Howard. His Regency house, **Colborne Lodge** (☎ 392-6916) *open Mon-Sat 9.30am-5.30pm, Sun noon-5pm)*, is near the s entrance of the park, overlooking Lake Ontario. Included in the original furnishings are Howard's watercolors of mid-19thC Toronto. The costumed staff demonstrates home crafts of the period.

Hockey Hall of Fame
Exhibition Place ☎ 595-1345. Map 2C5 Open Tues-Sun 10am-4.30pm. Subway: Bathurst, then #511 streetcar.
Those who count themselves fans of Canada's violent, graceful national game can revel in memorabilia associated with such past and present legends as Bobby Hull and the Great Gretsky. The first Stanley Cup is among the items on display.

Kensington Market
Map 4F3.
An enclave of ethnic food shops and stalls. See *Walks*, page 37.

Mackenzie House
82 Bond St. (nr Dundas) ☎ 392-6915. Map 5H3 ✗ Open Mon-Sat 9.30am-5pm, Sun noon-5pm. Subway: Dundas.
William Lyon Mackenzie was a newspaper publisher and the first mayor of the renamed city of Toronto in 1834. His frustrations in dealing with the powerful Family Compact ruling group drove him into leadership of the 1837 armed rebellion. It lasted only 6wks, and Mackenzie lived in exile for 11yrs in the US, where he continued to agitate for greater democracy in Canada. He was allowed to return after 1849, when governmental reforms were made. The house, Georgian in style and once one of a block of row houses, is furnished in the Victorian manner in vogue when Mackenzie and his family lived there in his later, more peaceful years. He died in 1861, and two of his daughters subsequently ran a boarding school there. Costumed guides tell the story and conduct demonstrations. It takes little encouragement for them to reveal the presence of the resident ghost.

Marine Museum of Upper Canada
Exhibition Place ☎ 392-6827. Map 2C5 ✶ Open Mon-Sat 9.30am-5pm, Sun noon-5pm. Subway: Bathurst, then #511 streetcar.
The ambitious and very competent Toronto Historical Board operates five properties around the city: *Fort York*, **Colborne Lodge** in *High Park*, *Mackenzie House*, *Spadina House*, and this, a repository of ships and artifacts charting the evolution of leisure and commercial shipping on the Great Lakes from the earliest days of the fur trade. The museum employs an 1841 military barracks associated with Fort York, not far away. Marvelously detailed model ships, nautical equipment and items salvaged from decommissioned boats crowd the rooms. In May, they wheel out the *Ned Hanlan*, a restored 1932 harbor tug, and invite visitors to clamber aboard. Children do so without hesitation. It's on the Canadian National Exhibition grounds, along with the *Hockey* and *Canada Sports Halls of Fame*.

McLaughlin Planetarium
100 Queen's Park (Bloor) ☎ 586-5736. Map 4G1 (with ROM or Gardiner Museum ticket) ✶ Open daily 10am-6pm, Tues, Thurs 10am-8pm. Subway: Museum.
The **Theatre of the Stars** has a dome more than 60ft across,

employing 80 projectors and hundreds of special effects to simulate shooting stars and black holes and the tapestry of the night sky. An **Astrocentre** reproduces the solar system in 3-dimension and invites the use of computer terminals and other interactive displays. And the **Laser Theatre** (*additional* ☎ *closed Mon*) gets the attention of young people with lightshows featuring music by the likes of Def Leppard and Bon Jovi.

McMichael Canadian Collection
Islington Ave, Kleinburg ☎ *893-2787* ☎ ▣ *Open May 1-Oct 31 Mon-Sat 10am-5pm, Sun 10am-6.30pm; Nov 1-Apr 30 Tues-Sun 11.30am-4.30pm.*

Highly recommended, if only as an excuse for a country outing, this museum preserves a corner of the Ontario wilderness that inspired the artists whose works are reverentially displayed inside. The collection, and the building in which it resides, are the result of the enthusiasm of the couple whose name they bear. They complement one another, with timbers and masonry as a backdrop for the deeply-felt paintings and sculptures of both Canadians of European background and native Inuit and Amerindians.

The landscape paintings are primarily by the Group of Seven artists (see *The arts*, page 17). Founders of the first school of uniquely Canadian painting, they were moved primarily by the unspoiled nature preserves and bodies of water of northern Ontario, and were a collective force on the art scene for three decades. Not that their work is interchangeable. At various stages, Tom Thomson worked in bright colors with Impressionistic strokes, Lawren Harris in sharply stylized forms, Clarence Cagnon in dreamy genre settings — and they were restless, experimental.

Superbly fashioned Inuit sculptures in black and green soapstone are much on view, as are prints and paintings by members of the Woodlands and Northwest Coast tribal bands. It feels warm and cared-for here, and more like a home than a chilly institution, and few people regret the modest trek required from downtown. A private car is best, taking Highway 400 N to Major Mackenzie Dr., then W to the town of Kleinburg. Public transit is possible, but takes longer and can be confusing.

Metropolitan Toronto Reference Library
789 Yonge St. (nr Bloor) ☎ *393-7196. Map 5H1* ▣ *Open Mon-Thurs 10am-9pm, Fri-Sat 10am-6pm, Sun 1.30-5pm. Subway: Bloor.*

Waterfalls, fountains, pools, and walkways whirl around a 5-story atrium, for this is not just another library. See *Walk 2*.

Metro Toronto Zoo
Highway 401 and Meadowvale Rd., Scarborough ☎ *392-5900. Map 7B4* ☎ ▣ ✱ ✇ *Open daily in summer 9.30am-7pm, in winter 9.30am-4.30pm. Subway: Kennedy, then Scarborough #86A bus, or Sheppard, then Sheppard East #85B bus.*

More than 4,000 creatures are exhibited in simulated natural habitats on a 710-acre zoological park about 1hr from downtown. It's well worth the trip, and most of a day should be planned, to allow a leisurely visit. Obviously the warmer months are preferable, when many of the animals run loose in open areas. But a winter trip is still worthwhile, for almost everything is viewable in the eight large pavilions, each filled with plants,

Ontario Place/Toronto

birds, mammals, reptiles, and even fish, characteristic of the regions of the world they represent.

Just inside the gate, mood-setting peacocks stalk imperiously across the path. There are choices as to how to proceed. A monorail skims for 25mins over the Rouge River valley, where North American animals are quartered. The Zoomobile tram provides a 45min overview. Both rides have commentaries. Or you can walk: blue footprints are painted on the paths, leading past each of the pavilions at the heart of the park. The circuit takes about 3hrs. At the Australasia pavilion, wallabies and kangaroos stare right back from their open pits, and the marine exhibits include lionfish, clown anemone and blue damsel fish from the Great Barrier Reef. The Americas are represented by polar bears, whose pools have underwater viewing windows, by flamingos, spider monkeys, jaguars, boa constrictors, armadillos, marmosets, and an aviary of tanagers and toucans.

Lowland gorillas, known to deliver mighty blows against the glass walls of their cages, are featured in the Africa Pavilion. Look, too, for the Saharan meerkat, a kind of gregarious mongoose that lives in colonies. The patriarch keeps constant watch for predators from the top of his rock pile while the family scavenges for food, whining and chattering. Then he changes guard with one of his sons. Nearby is the largest herd of African elephants in North America. After all that come the Indo-Malaya Pavilion, the Lion Trail, the Camel Trail and the Grizzly Bear Trail. Periodically, demonstrations are given of free-flying birds of prey, including bald eagles and great horned owls. Rides are available on two-humped camels.

All along the way, volunteers give directions and enthusiastically discuss the habits and characteristics of the creatures to which they are assigned. Visitors will exhaust themselves before the exhibits run out.

Montgomery's Tavern
4709 Dundas St. (Islington) ☎ 394-8113 ▣ Open Mon-Fri 9.30am-4.30pm, Sat, Sun 1pm-5pm. Subway: Islington, then Islington #37 bus.

The 1837 Rebellion was dispersed by government troops at Montgomery's Tavern, an attractive inn built in the prevalent Georgian style of the period. It has been restored to accept visitors, many of whom arrive expressly for daily afternoon tea.

Museum of the History of Medicine
288 Bloor St. W (St George) ☎ 922-0564. Map 4J1 ▣ Open Mon-Fri 9.30am-4pm. Subway: St George.

Four rooms in the Academy of Medicine building are given to fascinating displays of the medical arts dating to the time of leeches and magic potions and beyond.

Ontario Place
955 Lakeshore Blvd. W ☎ 965-7917. Map 2C6 ▣ ▣ ✱ Open mid-May to mid-Sept Mon-Sat 10am-1am, Sun 10am-11pm. For transit information ☎ 393-4636.

These remarkable connected islands just offshore from Exhibition Place defy classification. Part amusement park, part museum, Ontario Place has a movie studio, a stadium that holds both concerts *and* stock car races, elaborate playgrounds, a warship, the **Canadian Baseball Hall of Fame**... and that only begins to outline its diversity. From Lakeshore Blvd., one of the most arresting structures is a huge geodesic dome, the

Toronto/Ontario Science Centre

Cinesphere. It presents films in the IMAX format, with images 60ft high, and special effects that make participants out of passive viewers. A series of five elevated "pods" hold a variety of entertainments, including a 3-D cinema and a live theater for children. The canopied **Children's Village** has water slides, wading pools, trampolines, swaying bridges, and a treehouse snack bar. Two yacht marinas are part of the complex, as is the World War II destroyer HMCS *Haida*. Pedal and bumper boats are available for rent, and there is an island-to-shore shuttle craft.

The several restaurants range from mid-priced to ambitious, and there is an ample number of fast-food stands. Concerts in the Forum amphitheater have included symphony orchestras, ballet, and pop/rock entertainers of international stature. If all that isn't enough, they lay on such special events as an electrifying fireworks competition, comedy festivals, and stunts by daredevils and highdivers. (See *Calendar of events*.)

Ontario Science Centre
770 Don Mills Rd. (Eglinton) ☎ 429-4100. Map 6B3 ▨ ▬ ▬ ✱ Open daily 10am-6pm, Fri 10am-9pm. Subway: Pape, then Don Mills #25 bus.

All stops are pulled to render the world of science both palatable and comprehensible in this quadri-level playground. "Interactive" is a key word, with hundreds of exhibits that invite viewer participation. The images on a wall of more than 100 TV screens are controlled by the people in the camera's eye. Rainbow trout swim in aerated silos to demonstrate aquaculture. A laser ray burns a hole through a brick. Touch the Van der Graaf generator for a literally hair-raising experience. Step up to any of dozens of computer terminals to ask questions about communications, physics, engines. Operate the kinds of robot arms used in nuclear research. In the past, special exhibitions have focused on cars, china, wood, and science as employed in the arts. Movies for senior citizens are shown in the auditorium, and live demonstrations are always on tap. There's even a beer garden.

The four floors of the building step down the slope of a river valley, each unit connected by escalators and elevators. It can be a little confusing to negotiate, so a map is provided at the reception desk. Level 4 (the top, entry floor) has snack bars, a restaurant, souvenir shops. Level 3 has a cafeteria, presentation theaters and the temporary exhibition hall. Level 2 has permanent exhibits on space exploration, molecular structures, earth sciences and food production. Level 1 (at the bottom) examines technologies, communications, and transportation from steam engines to ships to automobiles. A good strategy is to descend to the lowest level and work up. Even an entire day is not enough to see it all.

Queen's Park
Map 4G2. Subway: Queen's Park or Museum.
A tranquil greensward below Bloor St. and E of the main campus of the University of Toronto. See *Walks*, page 37.

Royal Ontario Museum
100 Queen's Park (Bloor) ☎ 586-5549. Map 4G1 ▨ (▣ after 4.30pm Thurs) ▬ ✱ Open daily 10am-6pm, Tues, Thurs 10am-8pm. Subway: Museum.

As with most major museums, ROM is in a nearly constant state of flux, the latest manifestation of which was a long-term construction and realignment program completed in 1990. The frequent shifts and changes make a room-by-room description difficult, and what follows provides an overview of the nature and content of the several collections.

Art and science combine, with a noticeable emphasis on archeology. One exhibit plots the course of the archeological process, from hypothesis and research to fieldwork and analysis. A result of such efforts is the **Ming Tomb**, with its stone camels and guards.

Yet turn a corner and come upon a room full of live scorpions and tarantulas, or enter another and discover the reassembled fossils of a mastodon and a stegosaurus, rare stuffed birds and reptiles, a simulated bat cave, wildlife dioramas. A marked interest in Asia and the Middle East shows up in the statuary, coins and jewelry of the splendid Chinese Collection and in the *Caravans and Clippers* exhibit. Beyond these are ethnological displays illustrating the ways of Canadian Amerindians, rock and gem collections, medieval armor, musical instruments. Lack of space prevents many exhibits from being on permanent display, a problem expected to be solved over the next few years. Perhaps something will also be done about the too-often murky lighting and an apparent disjointedness in some presentations. Four shops sell jewelry, books, toys, pottery and sculpture reproductions. The adjacent *McLaughlin Planetarium* and *Gardiner Museum of Ceramic Art*, across the street, come under the ROM umbrella.

SkyDome
Front St. (John) ☎ *341-2770. Map 4F5* 🈯 *✗ Tickets and hours vary according to events scheduled* ♋ ≡ 🖳 *Subway: Union Station.*

Domed athletic stadiums are no longer a novelty in North America, but this one advanced the science one step further, with its rigid retractable roof of remarkable design and ingenuity. (The roof of Montréal's *Olympic Stadium* is of cloth and takes twice as long to winch into place.) Skydome is not to be confused with just any enclosed arena. It is 282ft from floor to ceiling, enough to cover a 30-story building, the roof weighs 11 tons, and the field alone could accommodate eight 747 jets. Seating sections move on tracks to reconfigure for different sports and events. This is the permanent home of the football Argonauts and baseball Blue Jays, and has been used for Aussie Rules football, basketball, cricket, opera, and rock concerts by such megastars as Paul McCartney, Elton John, and the Rolling Stones.

It is in the nature of such projects to provoke superlatives and statistics. SkyDome claims the world's largest scoreboard, and a television replay screen measuring 35 by 115ft. There are nine restaurants and lounges, 32 fast-food stands, a health club, and a 348-room hotel with 70 rooms and suites overlooking the field. Some 53,000 spectators can be seated for baseball, 50,000 for football and 60,000 for concerts and other events. When the roof is fully retracted in good weather, a hypnotic process that takes 20mins and involves three massive sections sliding into a nest at one end, 91 percent of the audience is exposed to sunlight. Eight miles of zippers hold the Astroturf carpeting together on the stadium floor. The 161 "SkyBoxes," leased by individuals and corporations, cost up to $225,000 a year, and the lessees have spent $100,000 to $400,000 to decorate their spaces. The cost of the entire project was $532 million when completed in 1989.

Tours are conducted 9am-6pm daily when not in conflict with scheduled events. They begin with a slick 20min film depicting the planning and construction of the stadium (*reservations* ☎ *872-1111*).

Spadina House
285 Spadina Rd. ☎ 392-6910. Map 6B3 ✗ Open Mon-Sat 9.30am-5pm, Sun noon-5pm. Subway: Dupont, then Davenport #127 bus.

One of the latest of historic homes to be opened to the public, the house was built for financier James Austin in 1866. Its fixtures, however, date from about three decades later. The original furnishings in the lush $2.5 million late Victorian, Edwardian and Art Nouveau collection provide a glimpse into the lives of the wealthy and their large domestic staffs in the days before income taxes. The enchanting garden, restored in period, has more than 300 varieties of plants and flowers in nearly six acres of parkland.

Toronto Islands
Map 2E6. Harbourfront streetcar from Union Station, then the ferry (☎ 392-8193) from dock behind the Harbour Castle Westin Hotel.

Opportunities for outdoor recreation in and near the city are almost inexhaustible. Occupying center-stage are the six small islands that nearly enclose the harbor off the downtown waterfront. Public lands are given over to swimming, fishing, sunbathing, picnicking, cycling and boating in summer, cross-country skiing and snowshoeing in winter. **Centreville** (☎ *363-1112* ✱ *open May 20-Sept 4 daily, May, Sept weekends only*) is a genteel amusement park for children. With not a bit of the usual screech-and-flash associated with the genre, it is an intentionally dated place that might have existed at the turn of the century, with a carousel and miniaturized old-time trains and automobiles for kids to ride. A petting zoo is there, and cable cars, bumper boats, a miniature golf course, and swan boats on the lagoon. Fine views of the city, too.

Toronto Stock Exchange
2 First Canadian Pl. (King) ☎ 947-4676. Map 4G4 ✗ Open Mon-Fri 9am-4.30pm. Subway: St Andrew.

The nation's busiest exchange offers tours, and a visitors' gallery provides views of the action on the trading floor, although much of it will be understood only by initiates.

Underground Toronto
Map 5H3. Subway: Union Station, Dundas, or Queen.

Toronto's version of a weatherproof city was a byproduct of the downtown construction boom that started in the 1960s, when planners were trying to find ways for people to travel around the area in comfort and safety. Local boosters claim theirs is larger than the one in Montréal, but that is a matter of opinion. It hardly matters, for few people have enough time to browse or dine in all its 1,000 stores and restaurants.

The underground complex began to come to fruition with the 1977 opening of the Eaton Centre, E of the new City Hall. Within a decade, it extended from the Atrium on Bay in the N, under Eaton Centre, Simpson's, the Sheraton Centre Hotel, First Canadian Pl., and on to the Royal York Hotel and Union Station on Front St. There are 3 miles of connecting tunnels, with entrances to the hotels and office buildings and access to seven subway stops. In theory, a visitor could arrive by train from other

HOTELS/TORONTO

parts of Canada or the US, check into a hotel, make business calls, cash travelers cheques, eat every meal of the day, buy gifts for the family, see a movie, drop into a nightclub, check out four days later and get back on the train — all without once stepping foot into the cold and slush of a Toronto winter. There are even trees down there, and the temperature hovers at a year-round 70°. The twists and turns can confuse, however, and making note of landmarks along the way is necessary, to avoid getting lost.

Yorkville
Map 4G1.
A trendy, upmarket neighborhood N of Bloor St. with scores of shops, restaurants and nightspots. See *Walks*, page 37.

Where to stay in Toronto

The desirability of Toronto as a vacation or business destination is greatly enhanced by the diversity of its lodgings. There is truly something for everyone, from grand hotels to clean, no-frills rooms at bedrock prices. For those who have always wanted to splurge on a dream hotel, this is the place to do it. While rates are high at such estimable hostelries as **Sutton Place** and the **Four Seasons**, they are no worse than at many less desirable hotels in the US and Europe, and prevailing dollar exchange rates make the actual cost 10-15 percent lower than it seems.

Try to arrange part of a trip over a weekend. Every hotel offers substantial discounts for Fri, Sat and sometimes Sun nights, at least during the slower months. That means reductions of up to 40 percent for half the nights of an average stay. Children can often share their parents' room for nothing extra. Even a tenuous connection with a recognizable corporation may bring a discount for a weeknight, and senior citizens can routinely get 10 or 15 percent off simply by asking. Snip a few more dollars off the cost by applying for a refund of the 5-percent room sales tax: before a visit, write or call **Ontario Travel** (*Queen's Park, Toronto, Ontario, M7A 2R9* ☎ *965-4008 or 1-800-268-4008*).

Hotels in all price ranges are concentrated in two central areas of the city. Residents tend to refer to all of the most important parts of the city as "downtown." That covers a lot of ground, however. For visitors, it is easier to think of downtown as the financial district, from the waterfront to City Hall, and midtown as the area around Bloor St., Yorkville. There are a great many motels and hotels scattered over greater Metro Toronto, but they offer no particular price advantage and are often distant from the places most people want to visit.

The larger downtown and midtown hotels have garage parking. Nonsmoking floors are often available. Swimming pools are common, as are simple or elaborate fitness facilities. Color TV and air conditioning are standard even in economy accommodations, as are private bathrooms. Room rates sometimes include complimentary breakfasts. A service charge may be added to checks for snacks and meals brought to the room: don't tip twice.

Lodging can usually be found on short notice from Oct-Apr. The crowded period is May-Sept, when warm weather attracts large numbers of tourists and visitors to the many trade fairs and conventions. During that time, it is wisest to make reservations

Toronto/Hotels

2-3wks in advance. When finding a room proves difficult, one source to turn to is **Accommodation Toronto** (☎ 596-7117). They represent 87 hotels in all price categories, and will endeavor to match callers with appropriate establishments, at no charge. An active bed-and-breakfast movement vies for attention, offering homey settings and lowish prices. See the end of this section.

Colleges and universities in the area have dormitory rooms available during summer. Possibilities are **Neill-Wyick College Hotel** (☎ 977-2320), **Victoria University** (☎ 585-4524) and the **University of Toronto** (☎ 284-3391).

Most of the hotels below provide toll-free telephone numbers. In some cases, these can be called from anywhere in North America; others are restricted to Ontario and Québec or the eastern US. Touch **1** before the rest of the number. When calling any of the non-800 numbers from outside Ontario, precede them with the Toronto area code: **416**.

Admiral at Harbourfront
249 Queen's Quay W (Spadina), Toronto M5J 2N5 ☎ *364-5444 or 800-387-1626 (Canada and eastern US)* ◐ *06-23361* ◉ *364-2975. Map 5H3* ⅢⅢ *157 rms*

Location: Harbourfront. Sheathed in blue glass, this perky newcomer is one of only two hotels in the Harbourfront development. SkyDome and the CN Tower loom to the N. The Pier 4 complex, of which the hotel is part, has three large restaurants. Pretty vistas of the harbor and offshore islands are the backdrop for drinkers seated on the Promenade Deck and in the lounge chairs around the outdoor pool. Rooms are pleasantly furnished, including minibar and TV with remote control.

Brownstone
15 Charles St. E (Yonge), Toronto M4Y 1S1 ☎ *924-7381 or 800-263-8967. Map 5H1* ⅢⅢ *110 rms*

Location: Midtown, near Bloor St. shopping center. Those who prefer to save their funds for purposes other than a place to sleep can do worse than this amiable little hotel off Yonge St. Recent remodeling has rescued it from a once suspect identity, and the very central location was always good. Rooms have TV and minibar, and the morning newspaper is placed by the door. Guests have access to a nearby health club.

Delta Chelsea
33 Gerrard St. W (Yonge), Toronto M5G 1Z4 ☎ *595-1975 or 800-268-1133. Map 5H3* ⅢⅢ *997 rms*

Location: Near City Hall and Eaton Centre. Very popular with families and tour groups, this isn't for those who prefer a sedate, unhurried pace. The atmosphere fairly crackles with energy, with much coming and going in the lobby. Its four restaurants are always full. Children have a supervised play center to permit parents a little adult quality time. A pool, sauna and billiards are among the other attractions. Moderate prices and good location keep the occupancy rate high.

Four Seasons
21 Avenue Rd (Bloor), Toronto M5R 2G1 ☎ *964-0411 or 800-268-6382 (Canada) or 800-332-3442 (US)* ◐ *06-23131* ◉ *964-2301. Map 4G1* ⅢⅢ *381 rms*

Location: In Yorkville, near Bloor St. shopping center and Royal Ontario Museum. From reception to departure, this is an operation as smooth as hot butter on glass. Every link in the Four Seasons chain operates to the highest standards of the hotelier's art, but this one is quite possibly the best of the lot. Housed in a contemporary highrise at the gateway to Yorkville, it softens the glass and steel exterior with the warmth of Asian floral motifs and reproductions of period furnishings. Mid to upper floors tender dazzling views of the city. The chambermaid checks each room twice a day, and food and beverages are available around the clock. Its Business Centre makes available computers and fax machines, and to tone up or come

52

down, there is an indoor-outdoor pool and a fully equipped health club. **Truffles**, the formal in-house restaurant, is accorded highest marks by local gourmands. None of this comes cheap, of course, but if cost is not primary, there isn't a better choice in town.

Four Seasons Inn on the Park
1100 Eglinton Ave. E (Leslie), Toronto M3C 1H8 ☎ *444-2561 or 800-268-6282* ● *06-966784* ⓕ *446-3308. Map 6B3* ▨ *568 rms*

Location: One mile from the Ontario Science Centre. It doesn't have the location and cachet of its celebrated downtown sibling, but then, they're riding different ponies. Here is a full-fledged resort in the outlying Don Mills district. The inner court has one pool for lap swimmers, a second deep enough for diving. Inside, next to the fitness center, is still another pool, this one heated. Guests have access to the adjacent **Park View Club**, which has covered tennis courts, squash, racquetball, aerobics classes and a Nautilus weight circuit. There is a supervised program for children aged 5-12 — games and swimming, all day, and their parents only have to pay for Junior's lunch. More? How about horseback riding or jogging on the trails of the adjoining 500 acres? The bedrooms, it must be said, are ordinary, presumably on the assumption that not much time will be spent in them.

Hilton International
145 Richmond St. W (University), Toronto M5H 2L2 ☎ *869-3456* ⓕ *869-1478. Map 4G4* ▨ *601 rms*

Location: In the heart of the financial district. Clearly oriented to the business traveler, especially in its location. Service standards and fixtures are at the high end of the middle range, short of luxury but more than merely comfortable. For dining, it has the retrograde **Trader Vic's**, as *faux* Polynesian as ever. The blue-suit brigade prevails in the **Barrister's Bar**, while a more relaxed crowd attends to piano music in the **Garden Court Lounge**. They can unwind further in the indoor-outdoor pool. Rooms look pretty much as expected from a Hilton, but are no less satisfying for that. Room service is always available.

L'Hôtel
225 Front St. W (University), Toronto M5V 2X3 ☎ *597-1400 or 800-268-9420 (Canada) or 800-828-7447 (US)* ● *06-218517* ⓕ *597-8128. Map 4G5* ▨ *616 rms*

Location: Next to the Metro Convention Centre and the CN Tower. An ideal businessperson's hotel, within a few blocks of every building in the financial district. Even standard rooms are exceptionally spacious, often with step-down sitting area, high ceilings and banked windows. (Rooms with numbers ending in 02 or 37 are largest.) Telephones are on the workdesk, where they should be, and room service brings breakfast as early as 6.30am. Computer ports are now installed in the rooms. As at most Canadian Pacific city hotels, there are three classes of service. Business class offers express check-in, free breakfast, and nightly turn-down service. Entrée Gold adds its own concierge. The health club has an indoor pool with doors opening to the patio in summer, a Universal weight circuit, exercycles and a rowing machine. With all this and generous weekend packages, it's a good choice for families, too.

Ibis ✿
240 Jarvis (Dundas), Toronto M5B 2B8 ☎ *593-9400 or 800-221-4542* ● *06-217814* ⓕ *593-8426. Map 5H3* ▨ *294 rms*

Location: A short walk from City Hall. Ibis doesn't disguise what it's about. The exterior could not be less ostentatious, guests carry their own bags, and not an unnecessary dollar has been spent on trappings. With that reduced overhead, they can offer comfortable rooms at a good price with either twin- or queen-sized beds. Each has cable TV, radio alarm clock and baths. Their unnamed restaurant serves workmanlike buffet breakfasts and lunches and *à la carte* dinners. One child under 12 can share its parents' room without charge. The resultant savings can then be blown in Eaton Centre, only three blocks away.

King Edward ⌘
37 King St. (Yonge), Toronto M5C 1E9 ☎ *863-9700 or 800-225-5843. Map 5H4* ▨ *318 rms*

Location: Financial district, near Union Station. The King Eddy was

Toronto/Hotels

built at the time that its namesake sat upon the British throne (1901-10) and it bears the stamp of that gilded age in all its structural details, rife with rose marble, gold leaf and burnished woods. The ceiling of the remarkable lobby is nearly lost in shadow, eight stories up, and one can easily conjure the royal party descending the ceremonial staircase. New owners pumped millions of dollars into its renovation, and the hotel now qualifies as a stop on the tourist circuit, even for those who cannot afford its steep prices. Those whose bank accounts can stand the assault have the use of a health club, all-hours room service, and diligent concierges of the Continental school.

Ramada Renaissance on Bloor
90 Bloor St. E (Yonge), Toronto M4W 1A7 ☎ *961-8000 or 800-268-8998 (Canada) or 800-228-9898 (US)* ● *06-23560* ⊗ *961-9581. Map 5H1* ⅢⅢ *256 rms*

Location: In the midst of Bloor-Yonge shopping center. Ramada, an international chain known primarily for its motels, has expanded its Renaissance subdivision, and the transformed former Plaza II hotel opened its doors in 1990. It is located next to Yorkville, with all the advantages of Fifth Avenue-style shopping, yet is also geared toward the businessman of the 1990s, with a full range of conference facilities, business center, private check-in and morning limousine service. There is direct access to the Bloor Park Club, a fully equipped recreational facility with indoor swimming pool, Nautilus gym, squash courts and even aerobic classes.

Royal York
100 Front St. W (York), Toronto M5J 1E3 ☎ *368-2511 or 800-828-7447 (US)* ⊗ *368-2884. Map 4G4* ⅢⅢ *1,412 rms*

Location: Opposite Union Station. As the "largest hotel in the British Commonwealth," warmth and intimacy can hardly be counted among its virtues. After all, if all rooms are occupied, it matches the population of many a good-sized town. Settle instead for its abundant array of shops and services, bedrooms that are entirely satisfactory if not striking, and *thirteen* restaurants and bars. One of the latter, the **Imperial Room**, is a showcase for internationally famous entertainers and music of the big band era. A fitness center with whirlpool is to be added in 1991. This is a place to keep in mind for those occasions when other hotels are fully booked.

Sheraton Centre of Toronto
123 Queen St. W (Bay), Toronto M5H 2M9 ☎ *361-1000 or 800-325-3535* ● *06-23681* ⊗ *947-4854. Map 4G4* ⅢⅢ *1,462 rms*

Location: Short walk to Eaton Centre and financial district. Only a monster of a hotel can underwrite such interior gardens as these, replete with hanging foliage, extensive flower-beds, stands of mature trees... and a 3-story waterfall. This Sheraton is, after all, the second-largest hotel in the city, and it doesn't shrink from its perceived responsibility to manufacture superlatives. Apart from the waterfall, it boasts the longest bar in town, with a view of City Hall and Nathan Phillips Square, and an 80ft pool that is partly inside, mostly out. A California-style hot tub is on hand. Those who want fancier perks and pampering than found in the standard rooms can upgrade to the more luxurious **Towers**.

SkyDome
45 Peter St. S (Spadina), Toronto M5V 3B4 ☎ *360-7100 or 800-268-9420 (Ontario and Québec) or 800-828-7447 (US)* ● *06-17677* ⊗ *341-5090. Map 4F5* ⅢⅢ *348 rms*

Location: Within walking distance of the theater and financial districts. The youngest of three Canadian Pacific hotels in Toronto (opened late 1989) has a feature that no other can claim: 70 rooms and suites that overlook the field of the spectacular SkyDome stadium itself. Obviously that has appeal for rabid sports fans — the Blue Jays and Argonauts play there — but the novelty itself is enough to hold anyone's attention. Guests assigned to one of the other 280 rooms won't feel deprived, for the management has loaded them with the extra touches and electronic doodads that travelers on expense accounts have come to expect. They include the morning newspaper with breakfast, 24hr food and beverage service, remote control TV, minibars. Many rooms have VCRs and Jacuzzi baths. The

Hotels/Toronto

goodies multiply on the floors set aside for Business and Entrée Gold categories.

Sutton Place Kempinski
955 Bay St. (Wellesley), Toronto M5S 2A2 ☎ *924-9221. Map 5H2* |||| *280 rms*

Location: *Near Queen's Park and University of Toronto.* Selecting a member establishment of the *Leading Hotels of the World* is a fail-safe decision. That prestigious association applies very high standards, and can be ruthless when any of their number fall behind the pace. Certainly no expense nor effort is spared to remain well above even these lofty expectations. The multilingual reception is impeccable, fixtures are tastefully opulent, and only the sourest curmudgeon can find fault with the lovely rooms, many of which have lawn-deep Oriental carpets on polished parquet floors. A butler is on call at all times. Shoe-shines and morning papers are complimentary. TV, minibar, robes and hairdryers, of course. An indoor pool, sauna and massage, naturally. The **Sanssouci** restaurant is exemplary. And a free limousine whisks guests to the financial district every workday morning.

Venture Inn
89 Avenue Rd. (Bloor), Toronto M5R 2G3 ☎ *964-1220 or 800-387-3933* ⓕ *964-8692 Map 4G1* |||| *71 rms*

Location: *Near Yorkville and the Royal Ontario Museum.* A college dormitory air is heightened by the squeaky-clean young staff. One of several Toronto entries of a growing budget chain, this one is noteworthy for its proximity to Yorkville. Rooms have firm beds, TV with pay movies, and not much else, but prices are very easy on the bank account.

Westin Harbour Castle
1 Harbour Square (Queen's Quay E & Yonge), Toronto M5J 1A6 ☎ *869-1600* ⓕ *06-22356* ⓕ *869-0573. Map 4G5* |||| *1,011 rms*

Location: *At the E end of Harbourfront.* Skillful marketing is repositioning this former Hilton from conventioneer warren to in-town resort. It has the necessary ingredients. The health club has free weights, a jogging track, three squash courts, a steam room, whirlpool, Universal machine, and an indoor pool that opens to a terrace in summer. But what distinguishes this from other hotels is the complete spa facility, which provides loofah-sponge baths, massage clinic, and restaurant menus of low-everything meals. Guests less paranoid about their belt sizes are tempted by the buffet lunch in the revolving **Lighthouse** restaurant, a two-tiered room 37 stories up. There are two other restaurants and two lounges, one with live music. Ferries for the Toronto Islands leave from the dock behind the hotel; a new streetcar loop makes the trip to Union Station in under 5mins.

Windsor Arms
22 St Thomas St. (Bloor), Toronto M5S 2B9 ☎ *979-2341 or 800-668-8106. Map 5G1* ||▮ *to* |||| *82 rms*

Location: *Quiet street in walking distance of Bloor St. shopping.* Were it not for its excellent restaurants, the **Courtyard Café** and the **Three Small Rooms**, this wonderful little downtown inn might have remained a cherished secret. Certainly its intimates would like to keep it to themselves. Included among the repeat customers are the kinds of celebrities who *don't* lay waste their rooms or court the paparazzi. A member of the admirable Relais & Chateaux group, the caring management strives to perfect *L'Art de Bien Recevoir* that is the goal of all its compatriots. Expect a quiet, almost placid, atmosphere with correct, not punctilious, service. Each room, often admittedly on the compact side, is distinctively furnished with handsome antiques, both European and Canadian. That is a requirement of membership, as is a room count less than 100. No fitness center, pool or Jacuzzi, but then, no tour groups or conventions, either. Do make time for afternoon tea beside the fire.

Bed and breakfast

The observations about B&B lodgings under that heading on page 101 apply here. Please review them before deciding to use the services of the referral agencies listed.

TORONTO/RESTAURANTS

Bed and Breakfast Homes of Toronto
235 Beverly St., Toronto, Ontario M5T 1Z4 ☎ 363-6362.
Full breakfasts at homes throughout Metro Toronto. Send a self-addressed envelope for a descriptive brochure.

Downtown Toronto Association of Bed and Breakfast Guesthouses
P.O. Box 190, Station B, Toronto, Ontario M5T 2W1 ☎ 977-6841 or 598-4562.
Twelve renovated Victorian homes with 25 available rooms. All are within 30mins of Eaton Centre by subway or bus. Three nights minimum preferred Apr-Oct. All homes are nonsmoking.

Metropolitan Bed & Breakfast Registry of Toronto
72 Lowther Ave., Toronto, Ontario M5R 1C8 ☎ 964-2566 or 928-2833.
About 30 homes. Credit cards sometimes accepted. Smoking is not allowed by most hosts, many of whom have pets. Descriptions of the homes are included in the brochure.

Where to eat in Toronto

Toronto is a culinary free-for-all. The phenomenon of star chefs and cuisines-of-the-week took hold in the self-indulgent Eighties and shows little sign of abating. Restless, impatient, insatiably curious young cooks observe no restrictions. They borrow ingredients and techniques from scores of national and regional styles and throw them together in multicultural pastiches. A single dish containing Cajun spices, Thai noodles, Chinese mushrooms, Mexican *cilantro* and Canadian venison (with perhaps a rhubarb *coulis* in a phyllo cup on the side) may not have been assembled yet, but it is only a matter of time. This manic experimentation and its eager acceptance by the public has spawned a global cuisine that may yet get its own name. Much of it can be arch and precious, a collective cleverness gone over the edge. What is surprising are the goodly number of bull's-eyes among all the thudding misfires.

The forum for this race to new frontiers is an updated version of the bistro. It is smaller and more casual than the Old World variety, with no tuxedoed retainers or flaming tableside preparations. Patrons no longer have to take assertiveness training to find out what good food is about. Staffs are not as stratified as they are elsewhere. The sommelier has nearly disappeared, and few places have captains occupying the chain of command between the *maitre d'* and the waiters. If part of the price for experiencing this new looseness is enduring its frequent silliness, no one said life was without flaw.

With all this going on, a favorite buzzword of Toronto restaurant critics is "accessible," as if a plate of food were an exercise in Joycean riddle. In the selections below, we've attempted to give an overview of what is available, from simple to ambitious, cheap to celebratory, from Far Eastern to Middle European, with most of the stops in between. Obviously, this is only a sampling, and a truncated one, at that. Toronto claims somewhere between 4,000 and 5,000 eating places. But the list points the way to fecund neighborhoods, past dozens of restaurants awaiting discovery. And please remember that restaurants are a chancy line of business — every year, more than 10 percent of restaurants fail.

It is possible to eat well on limited funds. In addition to ethnic eateries where prices are generally low, there are ways to try out the pricier emporia without emptying a wallet. Lunch is usually cheaper than dinner, sometimes by as much as 40 percent. Restaurants near the *SkyDome*, or in the theater district, have special menus before a baseball game and after the show. Weekend brunch, an entrenched tradition, is usually a few dollars less than a weekday meal. Some of the larger restaurants have lower-cost annexes, rooms in the same building with shorter menus and more casual environments. **Centro**, **Julien** and **Scaramouche** are three with that arrangement.

Liquor, wine and beer are expensive, but Canadian bottlings are less so and quite palatable; or buy wine by the glass instead of by the carafe. The standard tip is 15 percent, as is the provincial tax. Unfortunately, the tax is not usually stated separately on the check, so unless a pocket calculator is available, most people simply give 15 percent of the total. Larger restaurants are supposed to have nonsmoking sections. Should you need to know, the euphemism for toilet is "washroom."

Bamboo
312 Queen St. W ☎ *598-4656. Map 4G4* ||□ *to* ||□ AE ◉ ◎ VISA
West Indian informality and sensuality rule at this ramshackle club that grows steamier and more unpredictable as the night thumps on. Bamboo is a daily party for a crowd that is mostly young, usually hip, and sometimes exceptionally strange. Bands crank up around 10pm or whenever they can get themselves together. Their choice of sounds can be jazz, reggae, rock... and the unclassifiable. Since the Caribbean food repertoire is limited, the menu shares room with Thai. Noodle dishes are tops. Dinner at sunset on the roof patio is most agreeable. After that, see what happens.

Bangkok Garden
18 Elm St. ☎ *977-6748. Map 4G3* |||| AE ◉ ◎ VISA *Closed Sun.*
Thai is hot! In popularity, that is, and this is the place to see what all the fuss is about. Thai food is also hot in the spicy sense, but not always, and in subtle gradations. The menu ranks the degree of fire in each dish with one to five stars. Level three isn't too much for most people. The teak- and mirror-lined restaurant, illuminated at night by flickering candles, is a romantic setting in which to partake of lemon shrimp soup, *satay* or "warrior's curry." The waiters patiently describe and gently coach, even announcing how many chilies there are in each dish. This food is put together with delicacy and balance. Go with someone, preferably several someones, so more dishes can be sampled. Desserts are resistible.

Barberian's
7 Elm St. ☎ *597-0335. Map 4G3* |||| AE ◉ ◎ VISA *Closed Sat lunch, Sun lunch.*
When the urge for a beef booster strikes, there's no better place to mollify it than this old-timey downtown steakhouse. Join its regular coterie of two-fisted carnivores who like their T-bones and *filet mignons* unadorned and broiled precisely to order, and without *nouvelle* embellishments. Dark suits and silvered hair are much in evidence, youthful exuberance is not. An after-theater menu is offered from 10pm.

Boulevard Café
161 Harbord St. ☎ *961-7676. Map 4F2* ||□ ◎ VISA
Just about any gustatory need that might be imagined is targeted by this friendly café. It's open 7 days a week, serving sandwiches to 4-course meals. Brunch is bountiful and informal. In summer, an outdoor terrace adds to its appeal. A nominal Peruvian identity is announced by South American wall hangings and tables with handmade tile tops, and carried forth with such dishes from the owners' homeland as garlic shrimp and lamb *brochettes*. They aren't slavish about the connection, though, with burgers and such on the card. All in all, this is as gratifyingly low-pressure and good value as dining can get.

Beaujolais
165 John St. ☎ *598-4656. Map 4G4* ||□ *to* |||| AE ◎ VISA *Closed Sat lunch, Sun.*
Factory Chic prevails here, with the ceiling ducts, glass brick bar and

industrial carpeting. What the menu calls its Grand Beginning is hard to resist, a selection from the appetizer table at the door that skips around the continents with a bit of this and a taste of that. (Try eggplant-and-goat-cheese "*Oreos*" or *soba* noodles with marinated tuna, for two.) What we have here is another example of Toronto's infatuation with the Pan-Asian-Italo-Southwestern gastronomic frenzy. The menu fits the neighborhood, gingery Queen St. W. Dress and general atmosphere informal.

Le Bistingo
349 Queen St. W ☎ *598-3490. Map 4G4* ⅢⅠ *to* ⅢⅠⅠ AE ⊙ ⊙ VISA *Closed Sat lunch, Sun.*

There is the sense, in this *haute* bistro, of a steady, mature presence behind the kitchen doors. Little is seen of the usual flash and novelty, but that's not to say that what emerges is staid. Duck is a specialty, arriving in warm salads, as *confit*, or cloaked in brushstrokes of herbed honey. Warm apple tart in a reduced Calvados froth is the signature dessert. The cellar is carefully assembled, and many wines are available by the glass. A little pricey for many residents of the countercultural Queen St. neighborhood, Le Bistingo fills up, noon and night, with dressily casual sophisticates from all over the city. Reserve ahead.

Bistro 990
990 Bay St. ☎ *921-9990. Map 5H4* ⅢⅠ *to* ⅢⅠⅠ ⊙ VISA

Take someone with whom there is much to discuss. The rest of the effervescent crowd does, knowing that it will help pass the time awaiting the attentions of the elusive staff. A server finally stops by when patrons have committed the menu to memory... and proceeds to recite the day's specials, throwing prior decisions into chaos. Relax. This is a bistro, after all. (Casual enough that the bodybuilder at the next table suffers no embarrassment at drinking Diet Coke with his *pot au feu*.) And the food does arrive, in time, and makes the wait worthwhile. But do take a friend. Or a book. *War and Peace* would do nicely.

Centro
2472 Yonge St. ☎ *483-2211. Map 5H4* ⅢⅠⅠ AE ⊙ ⊙ VISA *Closed Tues.*

Santa Monica meets Tuscany in a place so "in" it almost hurts. There is the room — profoundly Post-Modernist, in desert tones with geometric Classical references. There are the trappings — a mesquite grill for designer pizzas and free-range capon. Handsome young waiters in aprons and wing collars ask, "How is the meal so far? about twice as often as necessary. Why go? Because the food is exceptional, if too chic for its own good. There is, for example, *tagliatelle* with smoked salmon, roast peppers, cream, vodka and caviar. Cute. Desserts are overblown. Nothing languid about the service — courses arrive too quickly, if anything. Don't go alone. Everyone is celebrating something, be it only their good fortune in being able to afford it.

Chile's Mexican Flavors
936 Gerrard St. E ☎ *465-1247. Map 5I3* ⅠⅠ AE ⊙ ⊙ VISA *Hours are changeable, so call. Closed lunch, Mon.*

Mexican restaurants aren't found in profusion this far N in the land of the Aztecs, so this family-run enterprise is to be treasured. Its dedicated owners, despite what must be considerable difficulty in finding proper ingredients, do an admirable job with one of the world's most complex cuisines. (More than 100 different kinds of chile peppers are routinely utilized in Mexican cooking, most of them unknown in Anglo-America.) They even bake their own *tortillas*, a tedious chore but absolutely essential to their success. The folksy, colorful setting is free of pretense.

Cibo
1055 Yonge St. ☎ *921-2166. Map 5H2* ⅢⅠ AE ⊙ VISA

There are other items on the menu, and some people actually order them. They are missing the point. Pasta is the reason to seek out this understated Rosedale eatery. Start, logically enough, with *antipasti*, a tempting selection. Daily specials — pasta, of course — represent the kitchen's best thinking of the moment. Many of the patrons know each other, which makes for a happy clamor. They can't get enough of the place, so even though it's open daily, expect to join the line of supplicants.

Another unassuming Italian, closer to midtown, is basement-level **Sisi** (*116A Avenue Rd.* ☎ *962-0011* ⅠⅠ). It is also small and very popular, and reservations are essential.

Restaurants/Toronto

Copenhagen Room
101 Bloor St. ☎ *920-3287. Map 4E2* ||| AE ◉ ◉ VISA *Closed Sun.*
This ideal lunch stop is part of the **Danish Food Centre** on Bloor St. At street level is a takeout shop and café, and downstairs, a more formal room. Smørrebrød is featured — Danish open-faced sandwiches heaped with imaginative edibles. Two are about right for most appetites. They aren't the exquisitely arranged creations that might be remembered from a visit to the home country, but their shaky claim to authenticity doesn't affect their taste. Dour waiters pour aquavit from bottles encased in blocks of ice. A chaser of icy Danish beer is advised.

Costa Basque
124 Avenue Rd. ☎ *968-0908. Map 4G1* ||| AE ◉ ◉ VISA *Closed Sun.*
An image of a romanticized Spain greets patrons. The center court is bracketed by seating tiers, tall trees with pinlights among their leaves arching over the tables. Salmon-pink walls and tile floors buttress the effect. While the name implies food of the Basque Country, the region that produces some of Iberia's best cooking, the dishes are less region-specific. The food isn't wonderful, just good enough, especially if gazing deeply into each other's eyes happens to be a higher priority.

Ed's Warehouse
270 King St. W ☎ *593-6676. Map 3E4* |||| AE ◉ ◉ VISA
Kitsch finds its definition here. A warehouse, indeed, it is full of huge fringed Tiffany lamps, massive semi-antiques, stained glass, statuary, and vases more than 6ft high. Most of the fixtures are the sort that were in brief fashion, never came back, and probably never will. Walls and columns are covered with autographed photos of movie stars of the first to fifth magnitudes. The food isn't much different from what many of us remember from the days before North America discovered cuisine. Say about 1959, for Parents' Day at the university cafeteria. Waiters are obviously instructed not to linger. An entire meal, appetizer to watery coffee, is served in under 30mins. Go for reasons that have little to do with eating: (a) for a giggle, (b) with kids, or (c) because everyone does, at least once. Coats and ties are required, for some reason.

Fenton's
2 Gloucester St. ☎ *961-8489. Map 5H2* |||| AE ◉ VISA
Always open except Christmas and New Year's Day, the fact is that locals think of Fenton's most fondly for only one meal — Sun brunch. And when they go, of the three areas available, they all want to be in the Garden room. That's understandable, for it is alive with the colors and mingled fragrances of oleander and hibiscus and other tropical blooms, all fed by TLC and sun (when there is any) streaming through the skylight. A meal there is a welcome escape from the gusts of winter and a revel in the release of spring. It doesn't hurt that the food is almost unfailingly tasty and mildly innovative, nor that desserts are irresistible indulgences as weekend dwindles into workweek.

The Great Wall
442-444 Spadina Ave. ☎ *961-5554. Map 4F3* ☐ AE ◉ ◉ VISA
At these low prices and open for every meal of the week, this would be a restaurant to remember even if the food *wasn't* so good. Too often, a menu that purports to scan several Chinese cuisines proves to have dishes distinguished by nothing more than the number of last-minute shakes of the chili oil bottle. They pull it off here, with toothsome versions of recipes with Szechuan, Peking, Shanghai and Hunan origins. Crabs in their shells with a generous glaze of the trademark black-bean-and-pork sauce make everyone's most-wanted list, followed closely by the tea-smoked duck. They have been known to close Mon and some holidays, so call ahead.

Another candidate for best cheap Chinese food is **The Eating Counter** (*23 Baldwin St.* ☎ *977-7028* ☐ *no credit cards*), on a largely residential street E of Spadina Ave.

Joso's
202 Davenport Rd. ☎ *925-1903 or 925-3911* |||| AE ◉ VISA *Closed Sun.*
"Tasteless," huffed one local critic. She wasn't talking about what arrived on the plate. Paintings and sculptural ceramics crowd the walls upstairs and down. Many of them were created by the owner, and his subject of choice is nudes, mostly female, some male, a few — um — together. Some first-time customers will agree with the critic, and parents will probably want to leave

Toronto/Restaurants

the kiddies at the hotel, but most seem to be amused by or indifferent to the arrays of improbable breasts and related anatomical parts. All that robust ribaldry aside, seafood is the specialty at this Adriatic trattoria, very fresh and prepared with a minimum of trickery. Cephalopods are paramount among the kitchen's concerns, and this is the place to discover that squid and octopus don't have to have the texture of inner tubes.

Julien
387 King St. ☎ *596-6738. Map 4F4* |||| AE ⊙ ⊙ VISA *Closed Sat lunch, Sun.*

This calming retreat is almost as notable for what it doesn't do as for what it does. No effort is made to incorporate elements of seven cuisines on one plate, and the food doesn't look as if it has been pushed and poked to turn it into Cubist collage. Waiters don't swoop, and the host himself isn't above filling a glass. Julien is French, and pretends to nothing else. Each table has white napery and flowers.

The grown men and women who comprise the clientele dress discreetly, not like their teenage children. The nightly *table d'hôte* includes soup or salad, a choice of main courses, and coffee or tea all for less than the cost of any *à la carte* item alone. Upstairs is a separate bistro, with a more limited but cheaper menu.

Metropolis
838 Yonge St. ☎ *924-4100. Map 5H4* ||⌑ *to* ||⌑ AE ⊙ ⊙ VISA *Closed Sun.*

The elements that constitute "Canadian" cooking aren't easily discerned by foreigners. Judged by this erstwhile diner in Yorkville, it means rabbit, lamb, country sausage, pork, and a predilection for root vegetables and maple syrup. Here, they are put together with flair and an awareness of recent trends. Call it "New Canadian." The kitchen uses domestically raised or gathered provender whenever possible, and breads and pastries are baked on the premises. The service tends toward ostentation in what is, after all, a somewhat scruffily informal setting. The food and easy-to-take tariffs offset that minor quibble.

Mövenpick
165 York St. ☎ *366-5234. Map 4G4* ||⌑ AE ⊙ ⊙ VISA

This New World outpost of a Swiss chain has the requisite Cantonal banners and alpine chalet motifs, decorative flourishes reminiscent of a middle-class ski resort. Service is efficient, but hardly warm. The selection of foods is broad and well-prepared, with a tantalizing display of guilty treats on the dessert table. In the heart of the financial district, it's busy at every meal, even more so at Sun brunch, when nonbusiness types show up from all over the city. Reservations are a good idea, although they keep the lineup of eager eaters moving fairly quickly. There's a smaller branch in Yorkville.

Palmerston
488 College St. ☎ *922-9277. Map 4G2* |||| AE ⊙ ⊙ *Closed lunch.*

Jamie Kennedy is the name most often uttered when gourmands are asked about Toronto's swelling cadre of celebrity chefs. His arena is surprisingly small for a reputation so large. The plain, almost ascetic look of the space and the unobtrusive demeanor of the front staff have the effect of focusing attention on the young maestro in his exhibition kitchen. Fair enough. Food, not the scene, is what's important here. What emerges is a revelation for the eye as well as the palate, and he handles with *élan* any cut of lamb or type of fish.

While Palmerston doesn't rank very high on the lovability scale, it loosens up markedly in the summer, when the patio is opened. Simple grills are then featured, and Kennedy doesn't regard hamburgers as beneath his dignity. Always reserve ahead.

Pink Pearl
120 Avenue Rd. ☎ *966-3631. Map 4G1* ||⌑ AE ⊙ ⊙ VISA

One of several establishments in a local chain of somewhat self-consciously upscale Chinese eateries, this entry is the most convenient for visitors, near Yorkville. It's also open every day, a fact that's useful to know in a town where the Christian Sabbath is still observed with some rigor. The menu flits through a spectrum of several regional cuisines: Hunan, Szechuan, Pekinese, Cantonese.

It is a gracious establishment, with lovely watercolors on the walls and substantial linens on the tables. European methods of service are observed, and there don't seem to be two menus, one for Westerners, one for Chinese. Wines are mostly French and somewhat dear. Beer goes at least as well.

NIGHTLIFE AND THE PERFORMING ARTS/TORONTO

Pronto
692 Mount Pleasant Rd.
☎ 486-1111 ▯▯ to ▮▮▮▮ AE ◉ VISA
Closed lunch.
At this consensus choice for best Italian, the toughest obstacles are getting a table and deciding what to eat. The first is solved by reserving 1-2 days ahead rather than just showing up. Closing your eyes and punching a finger at the menu is the easiest way around the second. That way you may wind up with something composed primarily of goat cheese, *porcini* and sun-dried tomatoes, but just because they're cliches doesn't mean they aren't good. This isn't just another hi-tech Milanese pasta house, either. Veal is special, and most fish and meats are merely grilled and served with minimalist sauces. Quibble? The din resulting from crowds in a room built primarily of steel and glass.

Rotterdam Brewery Pub
600 King St. ☎ 868-6882. *Map 4F4* ▯▯ to ▮▮▯ ◉ VISA
A few steps down from the street is a long room of stone and wooden beams, an opening in the ceiling revealing ranks of copper vats. This is a working brewery, and they take their self-appointed task seriously. The result is a beer-lover's nirvana, with a roster of 300 brands of imported and domestic brews, in addition to those made on the premises. There are daily lunch specials, a popular Sun brunch, and since it's near the **SkyDome**, low-priced dinners before athletic events.

Scaramouche
1 Benvenuto Pl. (off Avenue Rd.)
☎ 961-8011. *Map 4G1* ▮▮▮▮ AE ◉ VISA *Closed Sun, lunch.*
Those who seek novelty over substance needn't bother with Scaramouche. This is a classic restaurant, populated in the main by people of a certain age and income that permit them to ignore the side of the menu where prices reside. That isn't to say that the management is indifferent to fashion. They have a sidebar café that specializes in pastas for the younger set. In the main room, dishes follow restrained *nouvelle* conventions, the fish and meats lying on top of sauces rather than beneath them. Taste sensations are frequent, but using familiar ingredients, not the latest creature to arrive from the Asian Pacific without an English name. Add to the serenity a panorama of the city beneath a spangle of stars, and it becomes the perfect choice for a last-night farewell to Toronto.

Switzer's Delicatessen
322 Spadina Ave. ☎ 596-6900. *Map 4F3* ▯▯ ◉ VISA
It wasn't always an anachronism, this Jewish deli in the midst of the noodle shops and tea houses of Chinatown. Once, this stretch of Spadina was the heart of an Eastern European garment district. Whatever has happened outside, inside it hasn't changed. Nova Scotia salmon and *pastrami* and gefilte fish and bagels are one culture's soul food, as good here as any place w of Montréal and N of New York.

Tall Poppies
326 Dundas St. W ☎ 595-5588. *Map 4F3* ▯▯ AE ◉ VISA *Closed Mon dinner, Sat lunch, Sun.*
Creativity reigns behind the skillets of this ever-popular spot opposite the Art Gallery of Ontario. Dishes designated as the "Chef's Whim" are always worth a try, at least for nontimid diners. It all arrives as pretty as a picture. Decor is attractive, not distracting, and there is an outdoor court in back.

Telfer's
212 King St. ☎ 977-4447. *Map 4G4* ▯▯ to ▮▮▮▮ AE ◉ ◉ VISA *Closed Sat lunch, Sun.*
This ingratiating theater-district favorite satisfies many urges. Business lunches, preconcert drinks, or after-theater supper and dancing to a combo (*Thurs-Sat*). Meals are the borrowings from several cuisines that a visitor comes to expect, but they avoid excess. The room is high-ceilinged, with banks of plants, and upholstered armchairs. Nearby are the Royal Alex Theatre and Roy Thomson Hall.

Nightlife & the performing arts

With their pronounced Protestant ethic, Torontonians were long said to be more interested in work than in leisure. It's true that the city turns off its lights early. Bars close at 1am

Toronto/Nightlife and the performing arts

and don't open again until noon. Probably that will dismay only the younger adults, and there are many compensations.

Theater, for example. Toronto has at least 40 English-language theaters, which mount both *avant-garde* experiments and mainstream plays of high professional caliber. Such complicated and costly shows as *The Phantom of the Opera* and *Les Misérables* have been given lavish treatment.

Toronto's symphony orchestra, ballet companies and opera are world-class, and there is a steady flow of touring organizations from other parts of Canada and abroad. Its discos and rock clubs jam on as late as 4am, which should satisfy all but those who need not worry about making a living.

A cover charge is usually levied wherever live entertainment is on hand. In most cases it isn't confiscatory. A minimum number of drinks may be stipulated. Supper clubs and dinner theaters allow the option of paying to see the show without having a meal, but with a cover charge. Dinner-and-show packages aren't especially expensive, but then the food is rarely better than passable.

Tickets to most plays and concerts can be bought by phone from **TicketMaster** (☎ *872-1111*). Their lines are open Mon-Fri 9.30am-9pm, Sat 9.30am-6pm, Sun noon-6pm. Have a credit card ready. Half-price tickets to most of the same events can be purchased the day of performance at **Five Star Tickets**. Their booth is located either in the lobby of the **Royal Ontario Museum** (winter) or at the corner of Dundas and Yonge near the **Eaton Centre**. Sales are final and must be paid in cash. For information on all forms of nightlife, the most current sources are the Fri edition of *The Toronto Star* and the Sat issue of *The Globe and Mail*. *Now* and *Metropolis* are also useful, as is the monthly *Toronto Life*.

Bars are found in every permutation. There are credible imitations of British pubs, power bars, gay bars, cruising bars, university bars, bohemian bars, theater bars, jazz bars, sports bars, piano bars... and even bars in which you might have just a quiet drink.

Singles bars are thriving. Their habitués proceed with more caution than a decade ago, for all the well-publicized reasons, but that hasn't seriously derailed the age-old quest. Two of the first that come to mind are next door to each other — **Scotland Yard** (*56 The Esplanade* ☎ *364-6577*) and **Brandy's** (*58 The Esplanade,* ☎ *364-6671*). On a developing downtown street near **O'Keefe Centre**, they have music and comedy on an irregular schedule. Up in Yorkville, seekers of companionship favor **Bellair Café** (*100 Cumberland St.* ☎ *964-2222*) for its sleek Manhattan look; food and outdoor tables, a live piano-and-bass duo until 10pm, then disco dancing. Not far away, **Hemingway's** (*142 Cumberland St.* ☎ *968-2828*) has an extensive following, attired in everything from jeans and tuxes to mink.

Pubs, some of which must have been dismantled over there and reassembled over here, are encountered everywhere. Their names are right: **Spotted Dick** (*81 Bloor St.* ☎ *927-0843*), **Toad in the Hole** (*525 King St.* ☎ *593-8623*) and **Duke of Gloucester** (*649 Yonge St.* ☎ *961-9704*) are just three. Inside, with their etched glass, brass chandeliers, flowered carpets, and beer pumps, they do their all to evoke Albion. The **Duke of York** (*39 Prince Arthur* ☎ *964-2441*) ups its authenticity with bangers and mash and pints of Watney's. The **Duke of Kent** (*2315 Yonge St.* ☎ *485-9507*) is of the same mold.

Nightlife and the performing arts/

Two hotel bars with nightly piano music are **Club 22** at the **Windsor Arms** (*22 St Thomas St.* ☎ *979-2341*), a celebrity haunt, and **Bosun's** in the **Admiral Hotel** (*259 Queen's Quay W* ☎ *364-5444*), with a pleasing view of the harbor. **The Long Bar** at **Sheraton Centre** (*123 Queen St. W* ☎ *361-1000*) lives up to its name, and has a vista of Nathan Phillips Square and City Hall.

Cabarets and dinner theaters put on comedy acts, magicians, Broadway musicals, showgirls, and men dressed as showgirls. Most of the following are closed Sun and/or Mon. **An Evening at La Cage** (*279 Yonge St.* ☎ *364-5200*) has dinner and female impersonators. *A Little Night Magic* is the name of the magic and comedy revue at **Harper's** (*38 Lombard St.* ☎ *863-6223*), which includes performers with grand illusions and clever table tricks. **His Majesty's Feast** (*1926 Lakeshore Blvd.* ☎ *769-1165*) is one of those "historical" costume cabarets, with the requisite serving wenches, minstrels and mildly bawdy humor. The **Imperial Room** (*Royal York Hotel, 100 Front St. W* ☎ *368-6175*) is a throwback to the glossy supper clubs of a time now glimmering — the kind of place where Fred and Ginger might have twirled and tapped for the swells. Such big-time entertainers as Anne Murray and Tony Bennett appear there. Martin Short, John Candy, Dan Aykroyd and Rick Moranis, among many, got their start with the Second City troupe at **Old Firehall** (*110 Lombard St.* ☎ *863-1111*). The present comedy corps performs its set pieces on weekends and engages in often riotous improvisations Mon-Thurs. **Yuk Yuk's** is a comedy club empire with 16 units all over English Canada. Two are in Toronto, one uptown (*1280 Bay St.* ☎ *967-6425*) and one midtown (*2335 Yonge St.* ☎ *967-6425*). The mix of "name" comedians (Robin Williams and George Carlin have appeared) with neophytes, with no predicting what might appear any given night. There are screamers, misogynists, macho men, man-haters. Some are funny.

Dance clubs and discos are no more stable here than in any other city, so always call or check the newspapers to confirm hours and attractions. Entrance policies aren't usually exclusionary, but on busy nights there are lines at the doors, and regulars may be waved through before strangers. Most stay open until 2 or 3am, even though they must stop pouring liquor after 1am. **Berlin** (*2335 Yonge St.* ☎ *489-7777*) strives to suggest the glittery debauchery of its eponymous city of the 1930s. Its glossy crowd gladly forks over the steep admission charge, which discourages teenagers and pays for the live bands and professional dancers. The huge **Copa** (*21 Scollard St.* ☎ *922-6500*) hasn't missed a gimmick, with its banks of TV monitors, laser lights, fashion shows, live bands and free buffets. More than 1,000 people can be accommodated at a time. Anyone who remembers the Moon-landing will feel like an antique. **Down Towne Brown's** (*49 Front St. E* ☎ *367-4949*) has dancing seven nights a week to a DJ, spelled by live bands that get six-night gigs. Young crowd. No ageism at **Studebaker's** (*150 Pearl St.* ☎ *591-7960*). There are almost as many greyheads as there are youngsters. A real Studebaker takes the place of honor, a relic of the same Fifties epoch that saw the birth of rock 'n' roll. Most of the recorded music is of that time. Very animated, with no cover or inflated prices.

There is enough **jazz** to keep enthusiasts happy. Several hotels bring in groups on weekends, and jazz brunch is a staple. Check out the **Chelsea Bun** (☎ *595-1975*) in the **Delta Chelsea**, and the **Trader's Lounge** (☎ *361-1000*) at the **Sheraton Centre**.

Nightlife and the performing arts

...lubs irregularly schedule combos, but for jazz ...week, try **Albert's Hall** (*481 Bloor St. W* ...) for blues and some Dixie. **Café des Copains** (*48 ...on St. E* ☎ *869-0148*) has a restaurant upstairs, jazz ...no downstairs. **George's Spaghetti House** (*290 Dundas St. E* ☎ *923-9887*) is the oldest jazz spot in Toronto, featuring the popular Moe Koffman. **Meyers Deli** (*69 Yorkville Ave.* ☎ *960-4780*) has duos and trios after 10pm.

Rock/pop/country/folk are found all over, in cramped cellars, warehouses, above restaurants. For one of the hottest, see the entry for **Bamboo** in *Restaurants* (page 57). At the **Apocalypse Club** (*750 College St.* ☎ *533-5787*), music varies, from rock as nasty as it can get, to updated sixties folk-protest. **Birchmount Tavern** (*462 Birchmount Rd.* ☎ *698-4115*) has entertainers working the country music vein. **Club Bluenote** (*128 Pears Ave.* ☎ *921-1109*) is the place for top-drawer rhythm 'n' blues. **Spectrum** (*2714 Danforth Ave.* ☎ *699-9913*) has live concerts most nights, with a super lightshow.

Film has its major celebration in Sept with the annual **Festival of Festivals** (*information* ☎ *968-3456*), which showcases more than 250 new movies from around the world, from early July to the end of the festival. The giant Canadian cinema chain **Cinéplex Odeon** has its flagship facility in **Eaton Centre** (☎ *593-4535*), with 17 screens and the ability to shuffle programs according to demand. Serious movie buffs have a number of repertory houses from which to choose. They often program series of movies on a particular theme, be it a genre or the work of a single director or actor. Features change frequently. Among them: **Bloor** (*506 Bloor St. W* ☎ *532-6677*); **Euclid** (*394 Euclid Ave.* ☎ *925-8104*); **Fox** (*2236 Queen St. E* ☎ *691-7330*); **Harbourfront** (*235 Queen's Quay W* ☎ *973-4000*); **Kingsway** and **Nostalgic** (*both at 3030 Bloor St. W* ☎ *236-1411*).

Toronto's **dance** companies perform in a number of venues, both indoors and out. The **National Ballet of Canada** (☎ *362-1041*), with some 70 dancers, is the third-largest in North America. It has a classical foundation, but tackles modern works as well. In summer, it appears at **Ontario Place**; in winter, at the O'Keefe Centre. Contemporary forms are explored by the **Toronto Dance Theatre** (☎ *967-1365*). The new **Première Dance Theatre** at Harbourfront enjoys the company's presence most of the year, and **Dancemakers** (☎ *535-8880*) performs there too.

Classical music and opera are abundantly served. Blessed with a mighty reputation, the **Canadian Opera Company** (☎ *363-6671*) is also one of the largest in North America. Most of its performances are in the original language of the composer, but the company was one of the first to project librettos in English on a screen above the stage. Seven operas are staged each year at **O'Keefe Centre**. Of equal stature is the **Toronto Symphony Orchestra** (☎ *593-7769*), which appears in winter at **Roy Thomson Hall** and in summer at **Ontario Place**. The orchestra often teams with the **Toronto Mendelssohn Choir** (☎ *598-0422*), which has close to 200 singers, producing a heavenly sound that brings it into considerable demand around the world.

Other classical groups to look for are **The Canadian Brass** (☎ *967-1421*), the **Orford String Quartet** (☎ *861-8600*), **The Chamber Players of Toronto** (☎ *862-8311*) and the **Tafelmusik Baroque Orchestra** (☎ *964-6337*), which plays on original period instruments.

Shopping in Toronto

Even the most aggressively acquisitive shopper can't exhaust the possibilities here. Every reasonable need, and most frivolous ones too, can be met in a retailing environment that takes every step from deepest discounts in 3rd-floor walkups to hushed emporia so rarefied that it's boorish to inquire about prices. All the major international names are represented — Ralph Lauren, Hermès, St-Laurent, Turnbull & Asser, Bulgari, Jaeger, Charles Jourdan, Cartier and Vuitton, to drop a few. There is no particular advantage to buying a $600 sweater or $250 shoes here, however. Better buys, not for their cheapness but for their generally excellent quality, are Canadian crafts, antique country furniture, and clothes by native designers and bespoke tailors. Toronto shares leadership in the fashion industry with Montréal, resulting in wide selections of both men's and women's clothing as stylishly conservative or head-turningly visionary as might be desired. Mennonite quilts, Inuit sculptures and Amerindian weavings are delightful.

Keep receipts for all purchases. There is an 8-percent sales tax, but articles that are taken out of the province and cost $100 or more are exempt. Applications for refunds and additional information can be obtained from **Ontario Travel** (*Toronto M7A 2R9* ☎ *965-4008*). (Hotel room tax is also refundable: see **Hotels**, page 51.) Credit cards are widely accepted; personal checks drawn on out-of-town banks are not.

Despite continued resistance, much of it from the provincial government, Toronto's blue laws forbidding Sun shopping are crumbling. Stores in such tourist areas as Harbourfront are allowed to be open, and larger stores are either defying the ban or rallying support to have it repealed. As a rule, though, store hours are 9 or 10am-6pm Mon-Sat, with one late night until 8 or 9pm, usually Thurs. Eaton Centre, Simpson's and the stores of Underground Toronto stay open until 9pm Mon-Fri.

Shops are found everywhere, of course. But there are several highly attractive concentrations along particular streets and in enclosed malls where almost every want can be satisfied.

Eaton Centre is said to be the number one tourist attraction in Toronto, a claim proved by the throngs that course through it 12hrs a day. The enclosed 4-tiered mall harbors more than 300 shops and eating places, a 17-screen cinema, and the mother Eaton's department store (*open Mon-Fri 9am-9pm, Sat 9am-6pm, closed Sun*), which occupies nine floors. The complex runs three full blocks between Dundas in the N and Queen on the S and is connected to Underground Toronto and **Simpson's department store**, opposite on Queen. Goods are primarily mid-priced popular brands, with some luxury items.

Bloor St., E of Yonge and W beyond Avenue Rd., is home to two major department stores and many famous international retailers. The **Holt Renfrew Centre** incorporates the eponymous department store and 37 satellite shops on three levels. Among the latter are **Bally Shoes** and **William Ashley China**. It connects with the subway and **The Bay**, across the street. Walking W, dozens of stores offer the products of such luminaries as Burberrys and Ralph Lauren. Men's clothiers **Harry Rosen** (*#80*) and **Stollery's** (*#1*) are two to look for, as is **Creed's** (*#45*), representing a number of designers for women. **European Jewelry** (*#111*) carries Rolex and Cartier. High-profile single brand stores are numerous — examples include **Gucci**, **Georg Jensen** and **Marks & Spencer**.

Toronto/Shopping

Yorkville is bounded on the s by Bloor St., but has a different identity. Its stores are no less upscale, but they are a bit less glittery, more iconoclastic. A good place to start is **Hazelton Lanes** (*55 Avenue Rd.*), a relatively small 2-story mall that contains a number of "name" boutiques (**Hermès**, **Yves St-Laurent**) and many fine Canadian clothiers. Look for **Beaver Canoe** (casual and outdoor wear) and **Chez Catherine** (high fashion for women). Afterwards, browsing along Yorkville Ave. E to Yonge and then (one block s) w on Cumberland St. is rewarding, as much for the lively street scene as for the shops.

Queen St. W follows a different drummer, at least between John St. and Spadina Ave. The street signs are subtitled "Fashion District," and there are clothing options, from studded suede minidresses to vintage cloche hats to those filmy blouses that only the most confident or oblivious women can wear in public. But the street is hardly single-minded. It has affinities with New York's SoHo and London's King's Road — youthful, arty, quirky — and along its bumptious way can be found laptop computers, saxophones, chess sets, penguin pull-toys, military prints, compact discs, tofu burgers, and 53 of the 55 volumes of the complete works of Balzac. Many shops feature Canadian designers, including **Club Monaco** (*#403*), **Crise** (*#278*), **Le Château** (*#336*) and **Emily Zarb** (*#276*). For furs and leathers at near-wholesale prices, continue w and turn right (N) on Spadina. There are more than a dozen furriers between there and Sullivan St.

Harbourfront has many shops spaced between its restaurants and marinas, and nearly all are open on Sun. Two buildings in particular deserve attention. **Queen's Quay Terminal**, near the middle of the waterfront strip, is a converted warehouse that now shelters boutiques, crafts booths, a theater and restaurants. At the w end of Queen's Quay W is the new **Harbourfront Antique Market** (*closed Mon*), with more than 100 permanent dealers selling every imaginable object and collectible of the last 150yrs. Find estate jewelry, duck decoys, country furniture, silverware, art glass, and, as they say, "much, much more." Most accept credit cards. On Sun, at least 100 more exhibitors set up shop on the pier across the street.

Finally, there is **Honest Ed's Emporium**, at the corner of Bloor St. W and Markham St. Ed Mirvish, Toronto's most visible millionaire merchant, is a presence impossible to ignore. His empire includes the Royal Alex Theatre and several restaurants, as well as his retail enterprises, and Ed won't let anyone forget it. The font of his fortune is this sprawling store, covered with signs and racing lights only slightly less gaudy than downtown Las Vegas. There, he peddles low-end housewares and related products. Signs on the walls reflect the founder's idea of wit: "Please don't bother our help. They have their own problems." Nearby is **Mirvish Village**, a block of houses between Bloor and Lennox, leased by Ed to private retailers. Most exercise more restraint than their landlord, selling books, antiques, discount clothes. A walk w on Bloor is a plunge into ethnic Toronto, with seemingly a restaurant for every one of its 70 national groups.

Every human need can be satisfied in at least one of these malls and shopping districts, but here is a brief selection of stores that can fill special requirements.

Antiques

Allery (*322 Queen St. W* ☎ *593-0853*). Maps and prints, most more than a century old, and authenticated. Good prices. **Atelier**

SPORTS/TORONTO

Art and Antiques (*588 Markham St.* ☎ *532-9244*). Vintage folk art — wood carvings, weathervanes, duck decoys. **Labell's Toy Soldiers** (*100 Front St. W* ☎ *362-8697*). Military buffs, collectors and kids love these painted lead soldiers, some old, some new. Matchbox vehicles, too. **Louis Wine** (*848A Yonge St.* ☎ *929-9333*). Estate jewelry and silver. **Primrose Lane** (*1258 Yonge St.* ☎ *969-8855*). Specialist in Victoriana, including furniture, silver and china. **Sandy's Antiques** (*3130 Bathurst St.* ☎ *787-5230*). Substantial discounts on silver, much of it pre-1900.

Arts and crafts
Algonquians (*670 Queen St. W* ☎ *368-1336*). Amerindian masks, carvings and crafts. **Dexterity** (*173 King St. E* ☎ *367-4775*). Ceramics, furniture, glass and clothing. **The Guild Shop** (*140 Cumberland St.* ☎ *921-1721*). Canadian crafts in all materials, and a selection of Inuit sculptures. Run by the Ontario Crafts Council. **Inuit Gallery of Eskimo Art** (*9 Prince Arthur Ave.* ☎ *921-9985*). Antique and contemporary Inuit carvings, prints and wall-hangings. **Prime Canadian Crafts** (*229 Queen St. W* ☎ *593-5750*). Vintage and contemporary Canadiana, including pottery and folk art. **Sawtooth Borders** (*5 MacPherson St.* ☎ *961-8187; restricted hours, so call ahead.*). Antique quilts of superb quality.

Books
Bakka Science Fiction (*282 Queen St. W* ☎ *596-8161*). Claims to be Canada's largest seller of new and used sci-fi. **The Book Cellar** (*142 Yorkville Ave.* ☎ *925-9955, open Sun*). Across from the Four Seasons Hotel. International newspapers and magazines as well as books. **Can-Do Bookstore** (*311 Queen St. W* ☎ *977-2351*). Everything for the hobbyist and do-it-yourselfer: woodworking, cooking, crafts, plumbing, modelmaking and much more. **The Children's Book Store** (*604 and 597 Markham St.* ☎ *535-7011*). Author appearances and readings. Audio and video cassettes. **The Cookbook Store** (*850 Yonge St.* ☎ *920-2665*). Every cuisine, every taste, the books supplemented with videos and magazines. **World's Biggest Bookstore** (*20 Edward St.* ☎ *977-7009*. *Near Eaton Centre; open 7 days*). Perhaps the claim is hyperbole, but with 1 million volumes, there's little point in disputing it.

Sports

Auto racing
The grounds of the Canadian National Exhibition and nearby streets are the site in mid-July of the **Molson Indy** (☎ *595-5445*). Cars are of the Indianapolis 500 variety, rather than Formula One, and they reach speeds approaching 200mph. Tickets are available at varying prices for the several segments of the 3-day event.

Baseball
Apart from the bleats of purists who think baseball should be played on grass rather than carpet, there is no better facility in which to watch baseball than the splendid new *SkyDome* (*tickets and information* ☎ *595-0077*). Sightlines are exceptional and the retractable roof ensures that no games are called on account of rain. Not that poor weather and the considerably less

Toronto/Sports

desirable old Exhibition Stadium ever discouraged the fans of the Toronto Blue Jays. They are one of only two Canadian teams in Major League Baseball, and have been contenders for the pennant in recent years. Only hockey holds a higher place in the hearts of Torontonians.

Boating
Rowboats, canoes and/or pedalboats are available for rent at Ontario Place, at the pond in High Park, and on Centre Island, in the harbor. (See also *Sailing and sailboarding*, page 69).

Cycling
Toronto is an enthusiastic cycling city, with many miles of carefully laid-out routes in the city and its parks. One of the most popular is the 12-mile **Martin Goodman Trail**, which runs along the waterfront past Ontario Place and Harbourfront. High Park and the Toronto Islands are easily accessible. Bicycles are allowed on subway trains except during rush hours, and on Toronto Islands ferries, with some restrictions. Call the **Toronto Bicycling Network** (☎ *766-1985*) for updates on cycling news and special events. The parks department (☎ *392-8186*) provides maps of its trails, and free street guides and newsletters are available in bicycle stores. From May-Sept, bicycles can be rented on **Centre Island** (☎ *365-7901*) and at **McBride's** (*180 Queen's Quay W* ☎ *367-5651*).

Fishing
Lake Ontario has a substantial trout-and-salmon fishery, courtesy of diligent stocking by wildlife management departments. Scores of charter boats are available in and near the city for half- and full-day expeditions. Call **Ontario Travel** (*900 Bay St.* ☎ *965-4008*), or stop by their office for information on regulations and licenses. Unfortunately, Lake Ontario is badly polluted and caution must be exercised in eating any fish caught in it. The cheapest fishing is at the ponds in *High Park* and on *Toronto Islands*, both of which are open to casual anglers.

Fitness centers
Finding a place to work out isn't easy in a strange city, if the hotel doesn't have one. Many in Toronto do, or have arrangements for their guests with nearby health clubs. Three that have especially good facilities, with exercycles, weight circuits, pools and saunas are the **Harbour Castle Westin**, the **Sheraton Centre**, and the **Four Seasons Inn on the Park**. For other possibilities, see *Hotels* on page 51 or ask when making reservations. Otherwise, the **YMCA** (*20 Grosvenor St.* ☎ *921-5171*) allows use of its facilities for a low daily fee. Pay-as-you-sweat arrangements can also be made at the **Downtown Tennis Club** (*21 Eastern Ave.* ☎ *362-2439*) and at **Gold's Gym** (*675 Yonge St.* ☎ *962-9001*).

Football
Canadian football looks and plays very much like the American version, with minor variations in scoring, the number of downs, and the dimensions of the field. The local professional team is the up-and-down Toronto Argonauts, which plays at the *SkyDome* (☎ *595-1131*). There is some risk in even mentioning their existence, for attendance at Canadian Football League games is dwindling and there are repeated rumors of impending collapse. Montréal has already abandoned the sport. Part of the cause is the growing appeal of the gaudier American university

and professional game, beamed across the border on television
and radio from mid-summer to late Jan. The CFL season ends in
Nov with the Grey Cup championship.

Golf
The Canadian Open is held at **Glen Abbey Golf Club** in
Oakville (☎ *844-1800*). Municipal courses within Metro Toronto
are **Don Valley Golf Course** (*4200 Yonge St.* ☎ *392-2465*),
Humber Valley Golf Course (*40 Beattie Ave.* ☎ *392-2488*) and
Lakeview Golf Course (*Lakeshore Blvd. W* ☎ *278-4411*). All are
18-hole courses with inexpensive green fees. Don Valley is a par
71, the others, par 70. For information about other area courses
open to the public, call **Ontario Travel** (☎ *965-4008*).

Hockey
The Toronto Maple Leafs have been out of serious contention for
the Stanley Cup for more than two decades. That doesn't deter
their rabidly loyal fans from buying all the seats for every face-off
at ancient **Maple Leaf Gardens** (*60 Carlton St.* ☎ *977-1641*).
This, after all, may be the year. The hotel concierge may be able
to get tickets.

Horse-racing
Followers of both thoroughbreds and trotters are well-served.
Woodbine Race Track (*Highway 27 and Rexdale Blvd.* ☎ *675-6110*) hosts the legendary Queen's Plate in July. Its seasons are
late Apr-early Aug and Sept-Oct. Harness-racing, with both
pacers and trotters, meets three times a year at the venerable
Greenwood Race Track (*1669 Queen St. E* ☎ *698-3131*).
Mohawk Raceway (*Highway 401 W* ☎ *854-2255*) has an
enclosed grandstand for comfortable viewing of standard-bred
harness races in fall and spring meetings.

Running
Many of the same trails used for cycling (see above) are excellent
for runners. The boardwalk of the community known as **The
Beaches**, E of downtown on Queen St., is another possibility. For
advice, call the parks department (☎ *392-8186*).

Sailing and sailboarding
Boats and windsurfers dance across the harbor every warm day
of summer and into gray Oct. A favored push-off point is **The
Beaches** community E of downtown. Sailboards can be rented
there from **Wind Promotions** (☎ *694-6881*), located at the W
end of the boardwalk. A good source of information about both
sailing and sailboarding (or windsurfing) is the **Ontario Sailing
Association** (☎ *495-4240*).

Skating
Toronto makes the most (or the best) of its winters, with more
than 125 artificial and natural rinks. All are free. Perhaps the most
popular is the frozen reflecting pool in **Nathan Phillips Square**,
in front of the new City Hall, but there is at least one in every
neighborhood and many more in the parks (*information on
locations* ☎ *392-7251*). Most are open from 9 or 10am until
10pm Mon-Sat, until 6pm Sun. For indoor skating, there is a rink
at the **Hazelton Lanes** shopping mall in Yorkville.

Skiing
While there are a number of good hills with lifts within 2hrs of

downtown, there are slopes in town that can be satisfying and reduce expenditures of time and money. **Earl Bales Park** (☎ *392-8186*) is one option, with four short runs and rentals; **Centennial Park Ski Hill** (☎ *394-8750*) is another, with T-bar lifts and rentals. Those who demand greater challenges and have the time can call **Ontario Travel** (☎ *965-4008*) for suggestions. A delightful possibility for cross-country skiing is the *Metro Zoo* (☎ *392-5900*), where the whimsically named Zooski Trails curl around the animals. A fee is charged; they have rentals. *High Park*, **Tommy Thomson Park**, and the *Toronto Islands* are free and closer. Call the parks department (☎ *392-8186*) for advice. For ski conditions ☎ 963-2992.

Soccer
There's no telling how long the latest attempt at a professional soccer league will last, but the game known as football on every other continent can be seen at **Varsity Stadium** (*Bloor St. W and Bedford* ☎ *979-2186*).

Swimming
Lake Ontario, as noted above, is polluted, and its beaches often are closed as a result. The water is quite cold, too. Even so, there are many popular beaches, if only for a day in the sun. To the E of downtown is the aptly named **Beaches** community, with a boardwalk and sailboard rentals. For great views of the city while taking a dose of vitamin D in its most palatable form, the beaches of the *Toronto Islands* can't be bested. In addition, the parks department operates 50 indoor and outdoor pools in various venues (*for locations* ☎ *392-7259*). That might not be necessary for visitors, since most of the larger hotels have their own pools, which are usually much less crowded.

Tennis
The **National Tennis Centre** (☎ *665-9777*) on the York University campus is the setting every summer for the Player's Canadian Championship. For amateurs, there are free courts in several city parks and on the *Toronto Islands*, many of them illuminated for night play. Also, the **Ontario Tennis Association** (☎ *495-4215*) is a useful source. Call the parks department (☎ *392-7291*) for locations and hours.

Toronto for children

For all its recent press as Canada's first world city and the glossy cosmopolitanism that implies, Toronto remains, as it has always been, a family town. With its marvelous zoo, exciting theme parks and entertainments geared to the young set, no child ever need be bored. Some of the best of these are outlined here. For details, see *Sights and places of interest*, *Nightlife and the performing arts* and *Sports*; look for the ✱ symbol.

Amusement parks and zoos
At the very top of any list for parents with kids in tow must be the *Metro Zoo* and *Canada's Wonderland*. Each should be allotted the better part of a day because they have much to offer and are at some distance from downtown. In addition, there is the **African Lion Safari** (☎ *519-623-2620*). About an hour's drive W of Toronto, it is a drive-through game park where lions,

zebras, giraffes and many other species roam freely, some of them approaching to put their noses against car windows. Downtown, *Ontario Place* has rides and activities in its Children's Village, including an area where they can get deliriously soaked with hoses and water pistols. **Centre Island** has an intentionally old-fashioned amusement park and petting zoo. **High Park** also has a small zoo. The *Ontario Science Centre*, with its razzle-dazzle hands-on exhibits, is as entertaining as an amusement park, and educational, to boot.

Boat trips and rides

The ferry to the Toronto Islands has an unobstructed view of the skyline, and it's free. So are the glass elevators that shoot up the outsides of the **Harbour Castle Westin** hotel and the **Hilton**. There is a fee for the ride to the top of the *CN Tower*, but kids will never get higher off the ground without boarding an airplane. (It may be frightening to the very young.) Boats providing narrated 1-1½hr cruises of the harbor depart from several piers along Harbourfront. The **Wilderness Adventure Ride** at *Ontario Place* is a treat. And kids who have never seen one, get a kick out of the subway.

Events and entertainments

Harbourfront celebrates an **International Children's Festival** and has fireworks on Victoria Day, both in May. There are more pyrotechnics on Canada Day (July 1st) at Ontario Place and Harbourfront. In late July arrives the colorful **Caribana West Indian Festival**, with parades, music, and dancing in the streets. Various locations (☎ 925-5435). Mid-Aug sees the opening of the **Canadian National Exhibition**, with a carnival midway, rides, big-name rock concerts and an air show.

Shows and theater

In a category all its own is the **Tour of the Universe** (*☎ 364-2019, hours vary; call ahead*), at the base of the *CN Tower*. It simulates a 21stC spaceport, with employees acting as futuristic "commanders" and "pilots." There is a lot of hokum involved, which can prove irritating to adults who aren't in a playful mood, but the climax is a very effective "voyage" into space, fraught with danger and close calls. The **Laser Theatre** and **Theatre of the Stars** at the *McLaughlin Planetarium* provide a great spectacle for older children. **Young People's Theatre** (*165 Front St ☎ 864-9732*) and the **Puppet Centre** (*171 Avondale Rd. ☎ 222-9029*) offer a variety of winning productions. Reservations are usually required.

Montréal

To call Montréal a city possessed of a dual personality is a willful act of understatement. It is much more. Just when it seems to have arranged itself tidily under the aphoristic banners routinely assigned to it — "the Old Country next door" that is "big on life" — Montréal rears up and reveals yet another of its many aspects. Contrast and contradiction are the real rewards it grants to explorers of its variegated *quartiers*. True, it melds the comfort of the familiar with the tang of the foreign. At first look, the glass and steel towers of its commercial district may seem interchangeable with any middle-sized city on the American continent. Yet this is the second-largest French-speaking city in the world, a mighty distinction from Boston or Cincinnati. Hundreds of miles from the ocean, it is nevertheless a major port, gateway to the inland seas called the Great Lakes. In the very shadow of the pronounced modernity of its thriving downtown is a living remnant of the frontier settlement of three centuries ago. As New World Gallic as it undeniably is, with its French signs and names and *pâtisseries* serving bowls of *café au lait*, the city retains decidedly Anglophile neighborhoods and makes room for enclaves that live and breathe the Eastern European and Asian origins of their inhabitants. The only course is to settle back and revel in Montréal's diversity.

Montréal is an island, too, the whole of which constitutes a metropolitan area of 29 towns and cities and 2.8 million people. Over 65 percent are Francophone, 20 percent Anglophone, and the rest command some other first language. The ubiquitous city emblem seen hanging from lampposts reflects the origins of its first residents. The design combines a French *fleur-de-lis*, an English rose, a Scottish thistle and an Irish shamrock. In the classic pattern of immigration, they were soon joined by Germans, Poles, Slavs and Italians, and followed in more recent decades by West Indians, Chinese, Greeks, Latin Americans and refugees from south and southeast Asia. Given the inherent possible tensions, they show a remarkably high level of inter-ethnic tolerance.

A form of regional government extends train lines and public services well into the suburbs, so municipal boundaries blur. The part of the city that is of most interest to visitors, however, is relatively compact, and an enthusiastic walker can cover most of it in three days. It is dominated by Mont-Royal, simply "The Mountain" to residents. It looks taller than it is, due to the flat river plain from which it rises, and the illuminated cross at its peak is a landmark seen from every part of the city.

The British saw — and conquered — in 1760. Blvd. St-Laurent came eventually to be the north-south dividing line between French Montréal to the east and English Montréal to the west. There are still two school systems, one Catholic, one Protestant, as well as French and English universities. So while geographical demarcations have been overwhelmed by events, the Anglophone culture prevails in its traditional redoubts, despite streets now called Rue Crescent and Rue Mackay, while the Latin Quarter of St-Denis is as French as the Paris Left Bank.

Getting around

From the airports to the city
There are two principal airports. **Dorval**, which handles flights from the US and other parts of Canada, is 22km W of downtown. The **Aerocar** bus (☎ *514-397-9999*) makes the trip in about 30mins. It leaves Dorval every 20mins and stops at four large downtown hotels before its final destination, the **Terminus Voyager**, where there is a Metro station. The fare is moderate. Metered taxis cost twice as much, before tip, and limousines still more. Most international flights land at **Mirabel** airport, 55km NW of the city. The Aerocar operates on a similar schedule and its fare is about the same as for Dorval, despite the greater distance. Taxis and limousines are considerably more expensive, however. Cars can be rented at both airports.

Useful addresses/Montréal

Public transportation
The integrated bus and Metro transit system is superb. The Metro, in particular, is clean, safe, and swift and its routes are easy to understand. There are four lines in operation, with a fifth nearly completed. Where routes intersect, transfer to another line is free, as is transfer between connecting buses and Metro trains. Ask the bus driver for a transfer ticket upon debarking; in Metro stations, transfer tickets are dispensed from machines just beyond the turnstiles. The fare is for a trip of any length, not graduated according to distance. Buying a book of eight tickets reduces somewhat the cost of each trip. Bus fares must be paid in exact change, but Metro tickets are accepted. The trains run between 5.30am and about 12.30am, although bus schedules vary.

Taxis
For short distances, walk; for long trips, take the bus or Metro. In between, use cabs. While taxi fares are not exorbitant by current international standards, neither are they a bargain. A trip from downtown to such outlying attractions as the Olympic Stadium looks deceptively short on maps, but the meter clicks merrily away and the final bite can easily equal that of a good meal. Taxis can be hailed in the streets or found at stands outside hotels and train stations. Many are radio-dispatched, so they arrive fairly quickly if called from a restaurant or theater.

Private and rental cars
Stories of the devil-may-care habits of Québec drivers are overdrawn. In the main, they are courteous and orderly. Except during the morning and evening rush hours, traffic flows at tolerable levels. Major arteries are broad and well-marked, and only the streets of the historic district of Vieux Montréal are uncomfortably narrow. Parking lots and garages are not too expensive. Much downtown street parking is metered. Car rental is fairly expensive, but there are discounted weekend packages. Most large hotels have at least one agency office near their lobbies, and the concierge can make arrangements to have cars delivered. **Tilden** is the prominent company, associated with National Car Rental in the US, but the other major international firms are also represented.

Calèches
Horsedrawn open carriages are an anachronism in most modern cities, but somehow less so in Montréal, especially in the old quarter. They gather there at **Pl. Jacques-Cartier** and at **Dorchester Sq.** in downtown. The season depends on the weather. In winter, horses pull sleighs around the parklands of Mont-Royal, as romantic an enterprise as might be imagined. Prices are steep, but sometimes negotiable.

Useful addresses

Tourist information
The **Greater Montréal Convention and Tourism Bureau** (*1010 Ste-Catherine St W, Suite 410, Montréal, Québec H3B 1GS* ☎ *871-1595*) handles telephone and postal inquiries.
 Infotouriste is the main tourist office and handles in-person inquiries at 1001 Rue du Square-Dorchester, near Peel. There is a branch office in Vieux Montréal on Pl. Jacques-Cartier (*174 Notre-Dame E*), and another at Dorval Airport.

Montréal/Emergency information

American Express has Travel Service Offices in the downtown Bay department store (☎ *281-4777*) and at 1141 de Maisonneuve W (☎ *284-3300*). American Express offers a valuable source of information for any traveler in need of help, advice or emergency services.

Main post offices
1025 St-Jacques ☎ 283-2567
1250 University ☎ 283-2576

Telephone services
Daily events ☎ 352-2500 (English) ☎ 353-2000 (French)
Sports and recreation ☎ 872-6211
Road conditions outside Montréal ☎ 873-4121
Travel information (Québec) ☎ 873-2015
Weather ☎ 636-3026

Tour operators
Delco Aviation (Laval) ☎ 663-4311. Seaplane rides.
Grey Line ☎ 280-5327. Bus tours.
Guidatour ☎ 844-4021. Walks and "step-on" guides using client's vehicle.
Hertz Tourist Guides ☎ 461-0664. Walks, "step-on" guides.
Les Montréalistes ☎ 744-3009. Walking tours and "step-on" guides.
Save Montréal ☎ 282-2069. Several tours with preservationist architectural slant.
Step-on Guides ☎ 935-5131.

Emergency information

Hospitals with emergency rooms
Hôpital général de Montréal 1650 Cedar ☎ 937-6011
Hôpital Royal Victoria 687 Av. des Pins O ☎ 842-1231
Hôpital St Luc 1058 St-Denis ☎ 285-1525

Hospitals with poison centers
Hôpital de Montréal pour enfants (children's hospital) 2300 Tupper ☎ 934-4456
Hôpital Ste-Justine 3175 Côte Ste-Catherine ☎ 731-4931

Dental emergencies
3546 Van Horne ☎ 342-4444. Open 24hrs.

Pharmacy open 24hrs
Jean Coutu Drug Store 1370 Mont-Royal E ☎ 527-8827

Help lines
Animal emergencies ☎ 731-9442
Alcoholics Anonymous ☎ 376-9230 (9am-11pm daily)
Distress Centre (personal counseling) ☎ 842-7557
Referral Centre (questions about health, social services, welfare, open Mon-Fri 8.30am-4.45pm) ☎ 931-2292
Sexual assault ☎ 934-4504
Suicide-Action ☎ 522-5777
Traffic police (Sureté de Québec) ☎ 598-4141

See also *Emergency information*, page 26.

Tours Guides de Montréal ☎ 484-0104. Walks and bus tours in Montréal, Ottawa, Québec City and the Laurentian Mountains.

River trips
Croisières maritimes de l'Archipel Lachine Off 6th Ave. ☎ 367-2840. Variety of cruises featuring brunch, supper, night excursions and day trips; June 1-Sept 30.
Lachine Rapids Tours Victoria Pier, 105 de la Commune W ☎ 284-9607. White-water trip over the upriver rapids, end of Apr-Oct 1.
Montréal Harbour Cruises Victoria Pier ☎ 842-3871. 1-3hr cruises, May 1-Oct 15.

Libraries
Montréal Central Library 1210 Sherbrooke E ☎ 872-5923. Largest of 24 branches, with collections on history of French Canada. Open daily.
Bibliothèque Nationale du Québec Three locations: 1700 St-Denis ☎ 873-4553; 125 Sherbrooke W ☎ 873-0270; 449 de l'Esplanade ☎ 873-3064. Closed Sun, Mon.
Centre d'archives de Montréal 1945 Mullins ☎ 873-3064.

Local publications
The *Montréal Gazette* is the primary English-language newspaper. Its Thurs and Fri editions carry useful entertainment sections listing the week's concerts, theatrical performances and club schedules. *En Ville* is a free magazine distributed by hotels and is more complete than most examples of the breed. Hotel newsstands often sell major US and European newspapers and periodicals, but a better source is the **Maison de la Presse Internationale** (*550 Ste-Catherine* ☎ *842-3857 and other branches*). French-language papers are *La Presse*, *Le Devoir* and *Le Journal de Montréal*.

Orientation

The Island of Montréal has nearly 30 townships, with a number of parks scattered around its perimeter. Its major sights and attractions, however, are concentrated in the city itself. Most of Montréal is oriented toward the St Lawrence River, which forms the lower shore of the island.

With the exception of some of the residential areas around Mont-Royal, the streets follow a more-or-less regular grid plan. That is where some initial confusion may set in. Montréalers — amd *most* published maps — consider the river to be due s. By that reckoning, Blvd. St-Laurent, which divides the city in half, is a N-S street, while Rue Sherbrooke and Blvd. René-Lévesque are primary arteries running E-W. In geographical fact, though, the river at that point runs more nearly on a N-S course, so Blvd. St-Laurent actually runs almost E to W. No wonder the sun seems to be rising in the south! Don't fight it. Stand downtown and face the harbor. That's "south." Turn around. That's "north." Otherwise, not a direction will make any sense. However, to make the best use of space, our maps **8-11** and pages 76-77 show true north at the top of the page.

Most business and leisure activities take place in six distinctive districts. **Vieux Montréal** is where the city began. Neglected and run down for much of the present century, it began to be restored

Montréal/Orientation and walks

Montréal orientation map

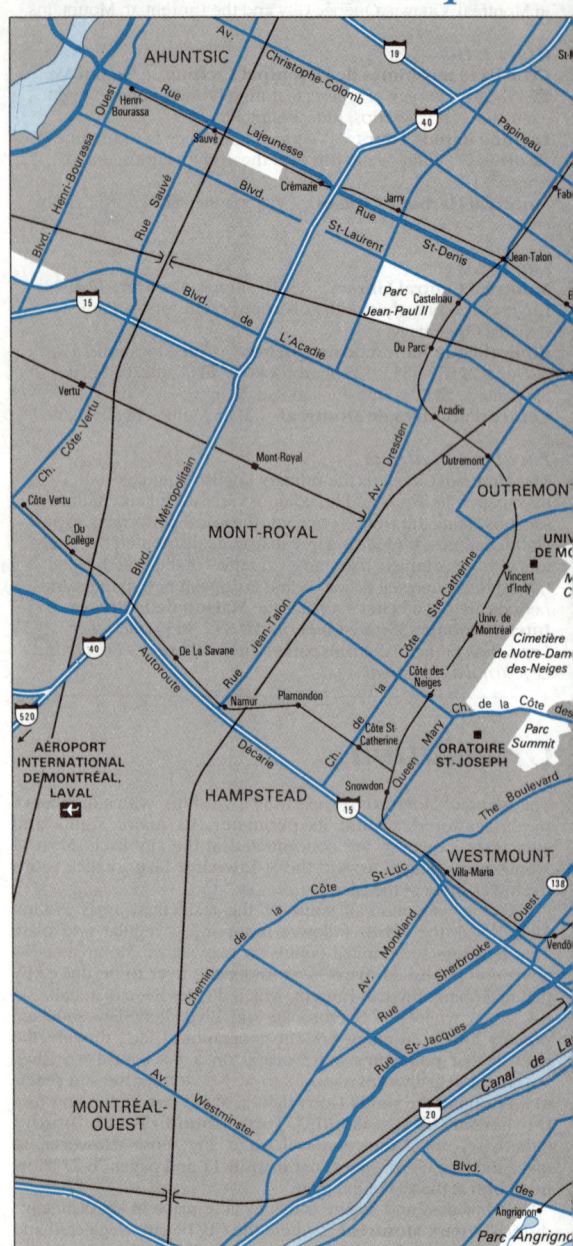

Orientation and walks/Montréal

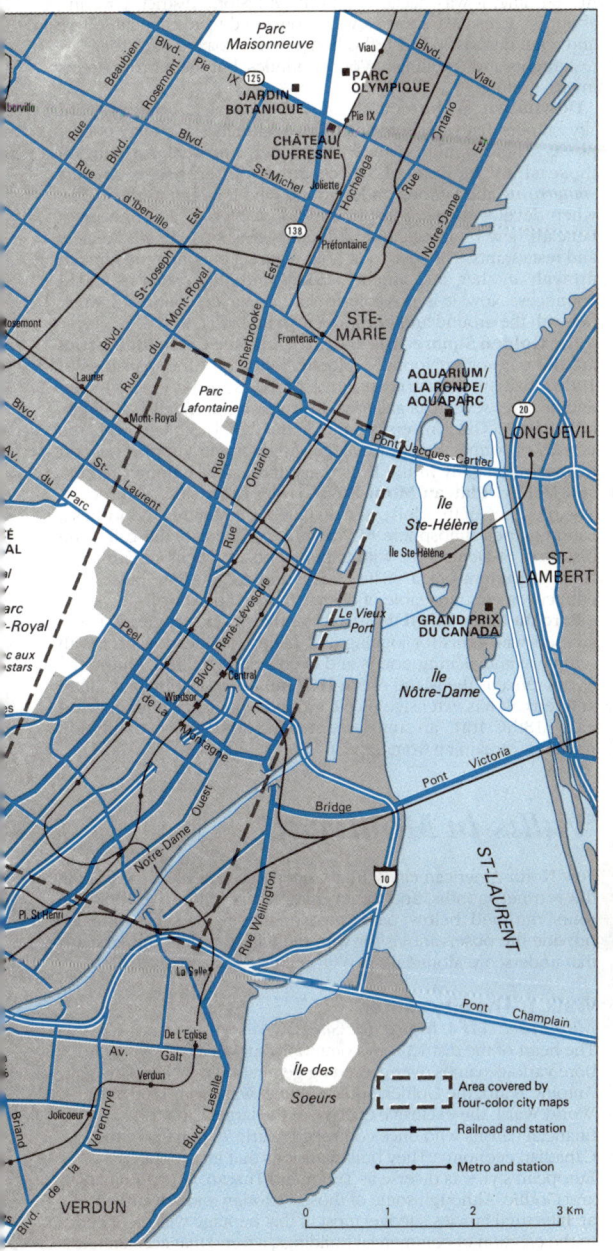

Montréal/Orientation and walks

in the 1960s, partly in anticipation of the Expo world fair in 1967. At that time, it was declared an official historic district, covering about 95 acres. Warehouses were converted to residential, office and retail purposes, and 18thC houses were coaxed back to life as restaurants and dwellings. Work continues, but the narrow streets invite strolling.

Downtown is the central business district, bristling with skyscrapers that yield here and there to churches and leafy pocket plazas. There is more than is immediately apparent, for beneath those shiny monuments to corporate enterprise is *la ville souterraine*, the famous underground city. It began in the 1950s, when developers were inspired to add subterranean concourses beneath new buildings and fill them with shops, movie theaters and restaurants. The idea took hold. One set of concourses linked up with another, and another. Hotels and Metro stations added entrances. Now it is possible to stay a climate-controlled week beneath the ground and never open an umbrella.

The **Golden Square Mile** and adjoining **Rue Crescent District** are the core of Anglophone Montréal. Some of the mansions of 19thC British industrialists and bankers survive along Rue Sherbrooke, several as galleries. Instruction is in English at highly regarded McGill University, and grand hotels sibilate with the echoes of former British privilege. Anglophone yuppies besport themselves nightly in the lively bars and eateries along Crescent and McKay. **Plateau Mont-Royal** is the other side of the coin. The presence of the Université du Québec à Montréal nourishes a Latin Quarter atmosphere of youthful exuberance, the cafés and bistros of St-Denis alive with experiments in rebellion. Farther N, Blvd. St-Laurent (a.k.a. "The Main") and Av. du Parc pulse with ethnicity, a groaning table of diverse foods and exotica.

Parc du Mont-Royal thrusts above the skyline, its green spaces crossed with trails for jogging and biking, its meadows set with sculpture and skating ponds and even a short ski run. Out in the St Lawrence is the island of **Ste-Hélène**. Accessible by bus, Metro and ferry, it has extensive picnic grounds, pools, an aquarium, an early 18thC fort, an amusement park, and active exhibition pavilions remaining from Expo '67.

Walks in Montréal

Few North American cities are as amenable to walkers, at least in the warmer months, and the evening hours hold no terrors. The tours outlined below pass most of the major sites, but also provide the observant visitor with the telling details and tableaus that underscore Montréal's rich diversity.

Walk 1: The city center
Maps 10F3-11F4. Metro: McGill.

The heart of the district now commonly known as the West End bore various names over preceding generations — New Town, St Antoine Ward, the Golden Square Mile. It was, from 1860 until World War I, the exclusive enclave of the largely Scottish financial barons who once controlled nearly 70 percent of the Canadian economy. They built mansions that incorporated European styles as diverse as Tudor and Tuscan, Greco-Roman and Gothic. Although some of those Victorian and Edwardian architectural fancies survive, most of that heritage was sacrificed to the erection of commercial buildings, a trend that accelerated with the skyscraper boom that began in the 1960s and has yet to abate. The district still contains streets of recycled row houses, however, as well as parks, museums, cathedrals, universities and multileveled shopping complexes.

To begin this tour, take the Union exit from the McGill Metro station. Directly opposite is the *Christ Church Anglican Cathedral*, a noteworthy Gothic Revival structure completed in 1857. Its backdrop is the **Maison des Coopérants**, a playful Post-Modernist office tower that incorporates angular Gothic conceits in its facades and twin "steeples" echoing those of the church. Beneath both buildings is a spanking-new subterranean shopping gallery, and the church is flanked by two venerable department stores, **La Baie** (The Bay) and **Eaton**. The entrance to Christ Church is on Rue Ste-Catherine. Its limestone interior and high wooden roof deserve a look, and organ recitals are scheduled some afternoons. After leaving the church, angle across Ste-Catherine toward Carré Phillips, a square containing a statue of Edward VII. Walk S on Union past **Henry Burkes et Fils**, the long-established purveyor of gold and silver jewelry and household objects. Turn W (right) on Blvd. René-Lévesque, which remains Blvd. Dorchester on some street maps and in the minds of Anglophones. Lévesque was the leader of the separatist-minded Parti Québecois in the turbulent 1970s and a hero to most Francophones. The 1st Baron Dorchester was Sir Guy Carleton, the British governor of Québec province during the time of the American Revolution.

At the far corner of University, on the right, is **Place Ville-Marie**, a massive 45-story skyscraper in a cruciform configuration intended to echo the cross placed on Mont-Royal by Jacques Cartier. Opened in 1959, it was the first structure to incorporate a large underground shopping mall, providing sheltered access as well to movie theaters, cafés, two railroad stations and three hotels. Its success prompted later builders to construct similar facilities, which, when linked together, resulted in the creation of the Underground City. Just past Pl. Ville-Marie is an esplanade with a fountain and three peaked glass roofs over the concourse below. To the N are seen Mont-Royal and part of the McGill University campus, and across the street is the **Hotel Reine Elizabeth** (Queen Elizabeth). Next to the hotel, on the same side, is the *Cathédrale Marie-Reine-du-Monde*, completed in 1894. This basilica is a replica (more or less) of St Peter's in Rome, but about a quarter the size of the original. On the right, across from the cathedral, is Dorchester Sq., rechristened from Dominion Sq. in a bit of political juggling to compensate the loss of the Baron's boulevard to René Lévesque. An inviting oasis in summer, with its old trees and benches, the square is one of several gathering places for the city's horse-drawn *calèches*. Bus tours of the city also start from here.

On the S of the square, across the open green space of **Place du Canada**, is the **Hotel Champlain**. Known, affectionately or not, as the "cheese grater," its resemblance to that kitchen implement is created by its rows of upturned semicircular windows. On the right side of Dorchester Sq. (while facing N) is the **Sun Life Building**, a wedding-cake structure built in successive layers during the 1920s, and the tallest building in the province until well into the post-World War II era. On the ground floor of the building at the NE corner of the square is an "**Infotouriste**" office. Walk across the square to bordering Rue Peel and continue N, past the Belgian restaurant **L'Actuel** and several foreign exchanges that compete with each other to offer

Montréal/Orientation and walks

the most attractive rates, occasionally better than those observed by banks. Turn left (w) on Ste-Catherine.

Near the next corner, at #1128, is a branch of the **Maison de la Presse Internationale** chain, which carries periodicals and newspapers from around the world. In this direction lies the trendy Rue Crescent district, full of tiny boutiques and art galleries and the cafés and pubs favored by Montréal's younger Anglophones. Turn right (N) on Rue Bishop, at the Church of St James the Apostle. In two blocks, across Rue Sherbrooke, is the Neo-Classical marble facade of the *Musée des Beaux-Arts*, the city's most important art museum. A large annex is under construction on the opposite side.

After visiting the museum, turn E along Sherbrooke past its concentration of expensive antique stores and galleries. The **Ritz-Carlton Hotel**, Montréal's epitome of Establishment luxe, lays on a correct British tea each afternoon in its summer garden, or in the wintertime Café de Paris. Proper dress is required to join its society custom. A little farther on, **Maison Alcan** has won prizes for its skillful blending of a modern office building with the 19thC residences fronting on Sherbrooke. Concerts and exhibitions are frequently mounted in its atrium.

Continuing on Sherbrooke, on the other side, is the entrance to **McGill University**. Its grounds are open to the public. At #690 is the *Musée McCord*, which specializes in Canada's ethnology. It reopens in 1991 after a long period of renovations and expansion. Turn right (s) on University for McGill Metro station.

Walk 2: Vieux Montréal *(Old Montréal)*
Map 9C5-E5. Metro: Square Victoria.

The evolution from trading post to commercial metropolis took place in this historic quarter beside the St Lawrence River, but by the 20thC, Old Montréal was in danger of total disintegration. Corporations moved away, residential neighborhoods sprang up to the N, and demolitions and major fires accelerated its decline. That trend was slowed in the 1960s, when the entire area was declared a landmark district and strict regulations controlled proposals to either raze or build. Although much remains to be done, deterioration has been arrested and continuing private and public restoration efforts now make a visit to the quarter virtually obligatory. Shops, cafés and taverns brighten its narrow streets, and the buildings constitute a living museum of 18th and 19thC native architecture.

Three Metro stations serve Old Montréal, but for this tour, start from the Square Victoria station, taking the St-Jacques exit. A statue of the long-lived Queen, inevitably crowned by a live pigeon, occupies the center of the plaza. The modern tower on the W side houses the *Bourse* (Stock Exchange). Visits to the 41st floor are permitted to those wishing to witness the largely incomprehensible pandemonium on the exchange floor.

Walk s, toward the river, on the left side of McGill. On the right are several examples of 19thC commercial and civic architecture, including, at #360, the former headquarters of the Grand Trunk railroad company. At the fifth street on the left is the Pl. d'Youville, one of the first public squares in Montréal. Turn left toward the 1903 firehouse, identified by its three arched doorways and the *Caserne Centrale de Pompiers* sign. Restored, it is now the **Centre d'histoire de Montréal**, a museum with 14 rooms containing audiovisual records of the city's development. If its scheduled renovations are complete, have a look inside, then turn left, past the front of the museum. On the S side of the

Orientation and walks/Montréal

square is the former **Hôpital général des Soeurs Grises**. Begun in 1694, the hospital was home to Mother Marie-Marguerite d'Youville, founder of the Sisters of Charity, or Grey Nuns.

Cross to Rue St-Pierre, bordering the hospital. At #118 is the **Musée Marc-Aurèle Fortin**, devoted to the career of the French Canadian landscape watercolorist who died in 1970. There are a few upscale shops on the ground floors of old warehouses being converted to luxury apartments. Return to Pl. d'Youville and turn right. A few strides along are the **d'Youville Stables**. First erected c.1740 and restored c. 1825, they were actually used to store potash, not horses. A low portal gives access to the tranquil inner courtyard, and on the left is the popular **Gibby's** restaurant, decorated in appropriate period style. It sets out tables in the court on warm days.

Continuing E on the elongated Pl. d'Youville, walkers encounter an obelisk marking the spot where French colonists founded Montréal in 1642. Led by the zealous missionary Paul de Chomedey, Sieur de Maisonneuve, they named their new town Ville-Marie. From there, the square is called **Pointe-à-Callières**, commemorating a governor who negotiated a peace treaty with the Iroquois Indians in 1701, ending a 14yr war. Next along this route is **Place Royale**, once a military parade ground and later the city market. Archeological digs at this site have produced a number of finds, some of which are on display at the Place d'Armes Metro station. Turn left into Pl. Royale, beside the old **Customs House** (1837), then left again.

At the next corner, by the L'Air du Temps jazz club, turn into Rue St-François-Xavier. At #453 is the 1903 Stock Exchange, now the **Centaur Theatre**, where English-language productions are mounted. Continue to Rue Notre-Dame, the first named street in Ville-Marie, laid out in 1672. Turn right (E). Soon, on the right, is the outer wall of the **Vieux Séminaire des Sulpiciens** (Sulpician Seminary). Begun in 1680, it is Montréal's oldest existing structure. The mechanism of the clock, seen through the seminary's iron gate, was originally made of wood and is said to be the oldest of its kind in North America (c.1700). Next to the seminary is the presbytery of the **Basilica of Notre-Dame**, which lies just beyond. This neo-Gothic church was completed in 1829 and seats 4,000 worshipers. Ornately carved woods and 14 stained-glass windows form the impressive interior, and a 5,772-pipe organ takes full advantage of the superb acoustics.

The **Place d'Armes** fronts the Basilica, contained by rather ponderous institutional buildings. On the N side is the domed **Banque de Montréal**, an 1847 Greco-Roman structure featuring a portico with six massive columns. A museum inside the bank (*open Mon-Fri 10am-4pm*) celebrates the expectable with a collection of currencies and piggy-banks. At this point, the tour can be broken off by walking N along the E side of the square, then down Côte de la Place d'Armes to the Pl. d'Armes Metro station. Otherwise, turn right (E) from the front of the basilica along Rue Notre-Dame.

The next intersection is Blvd. St-Laurent, which divides Montréal into E and W. Cross over. On the left is the new courthouse, a bleak contemporary intrusion that looms over the 1849 **Palais de Justice** it supplanted. The top floor and dome of the Palais date from 1891, the painted white stone of the addition in obvious contrast with the gray of the original lower floors. It now houses city offices, including a basement tourist office. Opposite the Palais is the **Ernest Cormier Building**, built in 1926, notable for its Art Deco lanterns and majestic copper doors.

Montréal/Orientation and walks

Old Montréal

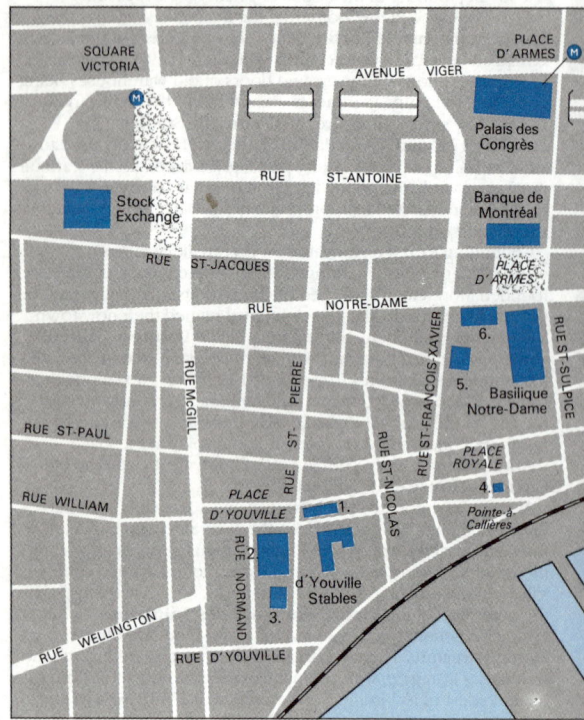

Next on the left is the small square with a statue honoring Jean Vauquelin, a naval hero who defended New France in engagements with the British in 1758-59. The park is overshadowed by the quarter's most august structure, the 1878 **Hôtel de Ville** (City Hall). In best Second Empire manner, it employs mansard roofs, squared turrets and robust Neo-Classical detailing in the facade, all seen to great advantage when it is illuminated at night. Charles de Gaulle, never one to let slip an opportunity to tweak Anglo-Saxon noses, delivered his "Long live free Québec" speech from the balcony over the front entrance in 1967. (He neglected to observe that he had several active separatist movements in his own country, and would have been outraged if a visiting Canadian statesman had ever shouted, "Long live the free Basques!" from, say, the Arc de Triomphe.)

Sloping down to the right is Pl. Jacques-Cartier, to which this tour soon returns. Continue along Rue Notre-Dame. Near the next corner is the handsome *Château Ramezay*, erected in 1705 as the home of the 11th French governor of Montréal and later the official residence of British Governors General. It was occupied by commanders of an invading American army in 1775-1776. Fully restored, it serves now as a showcase of

Orientation and walks

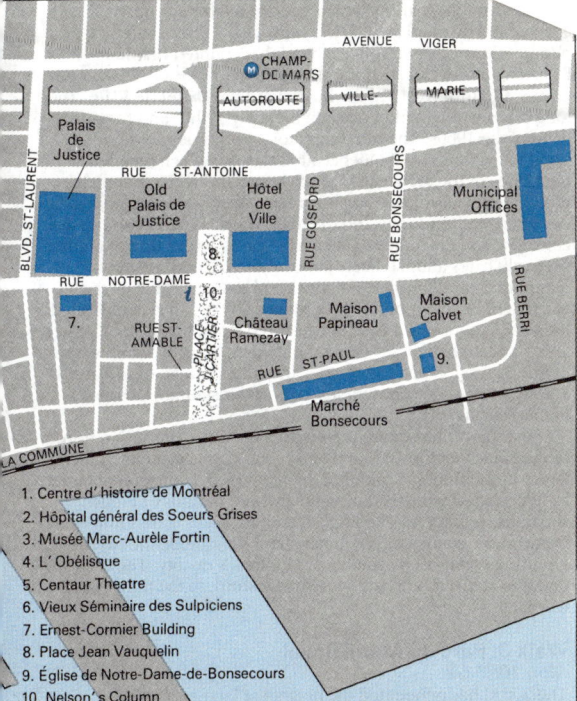

1. Centre d'histoire de Montréal
2. Hôpital général des Soeurs Grises
3. Musée Marc-Aurèle Fortin
4. L'Obélisque
5. Centaur Theatre
6. Vieux Séminaire des Sulpiciens
7. Ernest-Cormier Building
8. Place Jean Vauquelin
9. Église de Notre-Dame-de-Bonsecours
10. Nelson's Column

domestic life among the privileged in the early 18thC. One block more is Rue Bonsecours. Turn right and walk down the inclining street, lined with houses from the colonial period. The **Maison Papineau** at #440 was built in 1785 and was the birthplace of Henri Bourassa, founder of a Québec family that is still influential today. The exterior siding is of wood, fashioned to imitate stone. On the left is one of Montréal's best-known restaurants, **Les Filles du Roi**. The name refers to young women recruited by the French king in the 1660s to help populate the fledgling colony. On the corner is the **Maison Calvet** (c.1725). A superb example of a traditional French dwelling, it was restored in 1964 through the largesse of the owners of the Ogilvy department store. Fittingly, the ground floor is now a small shop, with an antique fireplace in its far wall. Across the street is the *Église de Notre-Dame-de-Bonsecours*. The founder of the sailor's church was Marguerite Bourgeoys, who led an order of noncloistered nuns in the 17thC. A statue of the Virgin stands atop the roof, her arms outstretched to welcome returning ships. On the site of two earlier churches destroyed by fire, the present chapel was completed in 1772. A tower with about 100 steps offers a good view of the harbor.

Turning right on Rue St-Paul, the long Neo-Classical building with the prominent dome is the **Marché Bonsecours**. It was used by the Canadian Parliament in the mid-19thC, but soon became a public market, which it remained for a century. Now it is occupied by municipal offices, and casual visitors are not permitted. At #295 was once a hotel that counted Charles Dickens among its guests. Continue another block to Pl. Jacques-Cartier and turn right, up the hill toward the **Hôtel de Ville**. The long plaza was a market place in the early 19thC, and remained so until the 1960s. The buildings along both sides are good, if abridged, examples of Québec architecture, which blended memories of the architects' French homeland with a pragmatic recognition of Canada's harsh winters. Steeply sloped roofs were designed to shed snow, and the thick walls helped keep out the cold. The square comes to life every spring with a flower market, sidewalk cafés and the lively atmosphere created by street entertainers and throngs of natives and tourists. Amid all the eateries of lesser ambition is **La Marée** (#404), an accomplished French restaurant in a carefully restored stone house. In summer, artists and craftspeople set out their wares (mostly unimpressive) in Rue St-Amable, off the W side, and hours can be easily spent among the cabarets, boutiques, bars and restaurants in the immediate vicinity.

At the top of the square is **Nelson's column**, erected in honor of the British victory at Trafalgar several years before the much larger monument in London. It has provided a convenient target for ideological vandals during heightened periods of French separatist sentiment. The English admiral gazes across Rue Notre-Dame at the statue of French navigator Vauquelin, the two being enduring juxtaposed symbols of Montréal's duality. The Champ-de-Mars Metro station is down Rue Gosford, to the right of the City Hall.

Walk 3: Parc du Mont-Royal
Map 10F2-G2.

The 20thC has penetrated the heights of Jacques Cartier's "*Mont Réal*" in the shape of a huge metal cross, lit at night by hundreds of bulbs. Erected in 1924, it commemorates the wooden crucifix planted there by de Maisonneuve in 1643. The hilltop has been preserved as parkland and much of it remains true to the original 1870 concept of landscape architect Frederick Law Olmsted, designer of New York's Central Park, which achieved an entirely natural look through careful planning. On the far side are two vast cemeteries — one French, one English — and a somber basilica with one of the largest domes in the world.

The park can be seen by taking a *calèche* from Dorchester Sq. or bus #165 from the Guy-Concordia Metro station, changing to the #11 bus, which has a stop at Beaver Lake. But it is best experienced on foot, if one *caveat* is observed. Only the reasonably fit will want to undertake the first phase of this suggested trek, that of hiking from the downtown district to the crest. Others are wise to take a taxi to the **Châlet de la Montagne** and pick up the walk from there. At the N end of Rue Peel is a flight of steps leading to a path that soon joins a marked jogging trail, rising toward the left and doubling back to the right. Shortly, on the left of the trail, are wooden stairs climbing into the trees. Take them. They seem unlikely ever to end, but they do, and the reward is a partial vista of the city below. Continue up the paved path, the Chalet de la Montagne coming into view on the right. At the chalet, bear left to the esplanade and its sweeping panorama — the city hemmed in the distance by the river, and it, in turn, by the Eastern Townships of the s bank. Still farther, on clear days, is the Adirondack range of neighboring New York State, and off to the left are the beginnings of the Laurentian Mountains. Muggers are not a common threat in the park, so this is also a good vantage at sunset or after dark, when the city is a jewel box of winking necklaces of light.

Circle around the far side of the chalet, taking the left (paved) fork at the next intersection. The way is shared with serious runners, amblers, cyclists and an occasional horse and rider. Slowly descending in direction, it soon comes to a stone building beside a large parking lot. This is the **Musée de la Chasse et de la Nature** (Museum of Hunting and Wildlife), (*open Tues-Sun 10am-5pm, closed Mon and Sept-May*). After a brief visit, continue in the same direction along the central path that crosses an open, rolling field serving as an outdoor sculpture garden. Down the hill is the **Lac aux Castors** (Beaver Lake), a name referring to the fur-trapping history of the region rather than to the actual presence of those once highly profitable animals. In summer, ducks paddle among the remote-controlled model boats and sailing ships, young lovers find themselves quiet shaded places, and families tend charcoal grills beside picnic tables. In winter, a rope-tow carries skiers up to the top of the gentle slope, and skaters twirl on the frozen lake. Follow along its near shore to the pavilion, where refreshments and rest rooms are available. Walk on past the pavilion to the edge of the double road called the Chemin de la Remembrance. A forest of headstones begins on the other side, the **Notre-Dame-des-Neiges Catholic cemetery**. The entrance is 50yds up on the right. Still farther in the same direction is the **Protestant cemetery**, notable for the splendor of its monuments and memorials that stand as proof of the greater economic power of its 19th and early 20thC occupants. Montréal's Anglophones and Francophones rest thus in their eternal peace, separate and slightly unequal even in death. The graveyards are open daily (*8am-5pm in winter, 8am-7pm in summer*). If the French cemetery is open (and after a *visit to the English one), enter and follow the paths downhill. If it is closed, turn left and take the sidewalk bordering the road, in either case heading toward the pointed green dome now visible in the distance. Just beyond the high wrought-iron main gate is a bus stop.

Those who still have energy to spare can continue along Chemin de la Côte-des-Neiges to the intersection with Chemin de la Reine-Marie. Turn left across Côte-des-Neiges and shortly arrive at the entrance to the grounds of *Oratoire St-Joseph* (St Joseph's Oratory), a fittingly imposing end to the walk. There is another coach stop near the entry. The #166 bus can be taken from there to the Guy-Concordia Metro station, or, with luck, an infrequent cruising taxi can be snared.

Sights and places of interest

Montréal has no great repositories of art and history to compare with those of New York, London or Paris. Even the larger historic buildings and museums require not more than an hour of any but a specialist's attention. That is not a fact to be mourned, and won't be by those who would rather spend their time shopping, strolling or observing the rhythms of the city from a table in a pleasant sidewalk café. There is easily enough to see to occupy a week's vacation, however, and keep in mind that smaller attractions are mentioned in the preceding section on walks, if not below.

Aquarium
*Île Ste-Hélène ☎ 872-4656. Map **13D5** 🔲 with ticket from La Ronde amusement park ✱ Open daily Sept-May 10am-5pm, June-Aug 10am-8pm. Metro: Île Ste-Hélène or Papineau.*
Penguins are the principal draw at this relatively small facility adjacent to **La Ronde amusement park**. Feeding is at 9.50am and 3.30pm. Tanks hold nearly 300 species of fish and reptiles, notably in a simulated coral reef filled with groupers, piranhas, clownfish, lobsters and moray eels. The dolphin show was closed indefinitely in 1990; call ahead to find out if it has re-opened.

Blvd. St-Laurent
*Maps **8C1-9D5**. Metro: Sherbrooke or Mont-Royal.*
Known to both Francophones and Anglophones as "The Main", this N-S avenue was the historic dividing line between the French East End and the English West End of the elongated metropolis. It remains the pulsing central artery of Montréal's best-known immigrant neighborhood. Novelist Mordecai Richler's rapacious Duddy Kravitz served his apprenticeship here among Greeks, Germans, Poles, Italians and Eastern Europeans. When the newcomers made their fortunes, or at least salaries adequate to move up to Outremont or the suburbs, their places were taken by newer waves of Portuguese, Indians, Thais, West Indians and Vietnamese. Their children return as predictably as puffins for their weekly ingestions of smoked meat, bagels, *borscht, bigos, pikilia* and *pla lad plik*. Nothing but a *bona fide* blizzard keeps them from their Saturday treks along what many consider to be the soul of the city. The nickname may have arisen from the fact that immigrants once tumbled off ships at the wharves in what is now Vieux Montréal and walked up this main street until they found lodging, work, and pockets of others of similar background. Some peeled off to establish the city's compact Chinatown, but most continued N, beyond Sherbrooke.

Between there and Rue Laurier is the most engaging stretch. St-Laurent isn't included on architectural tours, for its loft buildings and tenements are of largely shabby aspect. But it bristles with life, 24hrs a day, and the only danger is sensory overload. All-night clubs and avant-garde boutiques have staked their claims among the ethnic groceries, fish stores, discount clothiers and houseware stores. Purveyors of high-style furs and low-cost leathers insinuate themselves betwixt bakeries, delicatessens, jazz bars and hyper-trendy *boîtes* and galleries. Yet despite the presence of hipper-than-thou designers and periodic invasions of suburbanites and tourists, gentrification has yet to afflict The Main with the cute and predictable.

Canadian Centre for Architecture
*1920 Rue Baile ☎ 939-7026. Map **10G3** 🔲 ✱ Open Wed, Fri 11am-6pm, Thurs 11am-8pm, Sat, Sun 11am-5pm. Closed Mon, Tues. Metro: Guy-Concordia.*
This ambitious new museum and research center opened in 1989, its primary concern being the preservation and exhibition of drawings, photographs and other materials related to architecture. That mission admittedly makes it of specialized

Château Dufresne/Montréal

interest, and there are none of the whizz-bang, hands-on, interactive exhibits that other museums employ to engage visitors. The Centre is the result of a single woman's vision and drive. Phyllis Lambert had the advantage of being the daughter of the founder of the Seagram distillery empire, and the energy to see her project to its conclusion. That meant the commissioning of the dignified contemporary building that embraces a 19thC Second Empire manse in the western part of the city. It presents its best face to Blvd. René-Lévesque, but the entrance is around back. The collection includes more than 55,000 photos and 130,000 books.

Cathédrale-Basilique Marie-Reine-du-Monde
Blvd. René-Lévesque and Rue de la Cathédrale ☎ 866-1661 (rectory). *Map* **11F4** 🔲 *Open daily. Metro: Bonaventure.*

The first Catholic cathedral was on Rue St-Denis, in the heart of French Montréal. When it burned down in 1852, then-Bishop Bourget determined that the site of its replacement should be in the western part of the city. Presumably his intent was to serve his city-wide congregation more efficiently, although the opportunity to insert a bastion of the Roman faith in the very midst of the Protestant West End must have added a certain piquancy to his decision. His overwhelmingly Francophone flock protested the relocation to alien territory, delaying implementation until 1875, when construction finally was begun. Bourget had in mind a scaled-down replica of St Peter's in Rome. Church architect Victor Bourgeau resisted that plan with the understandable reluctance of an artist of integrity asked to reproduce the work of others. His replacement so botched the job, however, that he agreed to join the effort after it had begun.

The cathedral did not commence its liturgical life until 1894, a decade after Bourget died. The result is less a replication of St Peter's than an echo, only partly because it covers less than one quarter the area. Unlike the original, it is overwhelmed by nearby skyscrapers, and there is no sweeping colonnade embracing a great plaza at its approach, as in Rome. The facade is nonetheless impressive, with its Neo-Classical columns and triangular pediment forming the portico. The dome, or cupola, is 252ft high, compared to the 500ft of St Peter's, and is slightly more than half the diameter of its model. The row of statues standing along the cornice are of local patron saints, rather than the Apostles. The most compelling feature of the interior is the copper-and-gold-leaf copy of Bernini's *baldachin*, the canopy above the altar.

Château Dufresne – Musée des Arts Décoratifs
Sherbrooke E and Pié-IX ☎ 259-2575. *Map* **13D5** 🔲 *Open Wed-Sun 11am-5pm. Closed Mon, Tues. Metro: Pié-IX.*

Said to have 44 rooms, although it looks smaller, the undeniably luxurious residence was erected between 1915 and 1918 at the behest of brothers Oscar and Marius Dufresne. Prosperous citizens of what was then the independent municipality of Maisonneuve, they chose a muted Beaux Arts design, but had it executed in the emerging technology of reinforced concrete, not chiseled stone. Still only partially restored and largely empty of furnishings, it is now the home of the **Museum of Decorative Arts**. A handful of rooms are open, with only hints of its former opulence, mostly in carved paneling and architectural elements. The library, for example, is of decidedly Gothic inspiration, while the smoking room shows mock-Arabic traceries. A top floor gallery displays a modest and somewhat incongruous collection

Montréal/Château Ramezay

of modern furniture dating from the 1930s. Works by Marcel Breuer and Frank Lloyd Wright are included. While not worth a special trip, a visit to the château can be combined with one to the nearby **Botanical Gardens** or *Parc Olympique*.

Château Ramezay
280 Rue Notre-Dame E (Pl. Jacques-Cartier) ☎ *861-7182. Map 9D5* ▣ ✗ ⃒ *Open Tues-Sun 10am-4.30pm. Closed Mon. Metro: Champ-de-Mars.*

When Governor Claude de Ramezey commissioned this house in 1705, Montréal had only 1,200 inhabitants living in 152 dwellings. Given the often harsh and straightened circumstances in which most of them lived, his new mansion must have seemed very grand indeed. It does so even now, at least in some of the larger rooms furnished with imported tapestries and mahogany *boiseries* (carved panels) that provide an intriguing peek into the domestic life of an 18thC aristocrat of New France. From 1764-1849, it was the residence of the Governors General of British North America, interrupted by a brief occupation by American officers during the 1775-76 military occupation.

Prints, paintings and useful signs trace the history of the house and the city for which it was a focal point. The main floor has 12 rooms, and Ramezey needed them all, since he had 16 children. A stuffed beaver beside a richly embroidered greatcoat are emblematic of his participation in the lucrative fur trade. The subterranean floor has displays of housekeeping crafts and Amerindian artifacts.

Chinatown
Map 9D4. Metro: Place d'Armes.

The Asian enclave hunched around the intersection of Blvd. St-Laurent and Rue Lagauchetière seems to grow smaller, unlike those in New York and San Francisco. It is tidier than its counterparts, too, with the usual pagoda facades, neon Chinese characters, and roast ducks in its windows, but with far less refuse underfoot. Threatened by encroaching development, it survives for now as a refreshingly exotic oasis in an enveloping sea of modernity.

Christ Church Cathedral
Rue Ste-Catherine W and University ☎ *843-6577. Map 11E4* ▣ *Open daily 8am-6pm. Metro: McGill.*

Called the "flying church" and the "floating cathedral" because of the vast network of underground corridors and galleries beneath it, the Anglican cathedral was opened in 1859. Its design is understated, not flamboyant, Gothic, executed by Frank Wills of Salisbury, England. The original stone steeple was taken down in 1927 when it appeared to be threatening the structure of the building. A lighter aluminum replica was put in place in 1940. The most notable feature of the interior is the *reredos* behind the altar, carved stone depictions of seven scenes from the life of Christ. Organ recitals take place throughout the year.

Dow Planetarium
1000 St-Jacques (near Peel) ☎ *872-4530. Map 11F5* ▣ *Free show Mon night. Schedules vary; call ahead. Metro: Bonaventure.*

A splendid spectacle is provided by 100 projectors casting images on a dome more than 60ft across, hushed "oohs" and "aahs" attending the changing depictions of planets, nebulae and quasars. Presentations change periodically. Mon evenings, this "Theater of the Stars" displays the sky as it appears that very night.

Église Notre-Dame
Pl. d'Armes and St-Sulpice ☎ 842-2925. Map 9E5 ▨ ✗
Open early Sept-late June 7am-6pm, rest of year 7am-8pm. Metro: Pl. d'Armes.

Arguably Québec's finest testament to the potential of ecclesiastical architecture, this Catholic church was the masterwork of an Irish-American Protestant, James O'Donnell. Certainly it is surpassed by none of the 375 churches on the island of Montréal. O'Donnell is credited by many for the Gothic Revival of the early 19thC, a movement that veered sharply away from the Georgian and Greco-Roman Classicism of the preceding century. The style persisted for 75yrs in the face of a welter of revivalist and eclectic architectural notions. The exterior was completed in only 6yrs, in 1829, and the experience so moved O'Donnell that he converted to Catholicism, and was eventually buried here. The interior was another story, requiring a full 40yrs before completion. It was worth the wait. Wherever the eye falls is a wealth of detail, most of it intricately carved wood and exquisite joinery, often gilded and painted with a precision to challenge that of medieval artisans. Yet while the credit rests with its European progenitors, these walls are distinctively Québecois, robust in execution and resonant of their frontier Canadian roots. The project must have been a joy for Victor Bourgeau, the architect who was forced during the same period to execute a design for the Cathedral of Marie-Reine-du-Monde that he reportedly deplored.

Of particular interest are the high altar, a commission of the French artist Bourich, and the pulpit statues by Phillippe Hébert. The stained-glass windows, from Limoges, were installed in 1929. Prized for its acoustic clarity, the church is often the scene of jazz and classical concerts, including the famous Christmas recital of Luciano Pavarotti. Up to 4,000 people can be accommodated at worship or performance, washed by the majestic chords of an organ with five keyboards and 5,772 pipes. On special occasions, the 12-ton bell in the w tower peals over Vieux Montréal.

Église de Notre-Dame-de-Bonsecours
400 Rue St-Paul E (Vieux Montréal) ☎ 845-9991. Map 9C5
▨ ◄€ *Open Nov-Apr 9am-11.30am and 1-5pm, May-Oct 9am-5pm. Metro: Champ-de-Mars.*

Marguerite Bourgeoys arrived with de Maisonneuve in the 17thC to become Ville-Marie's first teacher. Soon after, she founded Canada's first religious order, the Congregation of Notre-Dame.

The existing 1772 church was built upon the foundations of the earlier 1657 version. Both have sheltered a wooden Madonna that gained a reputation for miracles, especially to mariners and fishermen who came to give it honor for saving them from accidents at sea; thus its name, the "Sailor's Church." Following its recovery after a theft, the original Madonna was locked away, and a replica was substituted. A small basement museum contains 58 miniature stage sets charting the life of Bourgeoys. An **observatory** above the apse is open to the public, with views of the old town, port and river.

Église de St-Enfant-Jésus
5039 St-Dominique ☎ 271-0943. Map 8C1. Metro: Mont-Royal.

Montréal/Île Ste-Hélène

The Main's only contribution to significant city architecture was begun in 1857 but achieved notability with the later addition of its richly sculptured neo-Baroque facade. Cherubim, angels and biblical figures gaze down upon quiet **LaHaie Park**.

Île Ste-Hélène
*Map **13D5**. Metro: Île Ste-Hélène.*

As part of Montréal's epic efforts in preparation for the 1967 Expo world fair, this island in the middle of the St Lawrence was doubled in size. That was not enough, so a second island was created from scratch with landfill — the **Île Notre-Dame**. Since then, the two have become prime recreational centers. Connected to the city by the Metro and the Jacques Cartier Bridge, Ste-Hélène has a thrill-happy amusement park, *La Ronde*, a small aquarium, an 1824 fort, swimming pools (and an old-fashioned swimming hole), restaurants and *pique-nique* grounds. In May and June it is the site of the **International Festival of Fireworks**; in winter, cross-country skiers and snowshoers brave the chill. Parts of the Expo exhibition grounds, *Man and his World*, remain and are being rehabilitated. They are marked by the skeletal frame of Buckminster Fuller's visionary **geodesic dome**. Île Notre-Dame has a lovely floral park, open mid-June to Sept, a track for Formula One races and a gigantic rectangular lake made for the '76 Olympics. The basin is a winter skating rink and a summer site for windsurfing and sailing.

For the exhibition and picnic grounds on Île Ste-Hélène, take the Metro to the Île Ste-Hélène stop, at the W end of the island. For La Ronde and the aquarium, take the Metro to Papineau, then the shuttle bus outside.

Jardin Botanique *(Botanical Gardens)*
4101 Sherbrooke E (Pié-IX) ☎ *872-1400. Map **13D5*** 🚋 *𝒦* 🍴
Greenhouses open daily 9am-6pm (7pm in summer).
Outdoor gardens open daily sunrise-sunset. Metro: Pié-IX.

No one appreciates flowers more than those living in regions with short growing seasons, and Montréal's superb Botanical Garden satisfies that need. Founded in 1931, it is among the largest in the world, boasting 73ha with 26,000 species of plants and trees, arranged in outdoor beds and groves and in nine greenhouses heavy with the scent of tropical blooms.

The open-sided sightseeing tram (🚋) provides a good overview of the exhibits. A recorded bilingual narration describes each section, from the rose garden with its signature "Montréal Rose" to the aquatic gardens afloat with lotus and hyacinth to the new Japanese gardens that opened in 1988. Audio cassettes can also be rented for self-guided walking tours.

One unmissable highlight is the **Japanese Pavilion**. The building displays works of art, and has periodic, shortened versions of the traditional tea ceremony (the real thing can take hours). Outside is a fascinating *bonsai* collection — artificially dwarfed trees more than 20yrs old and barely 1ft high. A particularly arresting specimen of this horticultural art is a spectacular American Larch growing from a rock. It is 152yrs old. One of the greenhouses, opened in 1986, features a waterfall that feeds a series of ponds displaying giant Amazon waterlilies. Another showcases *penjing*, the Chinese version of *bonsai*, and a third has more than 1,200 varieties of orchid. Special displays are arranged for Christmas and Easter. The **Parc Olympique** is a short walk from the front gate, giving an opportunity to take in the two major attractions in this eastern sector of the City.

Musée des Beaux-Arts/Montréal

Lachine Canal
☎ 283-6054. Map 11/5 ☒ Open daily sunrise-1am.
Early in the history of European Canada, it was believed that if a detour could be made around the turbulent Lachine Rapids of the St Lawrence River, a passage to the Orient might be discovered. The digging of a canal was first proposed in 1680 as a way for the fur brigades traveling to the NW to bypass the rapids. However, construction of a canal didn't begin until 1821. When work was completed 4yrs later, the waterway opened shipping between Montréal and the Great Lakes. Completed in its final form in 1925, the St Lawrence Seaway made the canal redundant only three decades later, and it was closed to navigation more than 20yrs ago. Now it is being transformed into a recreational resource, with cycling and skiing tracks along its banks. An **Interpretation Center** at 7th Ave and Blvd. St-Joseph in Lachine explains the history of the canal's development (*open mid-May to early Sept*).

Musée d'art contemporain *(Museum of Contemporary Art)*
Place des Arts ☎ *873-2878. Map* **9D4** ☒ ✗ *(for groups of 15-30). Check opening times.*
The museum and its post-1940 paintings and sculptures celebrated more than 25yrs of existence with the move from the Cité du Havre to its new facility in Place des Arts in 1991. That got it out of its former location in a remote waterfront district that never did develop as planners had hoped. A deservedly larger audience can now discover its admirable collection, which is dominated by Québec artists and other Canadians working in a wide variety of media.

Musée des Beaux-Arts *(Museum of Fine Arts)*
1379 Sherbrooke W (Crescent) ☎ *285-1600. Map* **10F3** ☒ ✗
☏ *Open Tues-Sun 10am-7pm. Closed Mon. Metro: Peel.*
Montréal's largest museum, erected in 1912 and expanded in 1975, is about to triple its gallery space with an ambitious annex extension on the opposite side of Sherbrooke. That can't help but be an improvement, for the present arrangement is marked by its sketchiness and fuzzy curatorial focus. Presumably this is due to lack of space, a deficiency most obvious when frequent temporary exhibitions are mounted. The opportunity to display a greater part of the permanent collection surely will flesh out exhibits in each department. In the meantime, expect tantalizing tastes of the arts of many cultures and epochs, and not comprehensive surveys.

Tickets are sold on the street-level floor. The museum shop offers books, souvenirs and a large number of Inuit carvings for fair, if steep, prices. A library holds more than 50,000 works, and lectures and educational programs are given in the auditorium. On the main floor, one flight up, are galleries devoted to European art from the Renaissance through the 18thC, and a display of Middle Eastern ceramics and glassware is cheek-by-jowl with a small sampling of antique Canadian furniture. The second floor concentrates primarily on Canadian artists, starting with 18thC portraiture. Scatterings of Amerindian and Inuit folk art are found among 19thC canvases with a pronounced emphasis on landscapes and genre paintings of Indians and farmers. Paintings by members of the Group of Seven (see page 17) illustrate the dominant Canadian artistic movement of the first half of the century, which bore a relationship to Impressionism.

Contemporary abstraction is represented by such painters as Jean-Paul Riopelle and Jean McEwen, supplemented by a few Rodin sculptures and the work of some British artists. The third (top) floor has a small number of lesser works by Picasso, Maillol and Henry Moore, among others.

Musée Marc-Aurèle Fortin
118 Rue St-Pierre (near d'Youville) ☎ *845-6108. Map 9E5 Open Tues-Sun 11am-5pm. Closed Mon. Metro: Square-Victoria.*

Temporary exhibitions of other artists are periodically mounted, but the permanent collection of this unusual museum is composed solely of works by Fortin (1888-1970). A prolific watercolorist, he sought to do nothing less than initiate a native Canadian school of landscape painting divorced from the dictates of European forerunners. Some think he succeeded.

Musée McCord *(McCord Museum of Canadian History)*
690 Sherbrooke W (University) ☎ *398-7100. Map 8E3. Metro: McGill.*

The province's principal ethnographical collection has long been housed in this 1905 building across the street from the campus of McGill University, of which it is part. It preserves elements of the arts and cultures of the four main aboriginal societies — the Inuit of the Arctic regions and the Amerindians of the west coast, central prairies and eastern woodlands. These intriguing artifacts will not be accessible to the public until sometime in late 1991 or early in 1992, when a major expansion project is due to be completed. Until then, temporary exhibitions are mounted in a variety of venues around the city.

Old Fort and David M. Stewart Museum
Île Ste-Hélène ☎ *861-6701. Map 13D5 Open daily 10am-5pm, except Sept-April closed Mon. Parades take place in summer at 11am, 2.30pm, 5pm. Metro: Île Ste-Hélène.*

Shortly after the war of 1812, a legitimate British fear of another American invasion prompted the Duke of Wellington to order the building of this moated fortress. It was completed in 1824 and became one of a string of St Lawrence fortifications.

The arsenal, barracks and blockhouses have low profiles, nestling behind high walls. A number of rooms, occupied by the David M. Stewart Museum, show an intriguing collection of maps, navigation equipment, furniture and kitchen implements of the era, as well as the expected antique weaponry and uniforms. There is a copy of the first book printed in 1776 in Montréal, by Fleury Mesplet, later the founder of the *Montréal Gazette*. In summer, on the parade ground in front, young people costumed as soldiers of the Fraser Highlanders and the *Compagnie Franche de la Marine* periodically perform drills to the skirl of bagpipes and pretend to repel attackers. The presence of the "French" force is still another smoothing of French-Canadian feathers, since the fort did not exist until long after New France had become English Canada, the real British army having withdrawn from the island in 1870.

A popular restaurant, **Le Festin du Gouverneur**, is in a restored building in the grounds.

Olympic Park See *Parc Olympique*.

Oratoire St-Joseph
3800 Chemin de la Reine-Marie ☎ *733-8211. Map 13D4*
Open daily 6.30am-9.30pm. Metro: Côte-des-Neiges.
Few people are undecided about this immense basilica positioned on the flank of the highest point in Montréal. For the faithful, its grandeur is suitably humbling for entry into the presence of their Maker. For others, its awesomely bulky dimensions are merely gloomy and ponderous. Large it certainly is. The huge dome is said to surpass in size all but those of St Peter's in Rome and St Paul's in London, although that feature, and the hilltop location, more often remind viewers of the Sacré Coeur in Paris' Montmartre. One Brother André, a lay brother in the Holy Cross order, was responsible for initiating the sanctuary project, starting with the small surviving chapel he erected in 1904. That accomplishment and his reputedly miraculous healing powers eventually led to his beatification, one level below sainthood. (St-Joseph is the patron saint of Canada and of healers.) He died in 1937 at the age of 91, never to see the completion of his vision, which took another 12yrs.

The basilica was begun in 1924 to the plans of architects Dalbe Viau and Alphonse Venne, while the interior was the commission of the French master Henri Charlier, who was responsible for the altar, crucifix, and sculptures of the Twelve Apostles. The result is primarily of Italian Renaissance inspiration, similar in outline if not in grace to the Duomo in Florence. A carillon with 56 bells, originally intended for the Eiffel Tower, was installed in 1955. With an elevation of 263m above sea level, the shrine has compelling views of the northern part of the island of Montréal.

Parc Angrignon and the Winter Zoo
3400 Blvd. des Trinitaires ☎ *872-2815. Map 13E4 to zoo*
Zoo open mid-Oct to late Apr 10am-5pm. Seal shows at 11am, noon, 1.30pm, 3pm, 4.30pm. Metro: Angrignon.
An important green space near downtown, the park has cycling paths, ski trails and picnic grounds. It also offers winter quarters to the animals of the **Montréal Zoological Garden** — more than 350 animals of some 60 species. Most popular are the seals, who perform at 90min intervals throughout the day. In summer, the zoo is at *Parc LaFontaine*. A **Fête des Neiges** — winter wonderland — is held from mid-Dec to mid-Feb, when the trees twinkle with lights and decorations and there is an ice-skating trail for adults and an illuminated ice slide for children.

Parc LaFontaine and the Summer Zoo
4000 Av. Calixa-Lavallée ☎ *872-6211. Map 8A3 to zoo*
Open daily 10am-sunset. Metro: Sherbrooke.
The warm-weather home of Montréal's zoo is the **Jardin des Merveilles** (Garden of Wonders) in this, one of Montréal's oldest parks. The animals are housed in an imaginative storybook village in which they illustrate fables and fairytales. In recognition of the city's cultural duality, half the park is landscaped in the English manner, the other in the more formal French style. Picnic areas border its several ponds and lakes, and there are seven tennis courts. In winter, when the animals are moved to *Parc Angrignon*, there are skating rinks and snowshoeing and skiing trails.

Parc Olympique *(Olympic Park)*
4545 Rue Pierre-de-Coubertin (Bennett) ☎ *252-4737 for general information, 253-3434 for baseball tickets. Map*

Montréal/Place des Arts

13D5 🚗 📷 ✗ (charge payable) ♿ 🅿 Open daily 11am-3.30pm. Metro: Pié-IX or Viau.

When the 1976 Summer Olympics were awarded to Montréal, there were relatively few existing facilities in which to hold its many events. Olympic Park was the solution. Just 15mins E of downtown, it contains a velodrome, stadium, and natatorium with several swimming pools. A retractable roof was deemed desirable for the flying-saucer-shaped central area, so an inclined tower now rears over it, from which 26 heavy cables winch back the heavy fabric covering. It is an ungainly structure, and the resulting effect is not unlike that of a giant stork leaning over a birdbath. The esthetic controversy that ensued was compounded by a decision to impose very stiff taxes, especially on cigarettes and on property owners, to pay for the billion-dollar enterprise. In many minds, "The Big O" became "The Big Owe."

Roger Taillibert designed the entire facility. Movable seating sections can be adjusted to accommodate 60,000-80,000 spectators. This allows for the very different configurations required for a baseball diamond (the Montréal Expos play here) or a soccer field, as well as for concerts, conferences and exhibitions. The roof, made of Kevlar cloth, measures more than 20,000sq.yds and weighs nearly 50 tons. It can be retracted or deployed in 45mins, when all is working as it should, which is not always the case. The signature tower, or mast, is 168m high and slopes at a 45° angle. (That compares to the 5.5° incline of the Leaning Tower of Pisa.) A funicular along the spine of the mast carries 90 passengers in 95secs to the observation deck at the top. There is a 35-mile view on a clear day. At the base of the tower is the **natatorium**, with a curved roof over its six pools on three levels. The general public can swim in the pool (☎ *252-4737 for information)*; bring bathing suit and towel. Beside the natatorium is the **velodrome**. The Cameroon hardwood surface of the bicycle track varies in angle from 13-48°. In summer, a shuttle bus service is provided between the Olympic Park and the nearby *Jardin Botanique* (Botanical Garden).

A few blocks to the N are the double pyramids of *Olympic Village*, where the athletes stayed in 1976. These are now private apartments and are regarded as highly desirable.

Place des Arts
175 Rue Ste-Catherine W (between Jeanne-Mance and St-Urbain) ☎ 285-4200 for information ☎ 842-2112 for tickets. Map 9D4 🚗 📷 Metro: Place-des-Arts.

Montréal's already impressive center for the performing arts is undergoing further expansion. Already in operation in the sprawling main building are four theaters and concert halls, ranging in size from the 2,982-seat **Salle Wilfrid-Pelletier** to the 138-seat **Café de la Place**. Due for completion in 1991 are a new home for the *Musée d'Art Contemporain* and another small theater. The prime venue for symphony concerts, dance, opera, drama and lectures, the center supplements its offerings with lunchtime events, which are often free. In winter, there is an outdoor skating rink.

La Ronde Amusement Park
Île Ste-Hélène ☎ 872-6222. Map 13D5 📷 ⚑ 🅿 ✦ Open May weekends 11am-1am; May 26-Sept 4 Mon-Thurs 11am- midnight, Fri, Sat 11am-1am. Closed Sept 5-April. Metro: Papineau, then shuttle bus.

St Lambert Lock/Montréal

Full of music, fireworks, parades and the kinds of hair-raising rides that tear endless shrieks from willing participants, this permanent fairground was another project of Expo '67. The double-tracked rollercoaster is said to be the highest in the world. It competes with the 20 water slides of the satellite **Aqua-Parc** in producing satisfying adrenalin rushes, as merrymakers allow themselves to be dropped from dizzying heights. (One slide is more than 75ft high and nearly vertical; tamer chutes also exist.) On Wed and Sat, ½hr musical revues from eight countries are presented, and there are daily performances by the resident circus, with animal and trapeze acts. Youngsters are entertained in a fairyland children's village populated with fanciful animals and animated wooden soldiers. During the **International Fireworks competition** in May-June, the pyrotechnics synchronize with stirring amplified music. All this, plus numerous snack bars and restaurants, and those fairly high admission fees, suggest that you schedule a whole-day visit.

Rue Prince Arthur
Map 8C3. Metro: Sherbrooke.
A cross street between Blvd. St-Laurent and the handsome residential Carré St-Louis, this was transformed into a pedestrian mall some years ago. Unabashedly touristy, most of the commercial tenants are restaurants, many of them Greek *brochette* factories with such imaginative names as *La Casa Grecque, La Caverne Grecque, La Cabane Grecque*.... In summer they set out white resin tables and chairs, the better to sip *sangria* and to watch the inevitable collection of street musicians, puppeteers, jewelry-makers and caricaturists drawn by the promise of all those plump tourist wallets. Few natives admit to coming here, but the low prices are difficult to resist.

Rue St-Denis
Map 8C2. Metro: Sherbrooke.
The blocks around the intersection of Rue St-Denis and Ste-Catherine are as French as Montréal gets, especially for those who spent even a few of their salad days on Paris' Left Bank. The presence of the large Francophone Université du Québec sets the tone. Thousands of students, professional and temporary, ensure the profitability of jazz clubs and student cafés that crowd the sidewalks. Youthful insights and revelations crackle in the air they share with the smell of *espresso* and the unmistakable fumes of *Gitanes* cigarettes. This is the *quartier latin*, scruffy and vibrant, as transitory as its New Age bookstores and holistic herbalists and as enduring as the eternal process of self-discovery. Walking N, up the hill, the street also travels up the economic and maturation scale. Scores of boutiques, storefront restaurants and yuppie bars crowd the way to **Carré St-Louis**, the city's most harmonious square of late 19thC row houses.

St Lambert Lock
Rt. 132 at E end of Victoria Bridge ☎ 672-4110. Map 13D5
Observation tower open daily May-Oct 9am-8pm.
Access for ships to the Great Lakes, in the heart of the continent, was desired from the earliest colonial days. Canals were dug to avoid the rapids and waterfalls along the way, but it was not until the middle of the 20thC that deep-draft ships were able to make the 2,300-mile voyage from the Atlantic Ocean to Lake Superior. Construction of the St Lawrence Seaway, a cooperative venture between Canada and the US, was completed in 1959. The entire

Montréal/Underground City

project took just 5yrs and includes 15 locks along its route that lift ships eventually to more than 600ft above the Atlantic sea level.

This lock is accessible from downtown Montréal, but only by car. Drive to the E end of Pont Victoria and take the exit marked "Écluses." Park in the "Observatory" lot. It's a short walk from there to the observation tower. Massive gates weighing 190 tons each rise and fall, the water in the lock draining and filling and draining again. Sometimes, it is only to allow a small pleasure craft through; at others, to raise or lower the huge ships (called "lakers") especially designed to ply this route. Often more than 700ft long, to carry maximum cargoes of grain and ore, they are still narrow enough to fit through the locks. A video monitor in the tower shows a short film in French or English describing the history and operation of the Seaway.

Underground City
Map 11F4.

Given Montréal's humid summers and frigid winters, the development of a weatherproof city *beneath* the city was a logical by-product of the downtown construction boom that began in the 1960s. It began with the first major skyscraper complex, Pl. Ville-Marie. While they were about it, the builders decided to install arcades for retail outlets beneath their building — a canny use of valuable ground and air space. Soon, other builders were doing the same thing, and passageways were punched through to connect them. By 1990, there were more than 12 miles of covered corridors and arcades, air-conditioned or heated according to season. The expanding Metro subway system, also begun in the 1960s, linked this hidden second city to outlying attractions, such as **Place des Arts** and the **Île Ste-Hélène**. The largest components of the "city" are below Pl. Bonaventure, Pl. du Canada and the originator, Pl. Ville-Marie. The present totals include 200 restaurants, 1,600 shops, 30 bars, 30 banks and 30 movie theaters wholly contained within the growing supermall. In addition, ten hotels, three department stores and both railroad stations have entrances to its underground walkways. It is therefore possible to leave a hotel, have lunch, see a movie, and even take a train to Toronto and back without once stepping outdoors.

This was an amoeba-like growth, however, created by private entrepreneurs and following no master plan; so the maze of promenades and atriums can bewilder even natives who turn off their regular routes, and it is necessary to make careful note of landmarks along the way. There are plans afoot to give some order to the complicated layout. In the meantime, there are worse things than getting lost down here — things such as driving rain... blizzards... sweltering temperatures....

Vieux-Port *(Old Port)*
On the waterfront, between Blvd. St-Laurent and Berri
☎ *293-5256. Map 9D5* ⇐ *Metro: Champ-de-Mars.*

The old piers at the base of Vieux Montréal are in the process of transformation from shipping to recreational use, a promise only partially realized so far. Cruises of the river and over the Lachine rapids depart and return here. The port is liveliest in summer, with flea markets, puppet shows, street theater and arts and crafts exhibitions. Focal point is the **Clock Tower** on Quai de l'Horloge, with 200 stairs up to an observation deck. Information about the harbor is displayed there. Cycles built for one, two, and even four riders are available for rent.

HOTELS/MONTRÉAL

Where to stay in Montréal

Fevered hotel construction over the last two decades has created a buyer's market in which visitors can nearly always obtain rooms in the price range and location they desire. Moreover, those accommodations represent bargains compared to their counterparts in the larger cities of the US and Europe, especially when taking into account the favorable exchange rates of major currencies against the Canadian dollar. Montréal's **Le Quatre Saisons** and the **Ritz-Carlton**, for example, maintain standards equal to those of their opposite numbers in New York, London and Paris, yet their rooms cost up to a third less. A remarkable number of mid-priced downtown hotels offer such enticements as swimming pools and health clubs. Away from the central core, tariffs are still lower, at no significant loss in convenience, and a strong bed-and-breakfast movement is present. Costs can be shaved still further. To fill their beds Fri through Sun, even the most opulent hotels offer weekend discounts. Most sweeten the package with free cocktails, breakfasts, parking, or sightseeing tours, a roster limited only by the imaginations of marketing directors. Many hotels allow children to stay free in their parents' rooms, or at a small supplement. During the week, businesspeople should inquire about corporate rates, and senior citizens are often eligible for discounts. Obviously, a little shopping is in order. An unusual but satisfying possibility in the Carré St-Louis area is **Institut** (*3535 St-Denis* ☎ *282-5121*), operated by earnest undergraduates of the Québec Institute of Tourism and the Hotel Trade.

Virtually all downtown hotels have garage parking, for which an extra charge is usually made. Increases in the corps of the health-conscious have inspired the installation of fitness rooms, which can range from bare spaces with a few exercise mats and a stationary bicycle to full-scale complexes with racquetball courts, weight circuits, jogging tracks and aerobics classes. Swimming pools are surprisingly common, and most are indoors. Complimentary morning newspapers in the guest's choice of French or English typically accompany room service breakfast or are left outside the door. Color TV is found even in moderately-priced hotels, often with cable and/or closed-circuit movies. All the lodgings listed here have private bathrooms. Most have eased access for disabled persons, and many have added ramps and specially modified rooms. Room rates do not include meals. There is no room tax at the time of writing, but a service charge is sometimes added. Be certain not to tip a room waiter twice.

A majority of the desirable hotels are located in the heart of the downtown district, along **Rue Sherbrooke** or in the **Rue Crescent** district. A few are found in the **St-Denis Latin Quarter**, on the slopes of **Mont-Royal**, or near the airports. Toll-free **800** numbers are provided by many hotels. In some cases, these can be used only within Canada. If an 800 call does not get through, the regular telephone number must be used, preceded by the Montréal area code, **514**.

Le Centre Sheraton Montréal
1201 Blvd. René-Lévesque O.
(Stanley), Montréal H3B 2L7
☎ *878-2000* or *800-325-3535*
⊙ *055-60719* ⊛ *878-3958*. Map
11F4 ⅢⅢ 827 rms 🖃 ⇌ 🖻 AE ⦿

Location: Downtown, near Dorchester Sq. No stinting on *this* lobby: It's an atrium 5 stories high, full of towering palms and other plantings, awash in light from the wall of glass facing the boulevard. A

Montréal/Hotels

pianist plays and cocktail waitresses circulate beneath the greenery. The hotel-within-the-hotel concept employed in many big-city Sheratons reserves the five top floors for fancier rooms and suites with their own check-in and a lounge serving free breakfast and afternoon tea. Given the full-fledged health club, five bars and three restaurants, there is no need to leave, but the lively Rue Crescent district is nearby.

Le Château Champlain
1 Pl. du Canada (Peel) Montréal H3B 4C9 ☎ *878-9000 or 800-268-9420* ⊙ *055-60048* ⊚ *878-6761. Map 11F4* 606 rms

Location: *Between the Windsor and Central Railway stations.* Inverted semicircular windows cover the sides of the slender 36-story tower, making it instantly recognizable by its nickname, "The Cheese-Grater." Nurse a drink in its penthouse lounge for one of the city's most arresting vistas. Those who stay for more than the view find commodious rooms equipped with in-house movie channels and minibars. Many are reserved for nonsmokers. Children under 17 are allowed free in their parents' rooms. They can pass time in the indoor pool, always a delight for youngsters, while the grownups have **Le Caf' Conc'** nightclub.

Château Versailles
1659 Sherbrooke O.(St-Mathieu), Montréal H3H 1E3 ☎ *933-3611 or 800-361-7199 (Canada) or 800-361-3664 (US)* ⊙ *055-267-412* ⊚ *933-7102. Map 10F3* 177 rms

Location: *Rue Crescent area, near the Musée des Beaux-Arts.* Beginning as a small European-style *pension* in the 1950s and expanding over the years into three adjacent houses, this is Montréal's most publicized in-city inn. Knockout decor is not to be expected, although a few antiques and artworks are scattered about the lobby area. Bedrooms are clean, plain, comfortable. The desk staff is eager to help with restaurant and theater reservations. Room-service breakfast arrives promptly.

La Citadelle
410 Sherbrooke O.(Durocher), Montréal H3A 1B3 ☎ *844-8551 or 800-263-8967* ⊚ *844-0912. Map 8D3* 199 rms

Location: *Near Place des Arts and shops.* One of La Citadelle's virtues is that a suite can be had for the same price as a plain double at competitors of its class. Few amenities are neglected. Food and beverages are available at all hours, and each room has minibar and remote-control closed-circuit TV. In addition to the indoor pool, guests can work out on Nautilus devices in the compact gym and wind down with sauna, steam room or massage. Continental breakfast is included when taken in the **C'est La Vie Café**, another saving, and the morning newspaper awaits outside the door. All this constitutes one of the better deals for business travelers on a tight budget.

Delta Montréal
450 Sherbrooke O. (City Councillors), Montréal H3A 2T4 ☎ *286-1986 or 800-268-1133* ⊙ *055-60954* ⊚ *284-4342 Map 8D3* 465 rms

Location: *Near downtown shopping and Place des Arts.* Although it has been on the scene since 1986, the paint barely looks dry. That can be counted as a measure of the management's commitment to proper maintenance, and attention to detail. Businesspeople are the obvious target clientele, with a center that provides copiers, computer modems, secretarial services and telecommunications. The executive on the go can pump up for the day's challenges in a large health club with exercycles and Universal weight circuit, an indoor lap pool and two squash courts, or mellow down in the outdoor pool, whirlpool, sauna or massage room. Families aren't neglected. A supervised game-and-crafts center keeps children busy for hours. Two restaurants, a jazz lounge and two Signature Service floors round out the attractions.

Le Grand
777 Rue University (St-Jacques), Montréal H3C 3Z7 ☎ *879-1370 or 800-361-8155* ⊙ *055-60223* ⊚ *879-1761. Map 9E5* to 737 rms

Location: *Next to the Stock Exchange, a walk to Old Montréal.* Once a Hyatt Regency, it retains that chain's flair for the dramatic, right up to the requisite revolving rooftop

Hotels/Montréal

restaurant. Although the location is less than beguiling — adjacent to highway exit ramps and elevated train lines — it's well placed for access to downtown offices and the respite of Old Montréal. Available to guests are a full-service spa and pool, common in the city's luxury hotels but not universal. The posh 25th floor is reserved for those willing to pay for private reception and free breakfasts and cocktails.

Holiday Inn Crowne Plaza
420 Sherbrooke O. (Bleury), Montréal H3A 1B4 ☎ *842-6111 or 800-361-6262* ⊗ *842-9381. Map 8D3* ▥ *489 rms* ▤ ▣ ⇌ AE ⊡

Location: Near Place des Arts. A multimillion-dollar infusion upgraded the once dowdy vertical motel to first-class, if not luxury, stature. That was necessary to compete with the cluster of upper-middle hostelries in the vicinity, and it succeeded. The pool is indoors, supplemented by whirlpool and sauna. Two executive floors with extra perks are available at modest surcharges. There are seven Holiday Inns in the Montréal area, including the **Holiday Inn Richelieu** (*505 Sherbrooke* ☎ *842-8581 or 800-465-4329*), near Carré St-Louis.

Manoir Le Moyne
2100 Blvd. de Maisonneuve O. (Atwater), Montréal H3H 1K6 ☎ *931-8861 or 800-361-7191* ⊗ *931-7726. Map 10H3* ▯ *262 rms* ▤ ⇌ ▣ AE ⊡

Location: Opposite The Forum sports and concert arena. Hockey and rock fans couldn't be better placed; others will think it a little too far w of downtown. That's the only drawback, and it does much to compensate. For the price of a single in one of the first-class hotels, get a duplex suite complete with dining room, kitchenette and balcony. Cable TV with closed-circuit movies and stocked refrigerators are included. Facilities include indoor swimming pool and garden, two saunas, bar and restaurant. There can't be a better choice for families or those planning a long stay who prefer not to spend it in a standard boxy room.

Le Meridien Montréal
4 Complexe Desjardins (Jeanne-Mance), Montréal H5B 1E5 ☎ *285-1450 or 800-361-8334* ⊕ *055-25268* ⊗ *285-1243. Map 9D4* ▥ *626 rms* ▤ ▣ ⇌ AE ⊡

Location: Across the street from Place des Arts. Roughly equidistant from the Latin Quarter, Rue Crescent and Old Montréal, this east-downtown area is within easy walking or Metro distance of all that Montréal offers. The concert halls and theaters of Place des Arts are a few steps away, and the hotel is often used as the headquarters of the International Jazz Festival. A glass tower erected in 1972, it is an integral part of a block-square complex of office buildings and subterranean shopping malls. An indoor pool hovers above the catacombs and beneath the rambling lobby. A nonsmoking floor is available, as is a special "Le Club Président" executive level with its own lounge and check-in.
(most rms)

de la Montagne
1430 Rue de la Montagne (Ste-Catherine) Montréal H3G 1Z5 ☎ *288-5656 or 800-361-6262* ⊕ *055-62157* ⊗ *288-9658. Map 11F4* ▥ *132 rms* ▤ ⇌ ▣

Location: Rue Crescent district. The management shows an almost bewildering number of faces to its public. The lobby has a pronounced Belle Époque/Art Nouveau character, exemplified by a fountain surmounted by a brass female nude butterfly with stained-glass wings. Businesspeople with a Continental flair populate the flamboyant **Les Beaux Jeudis** room, while their younger, up-and-coming cousins cruise **Thursday's** singles bar. Drinks and light lunches are also taken beside the rooftop pool, but excellent French cuisine and service are the attractions at the mezzanine **Le Lutétia**. And then there's the piano bar, the discotheque, the tea room, the boutiques... all this in a hotel with only 132 rooms and suites, many of them as eclectic as the rest of the place.

Montréal Bonaventure Hilton
1 Pl. Bonaventure (Mansfield), Montréal H5A 1E4 ☎ *878-2332 or 800-268-9275* ⊕ *055-24480* ⊗ *878-3881. Map 11F4* ▥ *393 rms* ▤ ⇌ ▣ AE ⊡

Location: Atop Pl. Bonaventure, next to the Central Railway Station. They like to think of it as a downtown resort hotel, and they almost have a case. From the street, the building looks like just another

99

Montréal/Hotels

skyscraper, the lower floors composed of offices and a convention hall. From the air, however, the top six floors form a hollow square around a garden terrace with brooks stocked with goldfish. For a memorable sensation, enter the indoor passageway and swim out into the heated pool — in a snowfall. Rooms either look out upon the cityscape or down into the garden. The restaurant **Le Castillon** receives high marks from local gourmands.
≢ ᕮ ≋ ❦ ♈ ♓ ☞ ♐ ♑

Le Quatre Saisons *(The Four Seasons)* 🏨
1050 Rue Sherbrooke O. (Peel), Montréal H3A 2R6 ☎ *284-1110 or 800-268-6282* ◉ *055-25142* ⊛ *845-3025. Map 8E3* ⫸ *300 rms* ▦ ⇌ ▣

Location: Near McGill University. This estimable Canadian-owned chain has 22 hotels in North America, with more on the drawing boards. They are routinely accorded the highest rank, and this one does full justice to that lofty reputation. This is contemporary luxe in a glass high-rise, not the Old World variety, but little is left to chance. Rooms are spacious and fully appointed, including complimentary closed-circuit movies, terry robes, minibar, bathroom hair dryer and scale. They'll even provide a room facsimile machine, on request. Nonsmoking floors are available. The 3rd-floor health club has a Keiser weight circuit. For an exhilarating change-of-winter-pace, plunge into the indoor pool, swim outside, then back, without leaving the water. Sauna, whirlpool and steam room are also available. Room service is on call round the clock. **Le Restaurant** is *the* site for power breakfasts, and power dinners, for that matter. Health-conscious diners can choose from an "alternative cuisine" card.
ᕮ ≋ ❦ ☞ ▣

Ramada Renaissance du Parc 🏨
3625 Av. du Parc (Prince-Arthur), Montréal H2X 3P8 ☎ *288-6666 or 800-268-8930* ◉ *055-60066* ⊛ *288-2469. Map 8D3* ⫸ *467 rms* ▦ ▣ ⇌ AE ◉

Location: Near Carré St-Louis. Comparable in all ways to competitors closer to the city center, yet with significantly lower tariffs, this hotel deserves careful consideration. Part of the La Cité complex, it has access to better sports and fitness facilities than any of them. The roster includes indoor and outdoor pools, squash courts, indoor running track, weight rooms, saunas, Turkish baths and whirlpools. There's even tennis, in summer. After a pressurized coat-and-tie day in the conference rooms of downtown towers, slip into jeans and relax in the funky *boîtes* and bars of St-Denis and St-Laurent.
≢ ᕮ ≋ ❦ ♈ ☞ ♐ ♑

La Reine Elizabeth *(Queen Elizabeth)* 🏨
900 Blvd. René-Lévesque O. (Mansfield), Montréal H3B 4A5 ☎ *861-3511 or 800-268-9143* ◉ *055-267584* ⊛ *514-861-3536. Map 11F4* ⫸ *1,016 rms* ▦ ⇌ ▣

Location: Downtown, above the main railroad station. Royalty and heads of state choose the "QE" as a matter of course. True, there are three or four hostelries boasting higher overall levels of luxury. None has a more central location, however, and the management endeavors to satisfy all but lowest-budget travelers. Recent renovation created three classes of accommodations: Entrée Première has comfortable rooms at relatively moderate tariffs; Entrée Silver and Gold lay on such extras as private concierge, separate elevator, bathrobes, free breakfasts, lounges, and special check-in service. The **Beaver Club** is the most celebrated of its several restaurants, a haunt of the power elite.
≢ ᕮ

Ritz-Carlton 🏨
1228 Sherbrooke O. (Drummond), Montréal H3G 1H6 ☎ *842-4212 or 800-268-1133* ◉ *055-24322* ⊛ *842-4907. Map 10F3* ⫸ *182 rms* ▦ ⇌ ▣ AE ◉

Location: Near the Musée des Beaux-Arts and Rue Crescent district. The famous black-and-white *porte-cochère* has sheltered members of the Establishment since 1912. They expect the ultimate in polished treatment, and get it. Nothing is overlooked at the Ritz, no caprice unattended. They once delivered pots and utensils to Sophia Loren's suite so she could cook her own pasta; a staff member officially witnessed the first marriage of Elizabeth Taylor and Richard Burton. Every room has remote-control TV, stereo, clock radio, electronic safe, umbrella, robes, minibar, lighted makeup mirror, hairdryer, bath telephone, and bathroom TV speaker to keep track of the morning news. All are of

Hotels/Montréal

ample proportion, so about the only thing that suites have is still more room and the extra furniture to fill it.

The ground-floor **Café de Paris** is not only a prime power breakfast site, but one of the city's best eateries. In summer, business is moved out into the garden, where afternoon tea is an obligatory event. This is still a bastion of dignity in an all-too-casual world.

⟰ ⚭ ⚘ ⚑ ▭ ♄ ♩

Bed and breakfast

As the term is employed here, "bed & breakfast" refers to rooms in private homes, not inns or *pensions* in the European sense. Reservations are made through several referral agencies, which attempt to match each client's needs with appropriate lodging. Accommodations range from spare, utilitarian rooms with the bath down the hall, to housekeeping apartments of engaging design and hotel-type comforts (except room service). Their primary appeal lies in their low prices. Even the most handsomely appointed rarely reach the top of our moderate price band.

But price is not all. Many guests could easily afford the fancy downtown hotels, but prefer the homey environment of a B&B, the opportunity to spend time with their Canadian hosts and their often international guests. The owner-hosts are an invariably gregarious, energetic lot, knowledgeable boosters of their city and storehouses of information and opinion.

A modest sense of adventure is required, if only because matchups between guests and hosts are made by telephone or mail. There is no guarantee that the resulting fit will be smooth, for there is not the relative certainty of expectation that one carries into a Hilton or a Holiday Inn. For that reason, it is important to be as precise as possible about requirements. Private bathrooms, for example, are available, but cannot be assumed. TV sets in bedrooms are the exception, not the rule, although there might be one in the front parlor. Hosts may forbid smoking, or pets, or children under a certain age. Some impose curfews. Most locations are within easy reach of public transit, but some outlying areas can be as distant as an hour from major attractions.

Reserving well in advance is always wise, especially in summer. As a rule, a deposit equal to one night's stay is required, the balance payable upon arrival. Credit cards are often acceptable, if only for the deposit, but not always and not all types. Given the inherent quirks and volatility of the business, the listing of agencies below should be regarded only as a first source.

A Downtown Bed and Breakfast Network
3485 Laval, Montréal H2X 3C8 ☎ *289-9749* AE ◉ VISA
Many homes are located near the Rue Crescent and Prince Arthur/St-Laurent districts. Parking usually available.

Bed & Breakfast de Chez Nous
5386 Brodeur, Montréal H4A 1J3 ☎ *485-1252 or 488-3149* ◉
About 30 residences, situated mostly in the residential quarters on the slopes of Mont-Royal rather than in the city center. Some efficiency apartments (self-catering) are available on a weekly basis.

Relais Montréal Hospitalité
3977 Laval, Montréal H2W 2H9 ☎ *287-9653* ◉ VISA
Full breakfasts, not just coffee and *croissant*, they say. Some accommodations are close to luxurious. Parking available

MONTRÉAL/RESTAURANTS

Montréal Bed & Breakfast
4921 Victoria, Montréal H3W 2N1 ☎ *738-9410* AE ◉ VISA
Said to be the first of the B&B networks, with a wide range of
accommodations in about 50 houses in all parts of the city.

Where to eat in Montréal

Trenchermen and gourmands rejoice, for Montréal has few
peers in North America for quality, value and diversity of dining.
With an avidity bordering on obsession, TV and the print media
chart the comings and goings of favored chefs, the opening of
new restaurants and the decline of culinary reputations. It is
undoubtedly due to the French heritage of a populace that cares
deeply about food and its preparation.

The tab for a taste of this good life can be surprisingly low. A
grand 4-course repast in one of the city's most expensive
restaurants handily matches a similar spread in New York for
taste and presentation, yet costs as little as half as much. More
good news: lunch in that same place is 25 to 60 percent less than
dinner, due to the widespread practice of offering steep
discounts at midday to attract businesspeople and shoppers.
Those visitors who can bring themselves to have their main meal
in the early afternoon, in the Latin manner, can sample the wares
of establishments that might prove otherwise out of reach. This
entails little sacrifice. Lunch menus are shorter, but with many
of the same dishes as on the dinner menu, and the animated
2-hour lunch is very much alive.

Given Montréal's prevailing cultural and linguistic
demographics, any food other than French can be regarded as
ethnic. That doesn't mean the rest of the world is neglected.
Immigration has brought able practitioners of many national
kitchens to join the feeding frenzy. Italian and Chinese
restaurants are especially favored, but many others, typically at
much lower prices, purvey Greek, Korean, Japanese, Middle
Eastern, Thai, Indian and Portuguese edibles.

Natives love their lowbrow fast foods as much as their turbot
and *entrecôte au poivre*, and arguments can arise over where to
find the best *chien chaud* (hot dog), pizza or *hambourgeois*. At
the top of this pecking order is a taste treat that expatriate
Québeckers yearn for above all others. It's smoked meat, a
delicatessen specialty similar to *pastrami*, but less fatty, and
distinctively flavored according to inevitably "secret" recipes. It
is served in a do-it-yourself heap of slices, with a stack of rye
bread and a plate of delectably greasy *pommes frites*.

There is an indigenous French-Canadian repertoire, too — a
home-cooking with roots in the colonial past and incorporating
such quintessential New World products as maple syrup. Among
the staples are a ground-pork paté, pork pie, baked beans, and
the ultimate regression to childhood, sugar pie. Discussions of
the last achingly high-calorie dessert narrow over whether it
should have nuts or not, a single crust or two, or be made of
brown sugar or maple syrup. No exploration of Québec is
complete without a sample.

There are a few quirks in local taste and practices. Salted
butter, not sweet, is the norm, even in the *haute* emporia. When
selecting a wine with dinner, the bottle is usually not opened
until the main course arrives, unless specifically requested
earlier. Most restaurants serve decent wines by the glass, which

Restaurants/Montréal

reduces waste and the final reckoning, especially since wine and liquor are heavily taxed. About a quarter of all Montréal restaurants allow patrons to bring their own wine, and nearby convenience stores cater to the practice. Look for the symbol of a red hand holding a bottle in store and restaurant windows, or the words *Apportez votre vin* (Bring your own wine).

Provincial laws require the posting of menus with prices outside every eating place. Tips of 10 percent are regarded as adequate in humbler establishments; 15 percent is the standard in those in the mid- to upper-range. Only extreme satisfaction with all aspects of a meal prompts the average Québecois to leave as much as 20 percent. Gratuities are easy to calculate, since the tax, listed separately, is 10 percent of the total. Price estimates in the entries below refer to dinner, not lunch.

Montréalers live for the weekend, not the workplace. That means reservations are essential Thurs through Sat for dinner at any restaurant of even middling achievment. For "hot" restaurants, the rule applies any time. Ordinarily, a call a few hours in advance suffices. Heaviest demand is between 8-9pm.

Cafés and snack bars

Cafés are resting places as much as anything. The most obvious are the many branches of **A.L. Van Houtte**, reliable serve-yourself operations featuring *croissants*, quiches, sandwiches and the founder's coffee. More traditional cafés, in tone if not in decor, typically offer a limited range of *croissants*, fruit tarts, quiches, and the like. Often notable for their excellent *espresso* and *café filtre*, they invite lingering and have loyal patrons of all ages and persuasions. They are found in greatest numbers in the **St-Denis/St-Laurent** area and in **Vieux Montréal**. Most are open every day, from early morning to late at night.

At the lower end of the food chain is the snack bar called a *casse-croûte*. The name translates, more or less, as "break bread," with hot dogs and baked beans or French fries the usual offering. They are scattered around the city, even in the tonier neighborhoods and tourist districts. To assuage pangs in anticipation of a grander meal later on, or when there isn't time to dawdle at a table, they're just the ticket.

L'Actuel
1194 Peel ☎ 866-1537. Map 10F3
▯▯▯ AE ◉ ◉ ▥ Closed Sat lunch, Sun, Mon.

Downstairs is a lively bar, upstairs the restaurant, crisp and uncluttered, with bare parquet floors and bentwood chairs. Ask for a window table overlooking Dorchester Sq. The house specialty is mussels. They come in several guises, inevitably accompanied by double-fried potatoes that approach perfection. Bountiful second helpings are also traditional. The waitress asks if you like your food spicy, as with the steak *tartare*, as tasty as can be found.

Bagel Etc.
4320 St-Laurent ☎ 845-9462. Map 9D4 ▯▯▯ to ▯▯▯▯ ◉ ▥ Open till 3.30am. Closed Mon.

Montréal bagels are thinner, crisper and better than the New York variety, which have the consistency of setting cement, and here is the living proof. The menu ranges beyond bagels to goulash and burgers, served by artistes who obviously have better things to do with their valuable time.

Beauty's
93 Mont-Royal W ☎ 849-8883. Map 8B1 ▯ No credit cards. Closed Sun in July-Aug.

On every native's list of musts for visitors is breakfast at Beauty's: the delicatessen as institution. No one mentions that the food can easily be duplicated in any of a thousand places across North America. Never mind. Bacon and eggs sound so much more exotic in French. Everything is fresh, including the

Montréal/Restaurants

orange juice. Arrive by 9am to be reasonably sure of a seat on Sun morning, when the faithful arrive by bike and Jaguar.

Boulevards
3435 St-Laurent ☎ 499-9944. Map 9D4 ⅡⅡ ⬛ ⬛

The rectangular island bar is the centerpiece, and it fills up after working hours with prosperous men in shirtsleeves and ties and women in short skirts and long jackets. There are many expressive Gallic shrugs and tosses of touseled hair, the faintest chuckles ricocheting off *moderne* black marble. The serviceable food is *nouvelle* Mediterranean in character.

Les Chenêts ⬛
2075 Bishop ☎ 844-1842. Map 10G3 ⅠⅠⅠⅠ AE ⬛ ⬛ ⬛

One reason why this is one of Montréal's priciest restaurants is apparent upon entering. Every wall is hung with phalanxes of expensive copper pans, and even the bar has a copper top. The setting of banquettes amid tones of warm brown is as classic as the entirely French menu. Specials are recited in either French or English by faintly bored waiters who look to have been around for years. Judicious seasonings and attractive presentations draw an older crowd that doesn't care to be startled. It's a suave, calming venue for special-event dinners, not daily bread.

Chez Delmo
211 Notre-Dame W ☎ 849-4061. Map 9E5 ⅡⅡ *to* ⅠⅠⅠⅠ AE ⬛ ⬛ *Closed Sat lunch, Mon eve, Sun.*

Stockbrokers and investment bankers who prefer their seafood precisely cooked and without trickery, flock to this fine old fish house in Vieux Montréal. Two long oyster bars with rows of wooden stools funnel diners into the main room in back, where fresh Dover sole and Nova Scotia salmon are high on the list of favorites. It's all cozily Old Guard and Old World.

Chez la Mère Michel
1209 Guy ☎ 934-0473. Map 10G3 ⅠⅠⅠⅠ AE ⬛ ⬛ ⬛ *Closed Sat lunch, Sun.*

The bar down below is the staging area for patrons awaiting their tables, and that time can stretch out on weekend nights. Upstairs, the several rooms have dark wood floors, white plaster walls and scarlet tablecloths. Trendy experimentation is not to be expected. Look instead for solid professionalism at both stove and table, as with rabbit *terrine*, lobster *soufflé*, and salmon and haddock with two sauces.

Dunn's ♥
892 Ste-Catherine W ☎ 866-4377. Map 9D4 ⅡⅡ *to* ⅠⅠⅠⅠ ⬛ ⬛ *Open 24hrs.*

Always included in episodes of the great smoked meat debate, Dunn's can argue that it is the ultimate deli in a town packed with the breed. Its windows are filled with such maddeningly delectable products as huge jars of pickles and garlands of sausage, calculated to stop passers-by in their tracks. Smoked meat (see also Schwartz's) is far from the only attraction. Classic deli sandwiches tower on the plate, joining myriad improbable but delicious components. Full dinners are available, too, along with potato *knishes* and cheesecake.

Elysée Mandarin
1221 Mackay ☎ 866-5975. Map 10G3 ⅡⅡ AE ⬛ ⬛ ⬛ *Closed Sun lunch.*

A tasteful display of Chinese ivory figurines and miniature musical instruments is arranged opposite the vestibule service bar. Add the high-ceilinged dining rooms, dark woodwork and European-style service and preparation, and it seems a throwback to the foreign enclave of Shanghai. Admittedly, this is not a lovable environment, for it is too correct for that. But neither is it the garish setting usually associated with Chinese restaurants, and it is serious, not gloomy. There is no sense that the largely Szechuan (not Mandarin) food is merely scooped from steam tables in the kitchen, and every indication that much of it is prepared to order. The *table d'hôte* lunch is a bargain.

Another stylish but younger Chinese restaurant of comparable achievement is **Le Chrysanthème** (*1208 Crescent ☎ 397-1408* ⅡⅡ), which features Szechuan and Peking dishes.

L'Express
3927 St-Denis ☎ 845-5333. Map 9C4 ⅡⅡ ⬛ ⬛

The white-hot bistro of the moment, L'Express is ablaze with shining faces that look to be on the verge of celebrity. It may be too hot not to cool down, the dining equivalent of the latest disco, but in the meantime, it shouldn't be missed by those who pretend to be on the cutting edge. The decor is rather stark, but everyone is too busy hooting and chattering to notice. Surprisingly, for a place so hip it could get away with serving pink bean curd and still be filled from breakfast to midnight, the food is usually pretty good. Make note of the address — it's between Roy and Duluth.

Le Festin du Gouverneur
Old Fort, Île Ste-Hélène
☎ 879-1141 *III* to *IIII* AE ◉ ◉ VISA

An ancient building within the Old Fort complex is the scene of re-creations of 17thC feasts, complete with serving wenches, musicians and jesters. The food is no more than acceptable, but it's the best dinner choice on a day trip to Île Ste-Hélène.

Fiesta Tapas ♦
479 St-Alexis ☎ 287-7482. *Map 9E5* *I* to *III* ◉ VISA

Lovers of the Spanish bar snacks called *tapas* need look no further than this outpost of Madrid in Vieux Montréal. The cellar setting is so authentic that one half-expects Sancho Panza to belly up to the bar and scarf down a selection of the more than 40 hot and cold *tapas* available. A common strategy is to order three or four and share with friends.

Les Filles du Roy
415 Bonsecours ☎ 849-3533. *Map 9C5* *III* AE ◉ ◉ VISA

The name refers to young women sent by Louis XIV to help populate Nouvelle-France. This 18thC building in Vieux Montréal is nearly as old as that migration, its stone interior walls lined with ancestral portraits, gilt-framed mirrors and antique sideboards.

Cocktails are served beside a crackling fire or at the marble bar, brought by fetching waitresses in sky-blue folk costumes with ruffled blouses. In such an ingratiating setting, who would be so mean-minded as to point out that the food is less than memorable?

Les Halles
1450 Crescent ☎ 844-2328. *Map 10F3* *IIII* AE ◉ ◉ VISA *Closed Mon lunch, Sat lunch, Sun, 1st 2wks in Aug, Christmas-Jan 6.*

The snug bistro setting is decorated with mock shopfronts intended to recall the lamented Paris market. It is a deceptive *petit-bourgeois* ambience, given the stiff tariffs, but the food is more than competently done, in ample portions. The waiters are pros who put on a good show of enjoying their work. Game and beef are emphasized, and the kitchen has a gentle hand with seafood, as in the *bouqueterie* of assorted fish. Sauces are light, not wimpy; desserts are huge. The parting gift of a bag of apples softens the shock of the check.

Henri II
1175 Crescent ☎ 395-8730. *Map 10F3* *II* to *IIII* AE ◉ VISA *Closed Sat lunch, Sun.*

This is the sort of unassuming cellar retreat that regulars keep to themselves. At the un-chic end of Rue Crescent, it crowds only 13 tables into a room decorated in warm grays and burgundy. Rolled napkins stand alert as rabbit ears in the wineglasses. Dishes arrive with alacrity, but not a rush, and the food is utterly without pretense. Expect the same three vegetables with every main course. Patrons are mostly satisfied, not transported, yet they return again and again.

Kam Fung ♦
1008 Clark ☎ 866-4016. *Map 9D4* *I* AE ◉ VISA

Dim sum is the reason and lunch is the time for this cavernous Chinatown landmark. Attendants push trolleys laden with curried shrimp balls or steamed dumplings or three-score other irresistible goodies along the aisles, pausing at each table to display and describe their contents. Diners eat until full — or, commonly, more than they should. Dinner isn't nearly as special.

Le Lutétia
1430 de la Montagne ☎ 288-5656. *Map 11F4* *III* to *IIII* AE ◉ ◉ VISA

The mezzanine dining room of the **Hôtel de la Montagne** does full credit to its whimsically iconoclastic surroundings. Profoundly Parisian in appearance and standards, it grabs the eye with arresting late Victorian/ Belle Époque details. The happy confusion is abetted by the splash of the lobby fountain and drifting accordion music. The kitchen makes many hits and few misses. One starter is a tasty *carpaccio* of smoked goose. Salmon is gently broiled, and on the side might be a tumble of haricots verts and cauliflower florets cupped in a *raddichio* leaf. A top choice for lunch or dinner.

Montréal/Restaurants

Maison Cajun House
1219 Mackay ☎ 871-3898. Map 10G3 ⅢⅠ AE ◉ ◯ VISA **Closed Sat lunch, Sun lunch, Mon lunch.**

"*Bonjour, y'all*," greets the picture of an alligator outside. The Creole-Cajun cookery of Louisiana has a historical connection with Canada, unlikely as that might seem. Long ago, Francophones from the Maritime Provinces were exiled to the bayous around New Orleans, where they then created America's most distinctive regional cuisine. It is ably replicated here, in well-spiced renditions that stop short of setting ears afire. It feels like a night on Bourbon Street. Do try *gumbo yaya*. The owner is from The Bronx, but don't hold that against him.

La Marée ⚘
404 Pl. Jacques Cartier ☎ 861-8126. Map 9D5 ⅢⅠ AE ◉ ◯ VISA

Fast food and vapid "continental" fare usually dominate in tourist districts. Vieux Montréal runs against that norm, with several admirable mid-priced restaurants and one or two — including this one — that are simply superb. La Marée is less expensive than some, and adds the bonus of a lovely 18thC house. At night, candlelight enhances the inherent romance of the setting; business lunches prevail at midday. French recipes form the core of the menu, with sauces made lighter for contemporary tastes. The staff is well-trained and unobtrusive.

Mazurka ✿
64 Prince Arthur ☎ 844-3539. Map 8D3 ▢ AE ◉ VISA

Even among the low prices of Rue Prince Arthur, this Polish entry stands out. A lunch of barley soup, bread and *pierogis* (ravioli-like dumplings filled with meat or cheese) costs less than a pack of cigarettes. They have offered *two* lobsters for little more than the price of *one* in a fish store. How do they do it? No one cares. Merchants, artists, students and "ladies who lunch" keep swarming back, hoping the management never hires a cost accountant.

Les Mignardises ⚘
2037 St-Denis ☎ 842-1151. Map 9C4 ⅢⅠ AE ◉ ◯ VISA **Closed Mon lunch, Sat lunch, Sun.**

The exterior isn't prepossessing. Beyond that door, however, lies what many believe to be perfection in dining. Certainly it comes close, from the warm greeting to the seamless service to the dazzling fabrications that issue from behind the kitchen doors. There is a master at work back there, owner-chef Jean-Pierre Monnet. His flawless presentations and artistry with diverse ingredients leave his guests breathless, groping for words to do justice to the experience. It can't be hurried, for all is done to order. The menu changes daily, according to what was available at market. The check is as impressive as the dinner. But then, this meal could not be bested this side of the Seine.

Moishes
3961 St-Laurent ☎ 845-3509. Map 9D4 ⅢⅠ AE ◉ ◯ VISA **Closed Sun, last 2wks July.**

Those who insist on spending serious money for a chop or steak on otherwise inexpensive Blvd. St-Laurent can take their credit ratings here. Moishes gets the trim new breed of up-and-coming executive as well as those of the older generation who didn't know about triglycerides until it was too late. All meats are cooked exactly to order; veal chops are memorable. Dills and pickled cabbage come with the bread basket. At lunch, the Junior rib steak with appetizer, soup, dessert and coffee costs substantially less than the same steak alone at dinner.

Oggi
108 Laurier W ☎ 272-9122 ⅢⅠ AE ◉ ◯ VISA **Closed Sat lunch, Sun lunch.**

Gentrifying Rue Laurier needed a place that was more than flash. It has it here, in a long room with a basic black-and-white scheme. The decidedly *nuovo Italiano* decor matches the comestibles. Sauces do not drench the pastas, they dress them, their component fresh herbs strongly in evidence. Restraint is apparent, too, in the salads and crisp vegetables with a mere whisper of extra-virgin olive oil. This spiffy trattoria should play well for years.

La Picholette ⚘
1020 St-Denis ☎ 843-8502. Map 9C4 ⅢⅠ AE ◉ ◯ VISA **Closed Sat lunch, Sun.**

Civilized dining with touches of wonderment pertain at this mid-Victorian house, built for an English lord in 1867, at the perimeter of the *quartier latin*. The gracious manner in which he lived has been preserved, with bronze figurines holding candelabra aloft in high-ceilinged parlor rooms. He almost certainly didn't eat this well, though, for a woman by the name of van der Berg is in the kitchen fashioning little miracles. She has an enviable knack for game — duck, venison, wild boar — with fruit sauces that complement, never cloy. Her amiable *maître d'* is helpful and not the least stuffy. There are only 65 seats, so advance reservation is advisable.

Pizza Pino
1472 Crescent ☎ *844-4477. Map 10F3*

All of young Montréal must pass this glassed-in corner of Rue Crescent and de Maisonneuve sooner or later. They drop in here as late as 3am for pastas, salads, or any of the 24 different types of individual pizzas. Many insist that the pizzas are the best in town, although they are less robust than most American versions.

Saint Honoré
1616 Ste-Catherine W. Map 10G3 **IIII** *Closed Sat lunch, Sun.*

Tricky to find — behind the Faubourg Ste-Catherine shopping mall — but worth the effort, the 130yr-old stone building once belonged to the Grey Nuns. There is nothing reverent about the current occupant. Your dashing owner-host recognizes that dining out is a social, not sacramental, event. Downstairs is a cozy upscale grill, upstairs, a more formal room with well-spaced tables and gray-green modern furnishings. While everything on the plate looks as good as it tastes, the chefs don't appear to have spent more time arranging the food than they did cooking it. A knowledgeable crowd of all ages appreciates that.

Schwartz's ♣
3895 Blvd. St-Laurent ☎ *842-4813. Map 9D5*

The Bill 101 sign outside may read "Chez Schwartz Charcuterie Hebraique de Montréal," but that doesn't alter what it is and long has been. This is straight Jewish delicatessen, plain and loud and doing business at the same stand for decades. What you want is a small plate of hand-carved smoked meat — listen up, now, *small*! — with an order of fries, a sausage-shaped pickle and a soft drink. It will feed two teenagers with galloping metabolisms. You say you want grace and elan? Don't go. A taste sensation? Dash over.

La Sila
2040 St-Denis ☎ *844-5083. Map 9C5* **IIII** *Closed lunch and Sun.*

With such traditional standbys as melon and *prosciutto*, *fettucini Alfredo* and *saltimbocca*, the owners obviously aren't making a play for the squid-ink-pasta-and-Perrier set. It hasn't a trace of trendiness. No flavor of the week, and the waiters look and act like waiters, not models between shoots. Diners can even hear themselves think. Note particularly the veal dishes. Prices are at the low end of the expensive range, but the special nightly *table d'hôte* comes in below that.

Le Taj
2077 Stanley ☎ *845-9015. Map 11F4* **III**

This Rue Crescent-area Indian can be packed at lunch and near-empty at dinner. The inexpensive luncheon buffet is one reason. Day or night, this is northern *mughlai* cuisine, prepared in three degrees of hotness. The one in the middle is spicy enough for those who don't think authenticity requires a seared tongue. The card includes several curries and lamb dishes along with tandoori specialties. Those who admire the attractive temple carvings might like to know that the owner has a shop in the **Ritz-Carlton Hotel**.

Tarte-Folie
4003 St-Denis ☎ *288-6103. Map 9C4* **III**

Even quiche-haters are drawn to this window display of several versions of that dish, which is supplemented by designer pizzas and fruit tarts. Inside, there are a couple of bright and chirpy rooms, with hanging lamps and raspberry trim and chairs. Some of the quiches have meat as well as vegetables, and most are exquisitely done. A bowl of *café au lait* is a perfect topper. Wine and stiffer drinks are available. Busiest on weekends.

Tulipe Noire
2100 Stanley ☎ *285-1225. Map 11F4* **I** *to* **III**

A wait is inevitable at this, one of the most popular of a hundred variations on the café-tearoom-luncheonette theme. Good-quality soups, omelets and sandwiches make it best for snacks, not full meals. Or, use it for a late *cappuccino* and a slab of one of the dreamy desserts.

Vent Vert
2105 de la Montagne ☎ *842-2482. Map 11F4* ▮▮ *to* ▮▮▮▮ AE ◈ ◉ ▨

Step down into a room of emerald and apple greens, which half-explains the name ("Green Wind?"). The front room is a glassed terrace observatory on the street. Adroit waiters bring food that observes modified *nouvelle* conventions but in ample, not niggardly, portions.

Nightlife & the performing arts

Montréal's reputation as Canada's ultimate party town is deserved. An average slow Tuesday can have a concert by the Montréal Symphony in Place des Arts, a dance recital at Victoria Hall, jazz at a club in the old quarter, heavy metal at the Forum, a Noel Coward play, and a *Folies-Bergères*-style musical revue. That's in winter. By June, Montréal kicks into overdrive. Apart from the scores of cafés and clubs catering to every taste, it brings on one festival after another, devoted, in turn, to Mozart, fireworks, jazz, bilingual comedy and film. To discover what's on, consult the *Montréal Gazette*.

The minimum drinking age is 18. Last call for orders can be as late as 3am. "Happy hour" is an institution, usually in effect from 5-7pm, but often longer, when cut-rate drinks and free snacks attract the decompressing after-work crowd. As a rule, patrons are expected to pay for drinks when they are served, but the bartender may accept a credit card for imprint, and run a tab that way. Exceptions are sometimes made in quiet places, or for customers with honest faces. A 15-percent tip is customary. Liquor is expensive and none-too-generously poured.

While bars and dance clubs are found in many parts of town, they are in greatest concentration in four distinct areas. Anglophones are most in evidence on **Rue Crescent** and adjacent streets. Speakers of French dominate in **Vieux Montréal** and in the **Latin Quarter**, which centers on **St-Denis** from Ontario N to Carré St-Louis. And increasingly active is the **Plateau Mont-Royal** district, incorporating the upper reaches of **St-Denis**, **St-Laurent** and **Av. du Parc**. As in the city's restaurants, dress codes are rarely in force, but blue jeans are sometimes cause for being turned away.

Policies change without notice. Always call ahead to determine what is scheduled that night, or, for that matter, whether the club still exists.

A cover or admission charge is often levied at places with live entertainment. It is rarely exorbitant and may include the first drink. At dinner-theaters and in the hotel nightclubs, the show may be included in the price of the meal, but show-only tickets are available. Tickets to major concerts, plays and sports events can be ordered by telephone through **Teletron** (☎ *288-2525*). Have a valid credit card handy. In-person purchases are made at **Ticketron** counters in **La Baie** store and **Pl. Ville-Marie**.

Bars are known less for mere elbow-bending than the proclivities of their habitués, be they jazz buffs, sports fans, or singles on the make. Food is available, but rarely memorable. King of the hill in the **Rue Crescent** district is **Thursday's** (*1430 Crescent* ☎ *288-5656*), prime hunting ground for the yuppie/preppie set. It is connected to **Les Beaux Jeudis** restaurant, a case of tail wagging dog. **Sir Winston**

Nightlife and the performing arts/Montréal

Churchill (*1459 Crescent* ☎ *288-0616*) has a sidewalk terrace, open in summer, enclosed in winter, and is great for all-season people-watching. After 5pm, the action shifts to the rambling pub down the stairs. Similar in style is nearby **DJ's Pub** (*1433 Crescent* ☎ *287-9354*), with its own front terrace and a small dance floor where the noon-8pm "happy hour" is very popular. Near-clones of the above are **Comforts** (*1195 Crescent* ☎ *861-0216*), **Rumors** (*2125 de la Montagne* ☎ *845-3607*) and **Dereks** (*1470 Crescent* ☎ *843-5697*). **Sam's** (*1458 de la Montagne* ☎ *842-8825*) has a terrace three floors above the bustle. Inside are booths and a dance floor.

Piano bars are another variation. The **New York Bar** (*2144 Mackay* ☎ *933-8444*) is the lounge of the **Abacus** restaurant, which means a happy marriage of Chinese bar nibbles and chrome-and-leather Manhattan ambience. **La Porte des Lilas** (*1473 Crescent* ☎ *284-0307*) has a Parisian flair, and a piano player Thurs-Sat.

Everyone is drawn to **Le Faubourg St-Denis** (*1660 St-Denis* ☎ *843-4814*) in the *quartier latin*. In good weather, tables are set out on the sidewalk, and no part of Montréal so evokes the Parisian Left Bank. The tables are behind glass in winter, and a fire crackles in the downstairs bar. Media types mix with academics at **Le Bistro St-Denis** (*1738 St-Denis* ☎ *842- 3717*), while **Beaux Esprits** (*2073 St-Denis* ☎ *844-0882*) is a refuge for couples more interested in each other than the surroundings. Those who prefer a livelier atmosphere go across the street to **La Côte à Baron** (*2070 St-Denis* ☎ *842-6626*). The food and service are variable, but these glossy folk have other pursuits in mind. **Lola's Paradise** (*3604 St-Laurent* ☎ *282-9944*) is a very hot after-midnight spot. The upstairs loft space is decorated, after a fashion, with Depression Era furniture and spotlighted flowers. Pretty people in cautiously fashionable duds mingle freely with those from the far edge, while the DJ spins anything he chooses over the excellent sound system — Benny Goodman to Roy Orbison. **Lux** (*5220 St-Laurent* ☎ *271-9272*) looks like a European notion of an American drugstore. Open 24hrs, it doesn't get intriguingly weird until after 2am, when the pale nightbirds start to bop through the doors.

At **discos and dance clubs**, conversation is in competition with thunderously amplified records and live bands. Gaining entrance is rarely a problem before 10pm. After that, lines often form and regulars may be ushered inside ahead of strangers.

The rear end of a tail-finned Cadillac is cantilevered over the entrance to **American Rock Café** (*2080 Aylmer* ☎ *288-9272*). The live music is of the early rock 'n' roll era. **Business** (*3500 Blvd. St-Laurent* ☎ *849-3988*) is as warm and welcoming as a prison exercise yard, all raw concrete and steel girders. Such neo-brutalism is "in," obviously, for it is packed with the trendiest young. Rap music is a staple. **Club Balatou** (*4372 Blvd. St-Laurent* ☎ *845-5447*) is a steamy, exotic enclave, a refreshing change from prevailing modes. Capable bands explore African and Caribbean roots, and their enthusiastic audiences are given plenty of hip room on the large dance floor. **Club Septembre** (*2015 de la Montagne* ☎ *849-4544, closed Tues*) throbs to pounding salsa and similar tropical rhythms for a largely Hispanic crowd. Electric dancers and frequent live bands.

L'Esprit (*1234 de la Montagne* ☎ *397-1711, open Thurs-Sat, with a Sun session for youngsters below drinking age*) looks like a funeral parlor because it once was. Inside, the only bodies are dressed to kill but very much alive. **Les Foufones Electriques**

Montréal/Nightlife and the performing arts

(*87 Ste-Catherine E* ☎ *845-5484*) is as off-the-wall as the breed gets, a *nouvelle vague* outpost with acts such as Screaming Tribesmen, Dysfunction and Tupelo Chain Sex. They are augmented by poets reading their unpublished odes, mimes, and whoever else might care to thumb their noses at the straight world. The city's biggest disco is **Metropolis** (*59 St-Catherine E* ☎ *288-5559, open Thurs-Sun*), with six bars and a 2,500sq.ft dance floor that is a writhing mass when the customers get their blood up after midnight. The Fritz Lang decor is underscored by an impressive lightshow. Elvis, Buddy Holly and the Big Bopper live on at **Studebakers** (*1255 Crescent* ☎ *866-1101*), and this is one dance club that has almost as many receding hairlines as acne cases. The waitresses even dress in cheerleader outfits.

A few large hotels have **nightclubs** with floorshows of the Las Vegas variety, wherein underdressed chorines prance around headliners and other performers. In another category are the **boîtes-à-chansons**, restaurants that showcase singers of the Edith Piaf persuasion. **Arthur-Café Baroque** (*900 Blvd. René Lévesque* ☎ *878-9000*) is a splashily elegant room of the Queen Elizabeth Hotel, where the fare is usually frothy, saucy musical revues. One show nightly Wed-Fri, Sun, two on Sat, with dancing after the show. **Le Caf' Conc'** (*1 Pl. du Canada* ☎ *878-9000*) is the Hotel Château Champlain's gaudy supper club, a mix of Moulin Rouge and Copacabana. Showgirls and chorus boys do their production numbers around a changing slate of comics, singers, magicians and jugglers. Two shows nightly, three on Sat; closed Sun. Reserve ahead; men must wear jackets. **Au Bistro d'Autrefois** (*1229 St-Hubert* ☎ *842-2808*) features singers in the French cabaret style (think Jacques Brel), but also might have jazz combos, blues shouters and theatrical groups. Performers come on around 10pm. Despite the annual **Just for Laughs Festival**, the **Comedy Nest** (*1234 Bishop* ☎ *395-8118, closed Mon*) is the only place in town that focuses entirely on comedy. There are no guarantees, of course, for one person's guffaw is another's affront. Wed night is reserved for newcomers. Reserve ahead. **Vieux Munich** (*1170 St-Denis* ☎ *288-8011*) comes as close to a replica of a Bavarian beer hall as can be found in North America. Waitresses in *dirndls* weave among the long wooden tables with platters of *wurst* or clutching impossible numbers of foaming mugs. Yodelers yodel, the big brass band oompahs polkas and waltzes with abandon, and in no time everyone is linking arms and singing at the tops of their voices. Weekends are liveliest, and it's so large that reservations are rarely necessary.

Montréal's enthusiasm for **jazz** predated the creation in 1980 of its 10-day **International Jazz Festival**. All modes are represented — Dixie, swing, blues, bebop, fusion — in hotel lounges, restaurant cellars and back rooms, and clubs, where the music is supreme. It can be heard every night of the week, although Thurs-Sat are best. Always inquire ahead.

They're serious about jazz at **L'Air du Temps** (*191 St-Paul E* ☎ *842-2003*), a longtime Vieux Montréal haunt. A good portion of available floor space is given to combos that often have five or more members. Attractions are changed frequently. Arrive by 9.45pm to get a seat; sets usually begin at 10.30pm. **Claudio's** (*124 St-Paul E* ☎ *866-0845*) is only a few steps away. Live music nightly except Thurs and Sun, and they often skip the cover charge. Downtown stalwart **Biddles** (*2060 Aylmer* ☎ *842-8656*) has "jazz and ribs" as its subtitle, and delivers on both counts. The barbecue sauce is of the honey-sweet variety, and the messy

Nightlife and the performing arts/Montréal

job of eating them contributes to the jolly informality, the better to attend to the mellow sounds of the Charles Biddle Trio. **Bijou** (*300 Lemoyne* ☎ *288-5508*) is another choice in Vieux Montréal, its artists fudging the line between jazz and soul. The club occasionally books comics and magicians. **Le Grand Café** (*1720 St-Denis* ☎ *849-6955*) squeezes in large combos and even bands, playing anything from swing to bluesy funk.

Montréal is on the North American circuit for every traveling **rock and pop** superstar group and vocalist. They book the biggest arenas and clubs, as do many Canadian talents. **Club Soda** (*5420 Av. du Parc* ☎ *270-7878*) defies categories. The monster concert hall and mega-bar hosts groups playing funk, soul, reggae, country, metal and blues. Even comedians show up. Most acts only stay around a night or two. When it isn't sheltering the Canadiens hockey team, the **Montréal Forum** (*2313 Ste-Catherine W* ☎ *932-2582*) is a major venue for rock bands of David Bowie and Rod Stewart wattage. **Spectrum** (*318 Ste-Catherine W* ☎ *861-5851*) is a converted movie palace for up to 1,000 music lovers. Groups appearing are not brand names, so tickets are usually lower than at Club Soda and the Forum.

All the Hollywood **movies** appear at the multiple-screen cinemas downtown. Showings usually commence at noon. There are about as many theaters showing movies in French as in English, and some have both, so find out before purchasing tickets. Repertory theaters show less commercial art films and classics. A few possibilities: **Cinéma Parallèle** (*3682 Blvd. St-Laurent* ☎ *843-6001*), **La Cinémathèque Québecois** (*355 de Maisonneuve* ☎ *842-9768*), **Conservatoire d'Art Cinématographique de Montréal** (*1456 de Maisonneuve* ☎ *848-3878*), **Cinéma V** (*5560 Sherbrooke W* ☎ *489-5559*), **Ouimétoscope** (*1204 Ste-Catherine* ☎ *525-8600*) and **Rialto** (*5723 Av. du Parc* ☎ *274-3550*).

The prime venue for **classical music, opera and dance** is **Place des Arts** (*information* ☎ *285-4200; box office* ☎ *842-2112*). Its two main buildings house three theater-concert halls. The largest, with almost 3,000 seats, is **Salle Wilfrid-Pelletier**, which hosts symphony orchestras, ballet and the opera, while the adaptable **Theatre Maisonneuve** and **Theatre Port-Royal** are employed for music and dance recitals, plays (usually in French), and concerts by touring pop and opera singers. Less regularly, performances are held in **Pollack Hall** (☎ *392-8224, closed June-Aug*) at McGill University, where most performances are free.

A rigorous touring schedule has brought acclaim to **Les Grands Ballets Canadiens** (☎ *849-8681*) in cities on five continents. When at home, the company, which explores both classical and contemporary dance forms, appears in the Salle Wilfrid-Pelletier and in summer performs for free in Parc LaFontaine. Created in 1980, the **Opéra de Montréal** (☎ *521-5577*) has garnered substantial prestige for such a short period of existence. It presents several productions during the Oct-May season, sharing Salle Wilfrid-Pelletier with the **Orchestre Symphonique de Montréal** (☎ *842-3402*). This orchestra has an international reputation and gives free summer concerts in outdoor arenas around the city. **Orchestre Metropolitain du Grand Montréal** (☎ *598-0870*) is the city's junior symphony, appearing in the Theatre Maisonneuve. Chamber music is performed by the **Société Pro Musica** and the **McGill Chamber Orchestra**, while serious 20thC music is the focus of the **Société de Musique Contemporaine de Québec**.

In dance, look for appearances by **Ballets Jazz de Montréal** and **Les Ballets Classiques de Montréal**. These are the principal companies, and not the full extent of cultural offerings.

Nearly a dozen Francophone **theaters** put on mainstream and avant-garde productions, but the choices are few for speakers of English. Only the **Centaur Theatre** (*453 St-François-Xavier,* ☎ *288-3161, closed Mon and June-Sept*) is a permanent venue of consistent merit. The Centaur mounts both popular and experimental productions, primarily with Canadian themes. **Dinner-theater** is another alternative, usually staging downsized Broadway retreads. Consult *The Gazette*.

Shopping in Montréal

The workmanship and diversity of Montréal's goods equal or exceed those of any city its size. Fashion and furs are paramount, for Montréal has always led the nation in their design and manufacture. Despite high duties, there is an abundance of imported products as well, notably English china and Scottish woolens. Collectors of art should pay particular attention to Inuit sculpture, carved from whalebone, antlers and walrus tusks, as well as the more familiar soapstone. None of it is cheap, but the artistry is commendable. Visitors seeking bargains will find the quest unrewarding, in the main, although some good buys can be ferreted out in discount lofts along Blvd. St-Laurent and in the Plateau Mont-Royal district.

The major department stores surround Christ Church Cathedral in center city, and boutiques of many local clothing designers are found along upper St-Laurent and Rue Laurier. Nearly 30 antique stores take up both sides of Rue Notre-Dame between Atwater and Guy. Art galleries cluster along Sherbrooke, near the *Musée des Beaux Arts*. Otherwise, finding just the right store requires advance planning and a lot of walking.

In general, hours are 9.30 or 10am-6pm during the week, but until 9pm Thurs and/or Fri. Most close at 5pm Sat and all day Sun. There are exceptions. Many stores in the Underground City stay open until 9pm Mon-Fri, and those in Vieux Montréal are often open Sun.

A provincial sales tax of 9 percent is applied to most purchases, but not to books, home furnishings, or to shoes under $125 and clothing under $500. Most stores take one or more of the major credit cards. US currency is widely accepted, but nearly always at rates inferior to those offered by banks.

For **arts and crafts**, try the **Centre du Céramique Poterie Bonsecours** (*444 St-Gabriel* ☎ *866-6581*), which has pottery and ceramics by Québec artisans. The affable staff of the **Eskimo Art Gallery** (*434 Sherbrooke W* ☎ *844-4080*) makes browsing a pleasure, and there are frequent special exhibits. The **Guilde Canadienne des Métiers d'Art** (*2025 Peel* ☎ *849-6091*) should be the first stop for those interested in blown glass, silver, ceramics, weavings, stained glass and other handcrafted objects of high order.

Attic Row is the name given to the concentration of **antiques and collectibles** shops along Rue Notre-Dame. Merchandise is generally cheaper than in the galleries on Sherbrooke. **Antiques Gisela** (*1960 Notre-Dame W* ☎ *937-7695*) traffics in teddy bears, dolls, trains and other toys dating from the late 19thC. **Antiquitou** (*2475 Notre-Dame W* ☎ *932-3256*) has old duck

Shopping/Montréal

decoys, country furniture and such offbeat objects as cash registers. They're used to people "just looking" at **Galerie Archaeologia** (*1486 Sherbrooke W* ☎ *932-7585*), which displays museum-quality artifacts from as early as the 4thC: urns, coins and statuary of Egyptian, Greek and Roman origins. A converted bank is put to appropriate use by **Henrietta Antony** (*4192 Ste-Catherine* ☎ *935-9116*) to showcase chandeliers, period furnishings, ornate mirrors and clocks, and copper and silver objects: three fascinating floors. In business for three generations, **Petit Musée** (*1494 Sherbrooke W* ☎ *937-6161*) has four levels of weaponry and armor, Greek and Roman archeological fragments, furniture and jewelry. Both Canadian country furniture and Art Deco are in stock at **Puces Libres Antiques** (*4240 St-Denis* ☎ *842-5931*), along with clocks, chandeliers and duck decoys.

This city of readers has **bookstores** (*libraires*) everywhere. Many are open 7 days a week, but those dealing in antiquarian books often follow unorthodox schedules. **Bibliomania** (*4685 Av. du Parc* ☎ *849-3175*) has new, used and rare books in both French and English. **Double Hook** (*1235A Greene* ☎ *932-5093*) is devoted exclusively to Canadian subjects or books by Canadian authors. Bright and crisp **Lexis Booksellers** (*2055 Peel* ☎ *848-9763*) purveys only English-language titles, while **Librairie Ulysse** (*560 President-Kennedy* ☎ *289-0993*) concentrates on travel books and videos. **Paragraphe** (*2065 Mansfield* ☎ *845-5811*) has a refurbished location, with an excellent selection in both French and English. **S.W. Welch** (*5673 Sherbrooke W* ☎ *488-5943*) deals in out-of-print books.

For **china and crystal**, there is no better source than **Birks et Fils** (*1240 Carré Phillips* ☎ *397-2511*), which presents such extensive selections of china, jewelry and silverware that it almost qualifies as a department store. Smart merchandizing and substantial discounts make **Caplan-Duval** (*6700 Côte des Neiges* ☎ *483-4040*) an appealing destination for those looking for Wedgwood and Royal Doulton dinnerware and Lalique and Waterford crystal. **Cadeaux Au Bon Marché** (*99 Chabanel W* ☎ *388-6564*) discounts china, crystal and silver.

While all the top European and American **fashion** designers are represented, this is an opportunity to check out homegrown clothiers, many of whom have made reputations abroad. **Alfred Sung** (*1455 Peel* ☎ *499-0963*) is one of Canada's most successful, with moderately-priced and couture lines for both men and women. Chantal Gagnon is featured at **Caboche** (*445 St-Sulpice* ☎ *285-1189*), with clothes for the career woman, and high fashion for those unconcerned with cost. **Fureur** (*4391 St-Denis* ☎ *844-7467*) sells deceptively simple styles by a Montréal designer, in a modishly bare showroom. The setting is so spare at **Parachute** (*3526 St-Laurent* ☎ *845-7865*) it looks as if they aren't selling *anything*. But they are — cutting edge fashions that get more than their share of attention. **Revenge** (*3852 St-Denis* ☎ *843-4379*) has no imports, just garments, by important Montréal designers, for both men and women.

The Hudson's Bay Company was chartered in 1670 to organize the fur trade, but didn't move into the retail business until the 1880s. Now **La Baie (The Bay)** (*585 Ste-Catherine W* ☎ *281-4422*) is one of Canada's most prominent chains of **department stores**, while retaining an emphasis on furs. **Eaton** (*667 Ste-Catherine W* ☎ *284-8411*), Montréal's biggest store, is undergoing updating intended to make it the anchor of an expanded mall along the lines of Toronto's Eaton Centre. Don't miss the glorious Art Deco lunchroom on the 9th floor. **Holt Renfrew** (*1300 Sherbrooke W* ☎ *842-5111*) is the upper crust of the chains, signaled by its proximity to the exclusive Ritz-Carlton; top-of-the-line merchandise at prices to match. **Ogilvy** (*1307 Ste-Catherine W* ☎ *842-7711*) is noted for its merchandizing pizazz, but the Scottish origins of the store are underscored by the noontime skirl of a bagpiper.

About 85 percent of Canada's **fur** industry is situated in Montréal. Everything from raccoon to sable is sold in department stores and scores of luxurious salons. **Alexandor** (*2025 de la Montagne* ☎ *288-1119*) enjoys an excellent reputation, as does **Desjardins** (*325 Blvd. René-Lévesque* ☎ *288-4151*), which is more than a century old. **Dubarry** (*370 Sherbrooke W* ☎ *844-7483*) and **McComber** (*440 de Maisonneuve W* ☎ *845-1167*) are also highly regarded. Look around first, but if prices are intimidating at other furriers, there may well be something within the budget at **Oslo** (*5149 St-Laurent* ☎ *270-2655*).

Sports

Auto-racing
The **Grand Prix Molson du Canada** is one of 16 races in the international Formula One circuit. Île Notre-Dame's refurbished **Gilles Villeneuve Circuit** (☎ *392-0000*) is the site of the three-day event. More than 130,000 spectators turn out for the spectacle of high-powered cars reaching speeds of 197mph. Held each year in mid-June.

Baseball
After hockey, Montréalers are wild about their Expos. The professional team is one of only two Canadian teams competing in US Major League Baseball. That isn't to say that the city's baseball history is short. Triple A teams, a notch below the major leagues, were in place, on and off, from as early as 1898. Such legendary players as Duke Snider, Don Newcombe, Roy Campanella and Jackie Robinson once played for the Royals. The Expos play their home games at **Olympic Stadium** (*season Apr-Sept* ☎ *253-3434 for information* ☎ *253-0700 for tickets*). It has a retractable roof which usually works, and is something of a tourist attraction in itself. Reservations may be made by phone, using a credit card.

Boating
A huge, rectangular artificial lake was created for the Olympic Games on man-made Île Notre-Dame. It now serves in summer for windsurfing, pedal boating and sailing. The **Société de l'Île Notre-Dame** (☎ *872-6093*) conducts a sailing school there, daily from mid-May to early Sept. In Lachine, between downtown and Dorval Airport, the **École de Voile de Lachine** (*2105 Blvd. St-Joseph* ☎ *634-4326*) rents boats and sailboards, and provides group and private lessons. Open mid-May to end of Sept.

Curling
Played on an ice court by teams of four, curling involves sliding a smooth, rounded, 38-pound granite stone with a handle, toward a series of concentric circles 38yds away. It is aided on its way (it is believed) by other players who sweep the ice in its path with a

broom. The stones stopping nearest the inner circle are given points. The sport was imported by immigrant Scots, where the popular winter sport has been played for at least four centuries. Curling is played by amateurs, usually the members of clubs devoted to the sport. Among these are the **Longue Pointe Curling Club** (☎ 254-2773), **Montréal West Curling Club** (☎ 486-5831) and the **Wentworth Curling Club** (☎ 481-6322). The nation's oldest is the **Royal Montréal Curling Club** (☎ 935-3411).

Cycling
Professional cyclists compete in the **Grand Prix Cycliste des Amériques** (☎ 879-1027) over a challenging 200km course through the streets and up Mont-Royal. Those who simply wish to ride for fun are pleased to know that the government maintains nearly 140miles of cycling paths on the Island of Montréal. They include rights-of-way along Lachine Canal and the St Lawrence Seaway, in Parc Angrignon, and on Rue Rachel between Parc LaFontaine and Parc Maisonneuve. Solo and tandem bicycles — even pedal vehicles carrying up to nine riders — can be rented in the Old Port at the **Jacques-Cartier pier** (☎ 844-9139) and on **Île Notre-Dame** (☎ 398-0634). Other possibilities are **Cycle Peel** (*6665 St-Jacques* ☎ 486-1148) and **La Cordée** (*2159 Ste-Catherine E* ☎ 524-1515). Cycling organization **Vélo-Québec** (*4545 Pierre-de-Coubertin* ☎ 252-3123) distributes guidebooks and brochures on cycling in Québec.

Fishing
Promising lakes and rivers for the angler are within a day trip of the city center. The Québec ministry for leisure, hunting and fishing (☎ 800-462-5349) can suggest locations.

Golf
Most golf clubs are private, but there are a few courses open to nonmembers. The entrance to **Golf Municipal de Montréal** (☎ 872-1143) is near the Viau Metro station, the only course (9 holes) accessible by subway. Each about 15mins from downtown, and requiring a car, are **Brossard Municipal Golf Course** (*4705 Lapinière, Brossard, exit 9 off Rte. 10 E* ☎ 676-0201), **Fresh Meadows** (*505 Av. du Golf, Beaconsfield, Rte. 20 W* ☎ 697-4036), **Club de Golf de Laprairie** (*75 Blvd. Taschereau, Laprairie, Rte. 10 E* ☎ 659-1908), and **Golf Dorval** (*2000 Reverchon, Dorval, Rte. 20 W* ☎ 631-6624). The Laprairie course has 18 holes, the one in Dorval 36, the others, nine.

Hockey
If there is a Canadian faith that crosses all ethnic and linguistic boundaries, it is hockey. Devotions are held in the secular temple, the **Montréal Forum** (*3213 Ste-Catherine W* ☎ 932-2582). There, the professional Canadiens periodically raise spirits and break Montréalers' hearts. The team started before the creation of the National Hockey League, which it has often dominated, winning the Stanley Cup 23 times in 60yrs. Its roster of immortals includes Maurice "The Rocket" Richard, "Boom-Boom" Geoffrion, Jean Beliveau and Guy Lafleur. The fervent followers of the Canadiens buy more than 14,000 season tickets every year, which leaves only 2,500 unpurchased seats. Games are played from Oct-Apr, with the playoffs in May.

Montréal/Sports

Horse-racing
Hippodrome Blue Bonnets (*7440 Blvd. Decarie* ☎ *739-2741*) is host to trotters and their drivers from around the world. Days for harness-racing vary with the season; call ahead. Post time is 7.30pm during the week, 1.30pm on Sun.

Rafting
Electrifying white-water rides over the rapids in the St Lawrence river are available from **Lachine Rapids Tours** (☎ *284-9607*). Their boats berth at **Victoria Pier** in the Old Port, near Rue Berri. Rain slickers and hats are provided, but expect to get wet anyway. Open from the end of Apr to the end of Sept. The trip takes 1½hrs and is not cheap.

Running
More than 10,000 runners, both professional and amateur, participate in the annual **Montréal Marathon** (☎ *879-1027*), held in Sept. Recreational runners train on the trails of Mont-Royal and the several larger parks, such as Parc LaFontaine and riverside Parc René-Lévesque.

Skating
Montréal has more than 150 outdoor skating rinks, 30 of them illuminated after dark, and 21 indoor arenas. **Beaver Lake** in **Parc Mont-Royal** is festive, and **Parc LaFontaine** and **Parc Maisonneuve** are popular. **Parc Angrignon** has two rinks and a 1-mile ice trail through the trees. The biggest rink is the former **Olympic Basin** (☎ *872-6211*) on Île Notre-Dame, and skates are available for rent; but the wind off the river can be piercing.

Skiing
Near **Beaver Lake** in **Parc Mont-Royal** is a modest downhill slope with rope-tow. It is suitable for beginners. Cross-country skiers and snowshoers use the trails of that park and those used for cyclists (see above) around the city. The *Botanical Gardens* have what they call an "ecology" trail through the grounds. Equipment can be rented on **Île Notre-Dame** (☎ *872-3376*) for cross-country skiing and at a number of sporting goods shops, including **Ski Dump** (*8366 St-Laurent* ☎ *384-1315*). The nearby Laurentian Mountains and the hills of **L'Estrie**, an hour's drive SE of the city, offer some of the best skiing in eastern North America.

Snowshoeing
Enthusiasts use the same trails as cross-country skiers (see *Skiing* above). For information ☎ 872-6211.

Soccer
What the rest of the world calls football has had about the same success in Canada as in the States — not much. That doesn't stop entrepreneurs from trying. In 1988, Supra de Montréal became the local entry in the 10-team Canadian Soccer League. Matches are played at **Claude-Robillard Centre** (*1000 Émile-Journault* ☎ *739-6266*). The season is late May to mid-Sept, Wed, Sun nights.

Swimming
The St Lawrence River has no swimming beaches, but there are many indoor and outdoor pools open to the public, and most of the larger downtown hotels have pools as well. **Olympic Park**

CHILDREN/MONTRÉAL

(*4545 Pierre-de-Coubertin* ☎ *252-4737*) has five pools open to the public. It's a little far E of downtown for visitors to go just for a swim, unless combined with a visit to the nearby *Jardin Botanique* and a ride to the top of the tower that winches up the retractable roof of the adjacent stadium. **Île Ste-Hélène** (☎ *872-6093*) has three large pools near the island's Metro station. For information on neighborhood pools operated by the city ☎ 872-6211.

Tennis
In an unusual arrangement, the annual **Player's International Challenge Tournament** has professional women tennis players competing in even-numbered years, the men in odd-numbered years. It's held at **Parc Jarry** (☎ *273-1515*) for 2wks in Aug. Amateurs have an ample number of courts available to them in summer, including those in **Parc LaFontaine** and **Parc Jeanne-Mance**. Further information from the Sports and Leisure line ☎ 872-6211.

Montréal for children

Museums and shopping pall quickly for youngsters. Mercifully, Montréal lays out many activities and attractions that are immensely enjoyable for both children and adults, so the need to provide them with diversions to their taste isn't a chore. For details, see *Sights and places of interest*, *Nightlife and the performing arts* and *Sports*; look for the ✱ symbol.

Amusement parks and zoos
Île Ste-Hélène is worth an entire day for families. Apart from its three swimming pools and acres of picnic grounds, it has a colonial fort with live "soldiers" and bagpipers, a small aquarium, an Aqua-Parc with exhilarating water slides (bring swimsuits), and *La Ronde amusement park*. This has 33 rides of varying degrees of adrenalin provocation, from mild to heart-stopping. Frequent firework displays augment live cabaret shows and exhibits, and the rather pricey admission ticket includes entrance to the aquarium with its ingratiating penguins. The city zoo moves from the summertime **Garden of Wonders** story village in *Parc LaFontaine* to its winter home in *Parc Angrignon*.

Boat trips
For all but the very young, the jetboat rides over the St Lawrence are thrilling, not frightening. Check with **Lachine Rapids Tours**. 1-3hr cruises of calmer but scenic parts of the river are available from **Montréal Harbor Cruises** (*Victoria Pier*, ☎ *842-3871*, *May-Oct*). Sure to please the adventurous child is the amphibious bus of **Amphi Tour** (*Old Port* ☎ *386-1298*, *May-end Oct*). It trundles up the streets of Vieux Montréal, then drives right into the water and pretends it's a boat.

Events and entertainments
What child doesn't like fireworks, the noisier and more explosive the better? Time a visit, then, for the **International Fireworks Competition** at La Ronde in May-June. A **Winter Carnival** seizes their imagination in Jan and early Feb, with hot-air balloons, clowns, dog sled and ice-canoe races, and much more. Various places. For information ☎ 800-363-0621.

QUÉBEC CITY/INTRODUCTION

Observation points
Take a horse-drawn *calèche* to the Chalet in **Parc Mont-Royal** for a spectacular view of the city and river that is especially dazzling at dusk. Or, scoot by swift funicular to the top of the tower of *Olympic Stadium* for 50-mile wraparound vistas.

Shows and concerts
The unique **Cirque du Soleil** (☎ *522-2324*) is a circus without animals, but the acts are so charming and inventive that no one minds. The **Children's Theatre** (*4626 Sherbrooke W* ☎ *484-6620*) mounts periodic productions at Victoria Hall. For 2wks around Christmas, **Les Grands Ballets Canadiens** (☎ *849-8681*) perform the evergreen *Nutcracker Suite*. Stargazers combine knowledge with wonder under the dome of the *Dow Planetarium*. Eyes are 20ft high on the 7-story screen that is employed by the **Imax Cinema** (*Old Port* ☎ *496-4629*).

Québec City

A more noble setting could not be conceived for a city that was destined to become the very soul of French America. Québec's steeples and turrets rake the sky from the formidable cliffs that rear over the northerly shore of the St Lawrence. The river, silvered by moonlight or high summer sun, makes a majestic sweep past Québec on its way to the ocean, bestowing an exhilarating panorama of sky and water and distant mountains. The treasure that is Québec was acknowledged when the only walled city north of Mexico was designated "a heritage of the world" by UNESCO in 1985.

Jacques Cartier was the first recorded European to stop at the spot, in 1535. It was left to Samuel de Champlain to put down roots. He built a small fort there in 1608, at the base of the sheer cliff that rose sharply to the high plateau that is now Vieux Québec. The city's most familiar landmark, the imposing Château Frontenac hotel, now looms over the constricted streets of gray stone houses, which date back to the 17thC.

Québec was the capital of Nouvelle France for more than 150 years, a status it retained despite almost constant conflict with the British, who wanted all of North America for themselves. Finally, in 1759, a decisive battle took place on the Plains of Abraham, southwest of the city. Both the French and British commanders were killed, but New France was subsequently ceded to England in the 1763 Treaty of Paris.

Fortunately for the city and the visitors who now revel in her every summer, colonization quickly moved west to Montréal, then to Toronto and beyond. Québec was left to thrive quietly, an island of French culture in an English sea, its distinctive character and boundless *joie de vivre* intact.

Basic information

Getting there and getting around
The airport is in Ste-Foy, only 12 miles away. While there are a few direct flights to US cities, most air travelers to Québec City fly into Montréal and make connections from there. VIA Rail has regular trains from Montréal and the trip takes a little over 3hrs. It

Basic information/Québec City

takes about that long in a car. The Voyageur bus line has service several times daily between the two cities.

Because the distance from the airport is short, a taxi ride isn't too expensive. The airport bus is cheaper and stops at selected downtown hotels, but the wait can be long between departures. Much of the city can be seen on foot, using taxis for long distances. Parking is quite limited, so those arriving by private car might prefer simply to leave it in the hotel garage until departure. All the major car rental companies have offices at the airport and downtown.

Road signs are in French. Explanations of these signs can be obtained from car rental agencies and automobile clubs, or from the Tourism and Convention Bureau (see *Useful addresses*). Driving in winter is not recommended. Québec is subject to very heavy snows, making driving conditions difficult and even perilous, especially for those not used to driving on ice. Streets can be very narrow and steep in the old town, made more so by banks of snow pushed aside by plows. Horse-drawn buggies, called *calèches*, found also in Montréal, are a romantic and appropriate way to see the old town. Keep *calèches* for sightseeing, however, and not transportation, as they are expensive.

Useful addresses
Tourist information
☎692-2471 or 651-2882. By mail, **Québec City Region Tourism and Convention Bureau** (*60 Rue d'Auteuil, Québec (Québec) G1R 4C4*). There is a visitor tourist office at the same address, and, in summer, information booths are found in several locations in old town. Also in summer, official bilingual guides on bicycles and motor scooters can be found, identified by flags with question marks. Just hail one and ask away.

Tour operators
Baillargé Cultural Tours ☎658-4799. Walking tours.
Grey Line ☎622-7420. Several bus tours of city and region, one of which includes a harbor cruise.
Maple Leaf Sightseeing ☎687-9226. Choice of bus tours.
S.T.E.P.O.N. Guides ☎654-0310. Guides use client's car.
Tours de Ville ☎687-9226. Bus and bus/cruise combination.

Local publications
The weekly English-language *Chronicle-Telegraph* is of limited use. Larger hotels and many newsstands carry newspapers from Canadian and US cities. French-language dailies are *Le Soleil* and *Le Journal de Québec*.

Emergency information
Police and Fire ☎691-6911.
Dental emergencies ☎653-5412 Mon-Fri, or ☎656-6060 Sat-Sun.
Health emergencies ☎648-2626. Calls are answered by nurses 24hrs.
Pharmacy (late) ☎623-1571. Open daily 8am-2am.
For **Auto accidents**, **car breakdowns** and **lost travelers cheques**, see *Montréal/Emergency information*, page 74.

Help lines
Alcoholics Anonymous ☎529-0015, daily 8am-midnight.
Distress Center ☎683-2153. Depression, emotional crises.
Pet emergency ☎647-2000, daily 24hrs.

Québec City/Orientation

Orientation

It may not seem so to tourists, who spend most of their time in the compact old town and immediate environs, but Québec is a sizeable city of more than 500,000 inhabitants, a busy seaport with two universities, and the seat of the provincial government. Much local revenue is derived from visitors, and the city goes out of its way to make them welcome. The year is segmented with celebrations and festivals, the most extravagant being the 10-day Carnival in Feb, with its riotous agenda of costume balls, flashlight parades, ice castles and snow sculpture competitions. It is overlapped by the **Festival d'hiver de Saint-Émile**, which begins in mid-Jan, and is followed immediately by a series of Olympic-level speedskating and cross-country ski races, hockey tournaments, auto and outdoor shows. In no time it is summer, which explodes with music festivals and street fairs almost weekly into fall.

Only a propensity for bad timing can deny the visitor at least a minor holiday, which is always an excuse for a little festive partying. Even with such misfortune, however, there is enough to this enchanting city to keep anyone occupied for days. At the very least, a long weekend should be allowed. With day trips along the St Lawrence and into the **Laurentian Mountains**, a full week is hardly enough.

Vieux Québec is a twin-level town: the older section down beside the water, the only somewhat less ancient upper quarter running w from the cusp of the sheer escarpment. The **Château Frontenac** (see *Hotels*) and other hotels and inns are in the upper town. Principal sights are *La Citadelle*, to the s, a fortress completed in 1832 and still an active military post; the **Basilique Notre-Dame** and adjacent **Seminaire**, founded in 1663; the **Musée du Fort**, with a scale model of the city; and the glorious **Terrasse Dufferin**, the broad promenade that runs along the edge of the cliff overlooking the river. In the lower town, reached by stairs or funicular, are **Place Royale**, a handsome square of restored 18thC buildings; **Quartier Petit-Champlain**, similarly refurbished and home to a lively melange of shops and bistros; the new *Musée de la Civilisation*; and the **Vieux Port**, a recycled wharf district of parks, marinas and markets. Outside the walls bordering the upper town are the *Hôtel du Parlement* of the provincial government and the **Parc des Champs-de-Bataille**. Along **Grande Allée**, the sw extension of Rue St-Louis, is a concentration of bars and restaurants. Most of the larger modern hotels are on this side of the wall, but within easy walking distance of the old town.

Sights and places of interest

A walk through Vieux Québec
Maps 14 & 15.

The pleasures of a stroll through Old Québec are precisely those of a similar *quartier* in Europe. The clopping of horses' hooves and the creak of *calèche* wheels echo off the stone facades of tightly-packed houses. Waiters dart among the tables beneath the bright awnings of sidewalk cafés. Darkened streets suddenly emerge upon dappled sunlit parks and plazas.

Pl. d'Armes is the customary starting point. Standing at the intersection of Rue St-Louis and Rue Fort and facing the river, the Château Frontenac hotel is on the right. It looms over all, a

Old Québec walk/Québec City

constant reference point from anywhere in the old town. Over to the left is the **Musée du Fort** (*10 Ste-Anne, map 15 C5* ☎ *692-2175, open daily*). A large model of the town as it was in 1750 is used in a fast-paced sound-and-light commentary on major episodes in its history. On leaving the museum, turn left into Terrasse Dufferin, bearing past the monument to Samuel de Champlain and then right along the promenade above the river. Street performers take advantage of this concentration of tourists. They might include a 5-piece Peruvian band, jugglers, folksingers, magicians, or the man who plays *Edelweiss* and the *Pachabel Canon* on the rims of water-filled brandy snifters.

Drinking in that fabulous view, continue to the end of the Château Frontenac and turn right up the stairs. Ahead is the **Parc des Gouverneurs**, a leafy enclave bordered on two sides by 19thC row houses. An obelisk honors both General James Wolfe and the Marquis de Montcalm, the victor and loser of the critical battle on the Plains of Abraham. Walk up Rue Mont-Carmel, the N border of the park, left on Rue Laporte, then right on Av. Ste-Geneviève. Several of the town's European-style inns are passed along the way, a collection with no counterpart in North America. Ste-Geneviève merges with Av. St-Denis. Follow it as it bends right.

At the intersection with Rue St-Louis, look left. Up there is the **Porte St-Louis**, the main gate in the town wall, which was first built in 1693 and reconstructed in 1878. Next to it is the **Poudrière de l'Esplanade**, a former powder magazine that is now an interpretation center (*open daily*) describing the city fortifications. Nearby will be found a gathering place of *calèches*. Straight ahead, a block away, is the main tourist information booth.

Turn right (E) on Rue St-Louis, a charming (although admittedly touristy in part) street of shops and appealing restaurants in some of the upper town's oldest houses. Turn left on Parloir. A short block down is the chapel of the **Couvent des Ursulines** (*12 Rue Donnacona* ☎ *694-0694, map 15 C4, closed Mon*). The convent was founded in 1642 by Madame de La Peltrie, who was dedicated to schooling Amerindian children. She compiled the first dictionaries of Native American languages.

Again, turn right. A few steps along is the entrance to the **Ursuline museum**, whose most bizarre artifact is the skull of General Montcalm. Bear left along what is now Rue des Jardins. Soon, on the right, is the 1804 **Holy Trinity Anglican Cathedral** (*#31* ☎ *692-2193, map 15 C4, open daily June-Sept, Tues-Sat rest of year*). Many of the objects inside and much of the woodwork were gifts of George III. Artists display their works in the courtyard in summer. As you continue, on the left are the gardens of **l'Hôtel-de-Ville**, the city hall. Turn right on Rue Buade. In one block, on the left, is the **Basilique Notre-Dame** (*#16* ☎ *692-2533, map 15 B4, open daily*), the cathedral of the oldest Roman Catholic parish in North America. Parts of it, including the bell tower and walls, date to 1647. The lamp in the sanctum was a gift of Louis XIV. Continue past the cathedral on Buade, turning right into the pedestrian alley of Rue Trésor. The way is lined with the drawings and prints of numerous artists. Although obviously geared to the tourist trade, some of the work is decently executed and might serve as a suitable memento. At the end of the alley, turn left on Ste-Anne.

This leads back to the Terrasse Dufferin. Look for the staircase on the left. Officially called the *Escalier Frontenac*, locals know it as the *Escalier Casse-Cou* (Breakneck Stairs). They descend, bearing right, into the **Quartier Petit-Champlain**, one of the earliest residential neighborhoods of Québec. In summer, the narrow streets swarm with tourists and those who wish to sell them something, but it is a happy, not tawdry, confluence, with many agreeable *boîtes* interspersed with stores selling souvenirs, crafts and clothing. Continue straight from the bottom of the stairs along Rue du Petit-Champlain, noting the entrance, in the house on the right, to the funicular that carries passengers back to the upper town. Watch for the stairs on the left near the end. Take them down to Blvd. Champlain. Turn left, past still more shops and cafés. This street, after a jog at the end, soon comes into Pl. Royale. Restoration is all but complete of the 3- to 4-story 18thC buildings that define the attractive square. They are dominated by the **Église Notre-Dame-des-Victoires** (☎ 692-1650, map **15** C5, open daily). The church was completed in 1688, restored after the English conquest of 1763 and again in 1969. A bust of Louis XIV in the center of the square is testimony to the epoch. Opposite the church is a wine store, in the 1689 **Maison Dumont** (*1 Pl. Royale*, ☎ 643-1214, map **15** C5).

Down the street, at the far right corner of the plaza, is an **information office** (*215 Rue du Marché-Finlay* ☎ 643-6631, map **15** C5, open daily mid-May to mid-Oct), the departure point for guided tours. Continue down Marché-Finlay and turn right to reach the **Batterie Royale**, the 1691 fortification with ten cannons that defended the young settlement. From there, wend back to the funicular.

Anima G
1037 Rue de la Chevrotière ☎ 643-6017. Map **14**D3 ▨
Open daily.

The 31st floor of the Complexe G building is an observation deck that provides incomparable vistas of the river, old town, the Citadelle and the surrounding countryside. The building is located behind the *Hôtel du Parlement*.

La Citadelle
1 Côte de la Citadelle ☎ 648-3563. Map **15**D4 ▨ ✗ *Open daily Mar-Oct; call to arrange visits Nov-Feb.*

Anticipating future American attacks after the War of 1812, the Duke of Wellington ordered this star-shaped fortress to be begun in 1820. It took 12yrs to complete and has never heard a shot fired in anger. Still an active military post, it is garrisoned by the Royal 22nd Regiment, the only fully Francophone unit in the Canadian Armed Forces.

The former powder magazine (1750) is now a museum, one of 25 buildings in the complex. Changing of the Guard is held daily at 10am, mid-June to Labor Day (early Sept). Tattoos take place Tues, Thurs, Sat, Sun in July-Aug at 7pm. Cannon salute from the Prince-de-Galles bastion daily, noon and 9.30pm.

Hôtel du Parlement
Av. Dufferin and Grande Allée E ☎ 643-7239. Map **14**D3 ▨ ✗ *Open daily June 24-Labor Day, Mon-Fri Sept-May. Closed June 1-23.*

What prideful Québecois choose to call their "National Assembly" is housed in this French Second Empire building dominating a hill just N of the St-Louis Gate in the city wall. Completed in 1886, its facade has niches with bronze statues of Québec historical figures. The debating chambers are open to the public when the Assembly is in session.

Maison Chevalier
60 Rue du Marché-Champlain ☎ 643-9689. Map 15C5. Open daily.

Three restored late 17thC houses, now an ethnology exhibition center administered by the **Musée de la Civilisation**.

Musée de la Civilisation
85 Rue Dalhousie ☎ 643-2158. Map 15B5 ◘ (◙ Tues). Open daily June 13-Sept 15, Tues-Sun rest of year.

Part of the Vieux Port redevelopment, near Pl. Royale, the very new museum is a striking architectural statement with a somewhat unfocused educational mission. Exhibits are interdisciplinary in character, changing frequently. Natural and social sciences are stressed, with a strong dose of the metaphysical, but not to the exclusion of other concerns. Examples of recent exhibition themes: "Memories that have forged the collective consciousness." "An essay on being and seeming." "How to function in a society based on the visual when we no longer have the use of our eyes." And so on.... Anyway, the lobby atrium is interesting.

Parc des Champs-de-Bataille
Map 14E3. Open daily.

These 235 acres of woods and meadows SW of the Citadelle were the site of the 1759 battle between the British and French that radically altered the course of North American history. Declared a public park in 1908, it incorporates the Plains of Abraham, where the blood of Wolfe and Montcalm was spilled along with that of many of their men. There is no biblical reference in the name: Abraham Martin was the man who was given the land in 1635. According to season, the park is used for picnicking, cycling, running, snowshoeing and cross-country skiing. Within its boundaries is the **Musée du Québec** (*☎ 643-2150, off map 14F2*), near the monument that marks the spot where Wolfe fell. It contains paintings, sculptures and related art objects from the earliest days of the colony to the present. Hours vary; call ahead.

Parc de l'Artillerie
2 Rue d'Auteuil ☎ 648-4205. Map 14B3 ◙ Hours vary: call ahead.

A French military site dating from the early 17thC, the complex occupies a position at the NW corner of the city walls. Its several buildings served a number of purposes over the years — as a barracks, a foundry, and an armament factory that made bullets for the Canadian Army until 1964. Restoration continues, but three buildings are now open. Of these, the **Redoute Dauphine**, begun in 1712, has exhibits of uniforms and relics that sketch military life during the French era. A reception and interpretation center has an oft-restored 1808 relief model of the city.

Port de Québec
100 Rue St-André ☎ 648-3300. Map 15B5 ◘ Hours vary: call ahead.

This modern exhibition hall on the waterfront of the enclosed Louise Basin contains four floors of displays illustrating the activities of the port in the 19thC. Shipbuilding and marine trade are emphasized. Audiovisual presentations and lectures are on offer. Afterwards, cross Rue St-André, go one block, and turn E on Rue St-Paul, a street lined with restored buildings housing galleries, antique stores and high-design furniture outlets.

QUÉBEC CITY/HOTELS

Where to stay in Québec City

There is little reason not to stay inside the walled old town, or at least within walking distance. A felicitous variety of modern high-rise hotels, inns and guesthouses covers every sybaritic desire or budgetary need. At whatever level of luxury (or lack of it), advance reservations are essential, especially in summer and during the Winter Carnival, as Québec's 8,000 rooms can fill up quickly. Should there be difficulty in finding lodgings, **ReservOtel** (☎ *800-463-1968*) is a reservation service for a number of area hotels.

Auberge de la Chouette
71 Rue d'Auteuil, Québec G1R 4C3 ☎ *694-0232. Map* **15C4** *10 rms*
Location: *Near the Information Centre and St-Louis Gate.* Those who dine at the ground-floor **Aspara**, arguably the city's best Asian restaurant, may not be aware that this is a true inn, with ten pleasant rooms upstairs. Each has a private bath, color TV, telephone and air conditioning, with antiques adding warmth to the otherwise ordinary furnishings.

Château Bellevue
16 Rue Laporte, Québec G1R 4M9 ☎ *692-2573 or 800-463-2617* ⓕ *692-4876. Map* **15C5** *55 rms*
Location: *Upper old town, on Parc des Gouverneurs.* Five attached row houses at the top end of the sloping Parc des Gouverneurs were gutted and rebuilt without altering the exterior. They are comfortable rooms, if uninspired, all but one with private bath. No dining room and no charm, but good value for low prices, and a desirable, fairly quiet location. Some have an excellent view, and those without view are a little cheaper. There are modest discounts Nov-Apr.

Château Frontenac
1 Rue des Carrières, Québec G1R 4P5 ☎ *692-3861 or 800-268-9420* ⓕ *692-1751. Map* **15C5** *550 rms*
Location: *On Terrasse Dufferin in upper old town.* In appearance, it resembles an outsized Loire Valley château, with its famous turrets, gables and spires dominating the skyline. The lower section was built in 1893, the squared high-rise tower with the green copper roof added three decades later. In recent years, there was a widespread perception that it was coasting on its reputation. Perhaps because of the competition of new luxury hotels in the town beyond the walls, a major overhaul has been undertaken. Bedrooms vary substantially in size, location, and state of cosmetic repair. Ask for one that has been renovated, with a river view. Briskly efficient, impersonal service is the norm. No health club.

Château de la Terrasse
6 Pl. Terrasse Dufferin, Québec G1R 4N5 ☎ *694-9472. Map* **15C5** *to 18 rms. Closed late Nov-Winter Carnival. No credit cards*
Location: *In upper old town, overlooking river.* Ten of the rooms have hypnotic river views and three have balconies in this converted turn-of-the-century house at the edge of the cliffside promenade. All have private baths, and color cable TV with English-language channels. The one suite has a kitchenette, and costs far less than a cramped single in one of the big hotels. No meals and no air conditioning (a factor only during a few weeks of high summer). At the price, it has very few rivals.

Clarendon
57 Rue Ste-Anne, Québec G1R 3X4 ☎ *692-2480 or 800-361-6162* ⓕ *051-3088* ⓕ *692-4652. Map* **15C4** *89 rms*
Location: *Center of old town, near City Hall.* While it insists on describing itself as Art Nouveau/Art Deco in style, those decorative details are confined to a few public areas. The building is even older than the Château Frontenac, and the bedrooms remain rather gloomy despite superficial primping. They aren't air conditioned, either. The location is good, rates are moderate, and there is a well-regarded restaurant downstairs, next to one of the town's best jazz bars.

Hotels/Québec City

des Gouverneurs
690 Blvd. St-Cyrille E, Québec G1R 5A8 ☎ *647-1717 or 800-463-2820* ● *051-31773* ® *647-2146. Map 14D3* ||||) *379 rms* ▦ ▭ ⇌ AE ●

Location: *Outside the walls, near Hôtel du Parlement.* A stark facade encloses an overwrought modernistic interior. Bedrooms are spacious and well-appointed, albeit with signs of heavy use none-too-swiftly scoured away. Oddly, the raw concrete walls somehow muffle, not amplify, sound. The in-house restaurant **Le Vignoble** has a tempting and inexpensive luncheon buffet. An adequate fitness center and heated indoor/outdoor pool round out the facilities.
⌂ ‡ 옷 ⩽ ❦ ♀ ■ ♫

Loews Le Concorde
1225 Pl. Montcalm, Québec G1R 4W6 ☎ *647-2222 or 800-223-0888. Map 14E3* |||||) *411 rms* ▦ ⇌ AE ●

Location: *Outside the walls, five blocks from St-Louis Gate.* It is difficult to forgive a structure of such surpassing ugliness when it blights an otherwise handsome neighborhood of Queen Anne row houses. Get past that esthetic affront and all the expectable first-class comforts and conventions are in place. Those who don't mind eating in a room that moves are treated to spectacular vistas from **L'Astral** rooftop bar/restaurant. Most rooms have excellent views. While it's a 15-20min walk from the heart of the old town, the bars and restaurants of the Grande Allée strip are close by. Guests can use a nearby health club, which has a pool and racquet courts.
⬅ ⩽ ❦ ➡

Manoir Ste-Geneviève
13 Av. Ste-Geneviève, Québec G1R 4A7 ☎ *694-1666. Map 15C5* |█| *to* |█|) *9 rms* ▦ *No credit cards.*

Location: *In old town, on Parc Jardin des Gouverneurs.* Its nine rooms are small, as is to be expected of a town house nearly 160yrs old. They are immaculate, though, kept so under the watchful eye of an owner/manager who has been in charge for more than 30yrs. No elevator, no room telephones, no food, and the TV carries only French channels, but all rooms have private baths and are air conditioned — and all that Vieux Québec has to offer is right outside the front door.

Québec Hilton
3 Pl. Québec, Québec G1K 7M9 ☎ *647-2411 or 800-268-9275* ● *051-3997* ® *647-6488. Map 14D3* |||||) *565 rms* ▦ ⇌ AE ●

Location: *Outside the walls, near Hôtel du Parlement.* Those unwilling to forego modern gadgets and conveniences for Old World charm need look no further. One of a trio of large, relatively new hotels within walking distance of Vieux Québec, this Hilton scores commendably high on all counts of efficiency and service.

Minibars, color cable TV and closed-circuit movies equip every room, with extra goodies available on the *Étages Plus* executive levels. Tour groups and conventioneers periodically throng the lobby. The health club and outdoor pool are among the few offered in the city. Upper floors have super views.
‡ 옷 ⬅ ⩽ ❦ ♀ ■ ♫ ➡

Bed and breakfast

Travelers who enjoy being closer to the natives and saving money in the process can arrange accommodations through several bed & breakfast agencies. Two possibilities are **Bonjour Québec** (*3765 Blvd. de Monaco, Québec G1R 1N4* ☎ *527-1465*) and **Apartments and Bed and Breakfast in Old Québec** (*35 Rue des Remparts, Québec G1R 3R6* ☎ *655-7685, map 15B4*).

When calling or writing, be as specific as possible about requirements — location, number and ages of children, bathrooms, TV, personal habits — to avoid disappointments. Many hosts, for example, do not allow young children, or smokers. Advance deposits are typically required, and credit cards may not be accepted.

One exemplary possibility is the B&B run by **Lyse & Raymond Brousseau** (*69-71 Rue Ste-Anne, Québec G1R 3X4*

☎ 692-1230, map **15**C4 ⬤ 💳). They have a pretty stone house (c.1700) near the City Hall. On the ground floor is their gallery of Inuit art, which merits a visit on its own. Upstairs are two apartments suitable for small families, one of which has a kitchen. They are made special by their decor, which is a mix of contemporary and one-of-a-kind antiques so enchanting that the 2nd-floor unit has been flatteringly featured in a glossy magazine. A minimum two-night stay and an advance deposit are required.

Where to eat in Québec

Québecois defer to no one in their love of fine food — not to Montréalers, and certainly not to Torontonians. No doubt due to their Gallic heritage, they elevate the act of eating to a plateau far higher than mere need. Visitors profit, and not one meal (with the possible exception of breakfast) need be anything but gratifying. Some will be memorable, happy marriages of setting, ambience and skill, to be recalled years later. Peak summer crowds and the Winter Carnival make reservations essential at the better and/or more popular restaurants and on almost any weekend.

The several schools of French cooking dominate, not surprisingly — bistros *haute* and *ordinaire*, formal explorations of the classical and *nouvelle*, even the indigenous cooking that had its origins in the challenges of merely surviving in New France. In those days, the need for abundant fare, simply prepared from ingredients easily stored over the long winter, gave rise to much use of pork, potatoes, beans, maple syrup and root vegetables. The resulting pork pies, ragoûts and sugar pies are still available, if not as widely as veal wrapped around goat cheese and sun-dried tomatoes.

After the French variations, Italian restaurants are most evident in Québec City, well ahead of the scattering of Asian, Central European and Mediterranean kitchens. Only a few are truly expensive, and the majority fall into the moderately-priced category and below. A 15 percent tip on the amount before tax is normal, but make certain that a service charge isn't already added.

Imported wines are expensive, making the somewhat cheaper Canadian bottlings worth a try. Domestic beers are excellent and go well with ethnic and bistro meals. Wine and beer can be purchased at supermarkets and the convenience stores (*dépanneurs*). For liquor and premium wines, an outlet of the government-controlled *Société des Alcools* must be found. There is a *Maison des Vins* on Pl. Royale in the lower town.

Aspara
71 Rue d'Auteuil ☎ *694-0232. Map 15C4* ⦀⦀ 🆎 ⬤ 💳 *Closed Sat lunch, Sun, Mon.*
They truthfully claim a *cuisine asiatique*, and proceed to skip around the Far East, with culinary stops in Thailand, Vietnam, Cambodia and a quick side trip to Taiwan. Would that they had stayed put with Thai cooking, which is superior to the others presented.

Under this heading are *mou sati* (pork brochettes with marinated cucumbers) and *poulet de Bangkok* (spicy chicken medallions). A 7-course sampler for two persons is appetizing. House wines are cheap, but that's about all that can be said for them. Upholstery and draperies

Restaurants/Québec City

are, incongruously, European, and the Victorian house dates back to 1845. The combination (and the cheap lunch) fills the place with businesspeople, sophisticates, couples, and families, for there is something here for everyone.

Aux Anciens Canadiens
34 Rue St-Louis ☎ *692-1627. Map 15C4* III *AE* ◐ ◉ *VISA Open daily.*

Very visible, and patronized largely by tourists, but that shouldn't discourage a visit, especially if one is interested in sampling more or less authentic traditional Québecois dishes. The restaurant is one of the oldest houses in the upper town, the low-ceilinged rooms on two floors hung with antique doodads and farm tools. It's like dinner at Grandma's house, even if she never braised rabbit in beer or baked duckling in maple syrup. And are those meatballs scented with cinnamon and allspice? There is a selection of native cheeses, but a caloric splurge is best saved for the sugar pie floating in heavy cream. This is stick-to-the-ribs stuff, satisfying and not a bit clever.

Café de la Paix
44 Rue Desjardins ☎ *692-1430. Map 15C4* III *to* IIII *AE* ◐ ◉ *VISA Open daily.*

Presumably the sauces are lighter than they were 30yrs ago. Otherwise, the dishes on this long menu might well be the same as they were in 1960. Not that this is to be deplored. In an age of the new-new-NEW, what a pleasure to see good old *coquille St-Jacques*, *escargots de Bourgogne*, lobster thermidor and *châteaubriand garni* (for two, of course). It's a step back from the gastronomic precipice, to let us savor what it was that we loved about French food in the first place. Although meats are featured and game often appears, the kitchen is especially adept with *fruits de mer*, and salmon in particular. The nightly *table d'hôte* is relatively easy on the budget, the light lunch even more so. Reserve ahead, for they rarely have room for drop-ins.

L'Échaude
73 Sault-au-Matelot ☎ *692-1299. Map 15B5* III *to* IIII *Closed Sat lunch, Sun eve.*

A *nouvelle* bistro to remember when wandering in the old port area or antiquing along Rue St-Paul. A little off the heaviest tourist trails, its custom is primarily local. They use the bistro convention of writing the daily menu on the mirrors — and even uninformed choices are likely to be flavorful and satisfying. You might get skate in browned butter, or rosy aromatic lamb. Evenings, it sheds the businesslike demeanor of the lunch crowd. Wines are pricey.

Faubourg St-Honoré
570 Grande Allée ☎ *529-0211. Map 14D3* III *AE* ◉ *VISA Open daily.*

The Grande Allée strip outside the walls is known more for its party mood and people-watching from terraces than for the quality of food to be found there. This is one of the better choices, by default, in a lovely old house *above* the Café St-Honoré, a popular fern bar. The menu is dictated by the availability of fresh seasonal ingredients, with the frequent gimmick of featuring the food of a specific country or region. Its convivial atmosphere and working fireplace are reasons to remember it on cold days.

Fleur de Lotus
50 Rue de la Fabrique ☎ *692-4286. Map 15B4* ☐ *to* I☐ *AE* ◉ *VISA Closed Sat lunch, Sun lunch.*

This tiny, largely unadorned room near City Hall packs them in at both lunch and dinner. They cover the same gastronomical territory as **Aspara**, with a comparable middling-to-good degree of skill. These Indochinese dishes, more than 20 of them, are about equally divided between the cuisines of three Southeast Asian countries, and again the Thai recipes stand out. Friendly reception by people who remember your face the second time. Top value for just a few dollars. Bring your own wine.

Le Marie-Clarisse
12 Rue du Petit-Champlain ☎ *692-0857. Map 15E4* III *AE* ◉ *VISA Closed Sat lunch, Sun.*

What a pleasure on a warm spring day to rest on this patio, a cool Chablis at hand, contemplating the passing parade. It's at the foot of Breakneck Stairs, where three car-less streets meet in the middle of the *Quartier Petit-Champlain*. A street performer will almost certainly be situated nearby — an accordionist, perhaps, to add a proper Parisian flavor to the scene. The daily special lunch doesn't cost much more than a couple of Big Macs with Large Fries. And if it's one of the catches-of-the-day, which

Québec City/Restaurants

L'Omelette
66 Rue St-Louis ☎ *694-9626.*
Map 15C4 🍴 AE ⦿ ⦿ VISA

Nothing special, just a coffee shop, really. But many of the inns in the immediate area serve no breakfast, and that meal is one to be avoided at the Frontenac down the street. The *café au lait* is good, with ready refills, and the *croissants* are fresh. There are ten kinds of omelets, and *crêpes* with strawberries, or peaches with ice cream. Linger over the morning newspaper, for there is no one silently urging you to be done and gone. It gets more rushed later in the day, as the crowds increase along old town's main drag.

Parmesan
38 Rue St-Louis ☎ *692-0341.*
Map 15C4 🍴 AE ⦿ ⦿ VISA

Flambéed *steak au poivre*! "Surf and turf"! *Duck à l'orange*! It is the 1960s revisited, when restaurants borrowed the same five dishes each from the French and Italian pantheons and called themselves "continental." The kitchen leans toward the Roman way of doing things, with *tortellini in brodo*, *fettucine Alfredo*, and *manicotti* stuffed with cheese and spinach. As conventional as it sounds, the pasta tastes freshly made, and the veal is of a select grade. Servings are large, and main courses come with vegetables and baked potatoes, so the appetizer and/or dessert can be skipped. An invariably convivial crowd is made more so by the strolling accordionist, whose music prompts certain patrons to leap to their feet and dance between the tables. Yes, it's a mass of dated clichés, but fun, when you're in the right mood. What the heck, you're on vacation.

Le Saint Amour
48 Rue Ste-Ursule ☎ *694-9259.*
Map 15C4 🍴 AE ⦿ ⦿ VISA
Closed Sun lunch, Mon lunch.

Here's a sophisticated retreat that lives up to its name. Romance breathes by candlelight and Victorian gas fixtures, with lace at the windows in the front room and in the all-weather terrace hung with plants. Two paddle fans whirr up by the roof, which can be retracted on clear nights. The attractive, knowledgeable crowd comes in jeans and polo shirts or dressed to kill. They are there to enjoy themselves, not to have a religious experience (see below). Game is one of chef Jean-Luc Boulay's strong suits, as with boned rabbit stuffed with chewy wild mushrooms, and the brace of quail, also boned, in a faintly astringent port sauce. The mouthwatering chocolate desserts are a must. Boulay is perfecting a culinary subgenre — hearty *nouvelle* — pretty as a still-life painting yet lusty with flavor. And they said it couldn't be done.

Table de Serge Bruyère
1200 Rue St-Jean ☎ *694-0618.*
Map 15B4 🍴 AE ⦿ ⦿ *Closed Sat lunch, Sun, Mon.*

If *everyone* didn't insist that this is the finest restaurant in Québec — some say in *Canada* — it wouldn't be mentioned here. But they do, so we must. Call a respectful three days in advance, don your best clothes, arrive on time. Those who are unknown to the gatekeepers are promptly ushered to the 3rd floor, above the main restaurant. It has the chill of Siberia, spacious and remote, with the hush of an ecclesiastical experience about to happen. The attendants are acolytes, there only to fill glasses and clear plates — and none too expertly. In time, orders are taken by a real waiter. He disappears, returning much later with the first course. A long time after that, he dashes through with the second. The first is already fully digested. At this rate, the 7-course "discovery" menu can last for hours. It is now apparent why the kitchen prides itself on only having one seating a night: it can't deliver the meal any faster. The food arrives exquisitely presented and very, very carefully prepared. But for someone who prowls the *nouvelle* frontier, M. Bruyère is remarkably lacking in daring. There are no surprises, at least for anyone who dines at this exalted level with any regularity. Even a robust mistake would be welcome. Perhaps things are more animated in the main room. That we'll never know. Two good meals can be had elsewhere for the same price, and the patrons aren't afraid to laugh out loud.

For the record, other levels in the complex house a tea salon and *patisserie*, a café, **La Petite Table**, a piano bar, and a wine-cellar dining room.

NIGHTLIFE AND SHOPPING/QUÉBEC CITY

Nightlife and shopping

Nightlife
As might be expected of a college town — the Université Laval is here — nightlife is vigorous, plentiful, and often raucous. Where it's all at is the **Grande Allée E**. The blocks between D'Artigny and Berthelot are bordered with stone houses converted to bars and *boîtes*, most with terraces or balconies on the street side, some with discos or music bars inside. One much-seen libation is a yard-long glass of beer so tall that it needs a wooden stand to hold it up and two bottles to fill it. Older revelers tend to move on to less frenetic hideaways in the old town, or down along the gentrifying streets of the port area.

The big summer event in early July is the **Festival d'été international de Québec**, ten days of mostly free open-air rock and jazz concerts, dance recitals, and other performance events held in such locations as the grounds of the city hall and the park just before the Grande Allée strip. In late June is the **Blue Nights jazz festival**, heard in concert halls, restaurants and on the streets of Vieux Québec.

Bars and clubs
Most tastes and proclivities are satisfied. Cover or admission charges are rare. A sometimes rapacious singles crowd prevails over the wan food at **Le Beaugarte** (*2590 Blvd. Laurier ☎ 659-2442*), while a barely older group with similar intentions gathers at **Café St Honoré** (*570 Grande Allée E ☎ 529-0211*), known to its habitués as "Saint-O."

Serious jazz fans are courted by the large combos at the reliable **Bar l'Emprise** in the **Hôtel Clarendon** (*57 Rue Ste-Anne ☎ 692-2480*): people actually go to listen. Nearby, **Le d'Orsay** (*68 Rue Buade ☎ 694-1582*) has a pubby look, with two bars and a small dance floor with a DJ; the mixed crowd can also eat out on the summer terrace in back, serenaded by a singer-guitarist. Young professionals shoot pool and chat each other up at the former workingman's retreat, **La Taverne Belley** (*249 Rue St-Paul ☎ 692-4595*). A nightcap can be savored to piano music, in the lounge of the **Château Frontenac**.

Discos
Discos are the usual youthful bedlam. Tri-leveled **Chez Dagobert** (*9600 Grande Allée E ☎ 522-0393*) cranks up its sound system to the edge of the pain threshold. The small disco at **Vogue** (*1170 Rue d'Artigny ☎ 529-9973*) is less frenetic. Down in the port area is **Le Tube Hi-Fi** (*139 Rue St-Pierre ☎ 692-0257*), whose dancers are a couple of years older and started in careers. Devoted disco darlings must travel to suburban Sainte-Foy to squeeze themselves into the biggest and hottest of them all, **Le Palladium** (*2327 Blvd. Versant N ☎ 682-8783*).

Shopping
Inevitably, there are enclosed malls, most of them in suburban Sainte-Foy and none of them especially noteworthy. For a gift, keepsake, or souvenir that can't be duplicated everywhere, most visitors have more luck (and fun) in the **Quartier Petit-Champlain**, at the bottom of Breakneck Stairs in the lower town. Local designers and craftsmen offer a variety of handmade goods, including jewelry, leather items, woven cloth, pottery and toys. **Rue du Petit-Champlain** (see *Walk* page 122) is the most productive place for making this kind of purchase.

EXCURSION/GASPÉ PENINSULA

Shoppers with a taste for antique crafts and contemporary native carvings — and the necessary discretionary income — should make a must of **Galerie Aux Multiples** (*70 Rue Dalhousie* ☎ *692-4434; smaller branch: 69 Rue Ste-Anne*). Quilts, duck decoys, old game boards, and small furniture pieces are ancillary to the collection of superb Inuit sculptures. For young antiques, folk art, and collectibles, browse nearby **Rue St-Paul**.

The Gaspé Peninsula

The province of Québec has been the Atlantic gateway to the heart of the continent since the first European explorers and traders sailed its waters in hopes of riches and a passage to Asia. It embraces the St Lawrence (St-Laurent) River all the way from its confluence with the Ottawa River to the ocean, a distance of more than 600 miles. The Gaspé Peninsula, which knuckles into the Atlantic above the Maritime Provinces, is a raw, elemental region entirely of itself, sharing only a language with the urbane citizens of Montréal and Québec City. Over much of its length, ancient blunted mountains fall directly to the shore, their feet laved by combers born off Portugal. In the interior are still higher peaks, traces of snow in their treeless upper reaches even in July. Deer, caribou and bears live there, and the clear tumbling streams are fairly choked with trout and salmon.

The usual starting point for a Gaspé excursion is Québec City. People driving from the US, especially from New England, may prefer to make the approach from the s, from Maine via Interstate 95, then N on Route 1 to the New Brunswick border, where it becomes Rte 17. Stay on that road to Campbellton, where there is a bridge to Pointe-à-la-Croix, then drive E on Rte 132. Since this is a circular tour, it can be read backward. See *Map **16***.

From Québec City, a driving tour around the perimeter of the peninsula and back to Québec takes a minimum of 4 days. That's not really enough: 5 or 6 days would be better, and 7 or 8 to allow at least a 2-night stay in the picturesque village of Percé, at the easternmost tip. This is not a trip to be undertaken from Oct-late Apr, when the weather can be fierce, and most motels and restaurants are closed. Even in summer, packing should allow for a sweater or windbreaker, for nights and the ocean breezes are cool. Tuck in a French phrasebook, too, preferably one published in Québec, for English is not as widely understood as in Montréal. Remember that use of seat belts is obligatory. Speed limits are given in km, so 60kph is slightly over 37mph.

Leave Québec City via the Grande Allée, (which goes through some name changes), driving W and staying with the Route 175 signs. In about 30mins, take the Pont (Bridge) Pierre-Laporte across the river toward **Rivière-du-Loup**. On the other side, pick up Rte 20, driving NE. This is a limited-access highway, passing farms and small towns of pleasant but not compelling aspect. Those with extra time available may wish to exit the highway at one of the several intersections, and pick up Rte 132, which runs closer to the southern shore of the St Lawrence. Along that route, the towns of **L'Islet-sur-Mer**, **St-Jean-Port-Joli** and **Kamouraska** invite brief exploration.

Rte 20 merges with 132 just beyond Rivière-du-Loup. That mostly 2-lane road bears the same number for the entire circuit of the peninsula. **Rimouski** is the last good-sized city heading E,

Gaspé Peninsula/Excursion

with little of interest to the traveler. Continue to the hamlet of **Ste-Flavie**. On the right will be the **Gaspésie Tourist Information Office** (*357 Route de la Mer* ☎ *775-2223*). It can't be missed, with its vivid green trim and crimson roof. Brochures, information and advice are available from the bilingual attendants inside.

🚗 They will surely recommend a stop at the **Jardins de Métis**, about 6 miles E on 132. Take their word, for these gardens are one of the major attractions of the entire peninsula. The entrance is on the left. One Elsie Meighen Reford developed the estate and its formal gardens, a lavish and thoughtfully planned display of more than 500 species of annuals and flowering shrubs. They are laid out in the English manner (more naturalistic than the French formal style), in six distinct settings. A brook runs through the property and past the magnificent rock garden. Ruby-throated hummingbirds whirr through the section called the **Allée Royale**, which is flanked by majestic peonies. Ms. Reford's large seaside villa is now a museum and a restaurant (good enough, but inevitably crowded). The gardens (☎) are open daily 8.30am-8pm from early June to mid-Sept.

Matane, about 30 miles NE, has the last ferry terminal to the N shore of the St Lawrence. The town is best known for its shrimp and salmon fisheries. As many as 3,000 salmon are known to migrate up the Matane River each year. This may be the place to stop for the night.

🛏 🚗 Among the limited possibilities are the **Motel & Hôtel Belle Plage** (*1310 Matane-sur-Mer* ☎ *562-2323* 💳) and the **Hôtel des Gouverneurs** (*250 Av. du Phare E* ☎ *566-2651* 💳 🏊 🍴 🐾).

But if time allows, a better stopping-place is **Ste-Anne-des-Monts**, about 53 miles E, then turn inland on the 299 road. The road slowly rises toward the **Chic-Choc** peaks, the continuation of the Appalachians that are the spine of the peninsula, and into the **Parc de la Gaspésie**, where one of the moose or caribou that roam these slopes might be glimpsed.

🛏 🚗 In about 25 miles is **Le Gîte du Mont-Albert** (*P.O. Box 1150, Ste-Anne-des-Monts, Québec G0E 2G0* ☎ *763-2288* 💳). The mountain lodge looks up directly at its towering namesake, **Mount Albert**, which is inevitably scored with streaks of snow. Accommodations, which are in the main lodge or outlying bungalows, are decidedly rustic. Cabins have summer camp furniture, painted plywood floors, bathtubs with claw feet, no TV. But there is plenty of hot water, a telephone, a fireplace, and chairs on the porch, for you to watch the sun fall, and inhale the clean alpine air. (Should a drink be desired along with the sunset, it's best to bring along the necessary supplies, since the bar in the lodge keeps unpredictable hours.) The attractive dining room there comes as a surprise, with its polished floors and crisp napery.

The lodge is part of a training program for young people intent on entering the hospitality trade. Service is by waitresses who are concerned with their clients' welfare, and the food is tasty and easy on the eye. The 5-course dinner is a bargain, and charitable guests will understand the occasional lapses and delays. Reservations for the lodge must be made in advance. Those who stay a full day have their choice of trout-fishing, hikes, helicopter-skiing, and treks to observe the caribou.

When leaving, return to the coast and continue E on 132. Now, the mountains start to crowd the sea and are soon plunging to the rock-strewn shore, and you pass a series of fishing and farming hamlets. At **Mont-St-Pierre**, there may be the startling sight of hang-gliders wheeling in the sky. This is one of the top sites for the sport in eastern Canada, due to the presence of favorable updrafts. Their launching pads are at the top of the mountain for which the town is named.

Excursion/Gaspé Peninsula

The **Motel-Restaurant aux Délices** is a lunch possibility, although unexceptional.

A picnic might be preferable, perhaps picking up a loaf of bread at one of the small bakeries and smoked salmon at the *poissonneries* spotted along the way. There is a picnic ground in **Mont-St-Pierre**, another just before **Grande-Vallée** (◆), a third a little beyond **St-Yvon**.

Drivers and their passengers grow accustomed by now to this juxtaposition of mountains and seascape. Details of Gaspé life become more apparent. The houses, for example, are sunburst yellow, royal blue, lavender, orange, pink or aqua. And these are not pale pastels, but undiluted hues straight from the tube. Perhaps they are painted thus as an expression of individualism. More likely, the colors are antidotes to the long gray winter, or even just a way to find home in a snowstorm. Watch, too, for the quirky lawn decorations — accumulations, really, that come close to constituting a form of folk art. Here, a shrine to the Virgin composed of driftwood and clam shells; there, a large black cormorant made of mussel shells, with a crab claw for a beak. One homeowner chooses to erect a miniature village of dwarfs, dollhouses, and bridges that go nowhere; another has a gaudy assemblage of pinwheels, cutout cartoon characters and lifesized fantasy animals of painted burlap stretched over wire armatures. Some of the naive displays are quite wonderful.

Ladders are affixed to roofs, to facilitate repair and snow removal. Large Canadian and Québec flags flutter from the ridgepoles. Although fast disappearing, there are still humpbacked ovens in some front lawns, with black iron doors to insert loaves of bread at one end and a chimney spout at the other to release the wood smoke. Long rows of stacked lobster traps are seen, often next to large drying-racks for cod. Men and boys sell crude ship models at the roadside — even the sails are wood. Logging trucks rumble by, for this is lumbering country, too. Black-and-white dairy cattle graze in rocky pastures, as do goats, sheep and horses. Québec City seems very far away. So does the rest of the world.

The road and the shore start to bend toward the s at **Rivière-au-Renard**, and a small decision must be made. Rte. 197 cuts inland toward the town of **Gaspé**, reducing travel time to the night's destination, **Percé**, by about 45mins. The more scenic route is to continue on 132. These are the forested Gaspé headlands, preserved as the **Parc National Forillon**. Apart from the thousands of sea birds that nest in its limestone cliffs each summer, there is the possibility of catching sight of the pelagic whales that pass here, as well as seals basking on offshore rocks. Boat cruises, hikes, horseback riding, skindiving and fishing trips are offered. Information is available at the **reception center** (*open daily June-Labor Day*), a couple of miles on 132 beyond the Rte 197 intersection.

At **Anse-au-Griffon** is the roadside **Manoir LeBoutillier**, an 1840 house built by a cod merchant, from the cargo of ships wrecked off that coast. Classified as an historic monument, it has a few relics and photos in an upstairs gallery. Its primary function is as a restaurant, with two dining rooms. Service is erratic and the food marginal.

Continuing, the road soon rounds the headland into a deep fjord-like bay. At the end is the town of **Gaspé**. This was where Jacques Cartier first stepped onto the mainland of the New World, in 1534. While the town is important economically to the

Gaspé Peninsula/Excursion

region, there is not much to interest a tourist, so press on toward Percé. Shortly before reaching the resort village, there is a first sighting of **Percé Rock** and **Bonaventure Island**, sitting in the ocean just off what could be the end of the world. Sky and sea seem to merge, and it is not difficult to imagine that one can make out the curvature of the earth.

Percé is just a few miles farther. The trip from Mont-Albert to Percé Rock will have taken 5-6hrs, a distance of about 220 miles. Perhaps because its development as a resort is fairly recent, Percé does not have the tatty, honky-tonk atmosphere that might be expected. The many motels strung out along the shore are just that: crisp and clean but unremarkable in themselves. What makes them unusual is their views of the most prominent feature of the near seascape — that Rock.

From the near end, it looms like the prow of a beached supertanker, its striated sides dropping straight from its flat top to the water nearly 300ft below. At low tide, it can be reached on foot, which everyone does. From the side, the Rock has a much different aspect. Over 1,400ft long, there is an arched hole piercing straight through the cliff at water level.

Farther out is **Bonaventure Island**, a bird sanctuary. It can be reached by ferry from the central wharf. (Park in the lot with the sign *Parc de l'Île-Bonaventure*.) The ferry leaves about every 20mins, and goes first past the Rock, then circles Bonaventure and docks to allow passengers to debark if they wish. (Another ferry will be along soon.) There are hundreds of thousands of sea birds, and although Bonaventure is known more for its numbers than its varieties, there are enough species to keep dedicated birdwatchers busy for a day. Included among them are double-crested cormorants, razorbills, puffins, kittiwakes, black guillemots, murres, and an estimated 50,000 yellow-headed gannets. Bring binoculars and sturdy shoes.

One of the first motels on the road into Percé is the double-decked **Auberge Les Trois Soeurs** (*Percé, Québec G0C 2L0* ☎ 782-2183 or 800-361-6162 ▢). It has a pleasant staff, a laundry room, and a beach with an unobstructed view of the "prow" end of the Rock. Farther along the road, past the village center, is the **Hôtel La Normandie** (*Percé G0C 2L0* ☎ 782-2112 or 800-463-0820 ▢). Its rooms are only slightly more expensive, and it is more stylish than others in town. A broad lawn leads down to the beach, with its view of the side of the Rock and Island. Both no-meal and Modified American Plan (breakfast and dinner) rates are available. The all-you-can-eat breakfast buffet is a real bargain.

Another breakfast choice might be **Biard Betty's**, near the town center on the main road. This buffet is for those who believe that the first meal of the day is the most important, and the cost is very low. The lunch and dinner buffets are neither as good, nor such a bargain.

Better, take the midday meal — exceptionally well-done for the low price — at the **Maison du Pêcheur** (*Pl. du Quai* ☎ 762-5331). A tidy place with a full bar, next to the ferry wharf, it has as pleasant a serving staff as might be asked. A meal might be creamy carrot soup, a whole cold lobster, or mackerel in a delicious tarragon bearnaise sauce, followed, of course, by sugar pie. All of it costs little more than the lobster alone purchased in a store. Don't miss it.

The gastronomic event of the entire excursion still awaits. Get directions at the motel for **L'Auberge du Gargantua** (☎ 782-2852 ▢). It's up the road called the Route des Failles, which intersects with 132 at the s end of town, and rises steeply to a peak that overlooks a stunning panorama of the empty fastness of the interior. Ridge follows mountain ridge until they fade into the mists, like a Japanese painting.

Dinner in the restaurant is less tranquil. It is owned and very actively run by an ebullient ferret of a man on the golden side of 70. He brooks no lip from employee or patron. "I'm busy," he says to a man who asks for a drink while waiting for a table, but in due course suggests a "Petit Gargantua."

Excursion/Gaspé Peninsula

That mild-looking concoction is made with five liqueurs. When a table becomes available, the proprietor sits down with his guests to take their order. What follows is a wonderment. Plate #1: vegetable and pasta salads, olives, cornichons, pâté and periwinkles (sea snails); #2: tureen of vegetable broth; #3: lobster, fish or beef with side dishes; #4: a dazzle of desserts. All is skillfully wrought, of that delectable order that sends eyes rolling back into heads in pleasure. The check is high for these parts, especially with wine and after-dinner brandy. It's worth every penny. When they leave, all the children get lollipops.

Those less intent on eating can hike from the inn up the Route des Failles to **La Grande Crevasse**, although the views from the inn itself will satisfy most people.

The next stretch, from Percé to **Carleton**, is about 170 miles. Very quickly, as the road bends W, the terrain flattens into a broad coastal plain. The mountains, so omnipresent on the northern shore, are no longer visible. After about 30 miles of contiguous towns and tawdry built-up areas, large dairy farms and neat little rural communities take over. The beaches are more accessible along this coast, and composed more of red sand than of rocks. English place names are frequently seen — Chandler, Newport, Hope Town, New Carlisle — for this part of the peninsula was settled by loyalists to the English Crown who fled the United States during and after the Revolution.

If departure from Percé was made after lunch, **Carleton** is a convenient overnight stop.

Two good motels stand next to one another, near the center of town: **Le Manoir Belle-Plage** (☎ *364-3388*) and the **Baie-Bleue** (☎ *364-3355*). Both have restaurants and ordinary but comfortable rooms. The Belle Plage isn't air-conditioned; the Baie-Bleue is, and has a heated swimming pool, giving it the edge in desirability.

But if it is still early, continue on 132. (Those who wish to go S into the US can turn onto the bridge at **Pointe-à-la-Croix**, picking up Rte 17S in New Brunswick.) **Restigouche** is the next town and is the center of the Micmac reserve. Some of their handicrafts are for sale there.

Matapédia, about 45 miles from Carleton, is a likely place for a lunch break.

Café l'Entracte (*Rte 132* ☎ *865-2734*) is the usual choice, featuring home-cooking and a terrace.

Beyond Matapédia, 132 turns inland, following a wide, shallow river of the same name. On the right are the last of the Chic-Choc Mountains, and the tumbling river is known for its excellent salmon fishing. Anglers camp along the banks, amid stands of fir and birch and aspen, to cast dry flies, either in hip waders or from boats. The prettiest part of the valley starts at **Causapscal**, marked by its two covered bridges. Should it now be time to stop for the night, the town of **Amqui**, is only 15mins away.

Its **Motel Val-Moni** (*340 Blvd. St-Benoît* ☎ *629-2241*) has 80 air-conditioned rooms, some with whirlpool baths, a pool and a bar-restaurant.

At **Mont-Joli** (formerly Ste-Flavie Station), 44 miles on, it is about 210 miles to Québec City, the last part of the trip on Highway 20.

Index

General index: 135 **List of street names: 143**

Individual hotels and restaurants have not been indexed, because they appear in alphabetical order within their appropriate sections. However, the sections themselves are indexed. Similarly, streets appear in the list on page 143 and not the index, with a few notable exceptions, such as Blvd. St-Laurent and Golden Square Mile, which are indexed as well.

Page numbers in **bold** type indicate the main entries. *Italic* page numbers refer to the illustrations and maps.

A

Abraham, Plains of, 10, 118, 121, 123
Accidents, automobile, 26
Addresses and telephone numbers:
  Montréal, 73-5
  Québec City, 119
  Toronto, 30-1
Adirondacks, 85
African Lion Safari, 70-1
AGO *see* Art Gallery of Ontario
Air Canada, 22
Air travel:
  getting to Canada, 22
  Montréal, 72
  Québec City, 118
  Toronto, 29, 30
Airports:
  Dorval Airport, 22, 72
  Lester B. Pearson International Airport, 22, 29
  Mirabel Airport, 22, 72
  Ste-Foy Airport, 118
  Toronto Island Airport, 30, 34
Alcohol:
  duty-free allowances, 22
  lower age limit, 26
  taxes, 23-4
Algonquin Park, 17, 18
Alien Registration Cards, 21
All That Jazz Festival, 28
Ambulances:
  Montréal, 26
  Toronto, 26, 31
America, 13-15
American Express:
  American Express Canada, 31
  MoneyGram (R), 24
  postal services, 24
  Travel Service Offices, 74
  travelers cheques, 21-2, 26
Americas Cycling Grand Prix, 28

Amerindians, 15, 49, 91, 92
Amqui, 134
Amtrak, 22
Amusement parks:
  Montréal, 117
  La Ronde, 86, 90, 94-5, 117
  Toronto, 70-1
André, Brother, 93
Anima G, **122**
Anka, Paul, 14
Antique stores:
  Montréal, 112-13
  Québec City, 130
  Toronto, 66-7
Appalachians, 131
Aqua-Parc, 95
Aquariums:
  Île Ste-Hélène, 90
  Montréal, **86**
Architecture, **18-21**
  Canadian Centre for Architecture, 86-7
Arnold, General Benedict, 10
Art galleries:
  Art Gallery of Ontario (AGO), 33, 36, **39-40**, 44
  George R. Gardiner Museum of Ceramic Art, 33, 37, **44**, 49
  McMichael Canadian Collection, 39, **46**
  Musée d'art contemporain, **91**, 94
  Musée des Arts Décoratifs, **87-8**
  Musée des Beaux-Arts, 80, **91-2**
  Musée Marc-Aurèle Fortin, **92**
Arts, **17-18**
Arts and crafts stores:
  Montréal, 112
  Québec City, 129-30
  Toronto, 67
Astrachan, Anthony, 28
Austin, James, 50
Auto-racing, 28
  Montréal, 114

  Toronto, 67
Aykroyd, Dan, 14, 63

B

Ballet, 17
  Montréal, 111, 112
  Toronto, 64
Banks, 24
Banque de Montréal, 18-19, *19*, 81
Bars:
  Montréal, 108-9
  Québec City, 129
  Toronto, 61-3
Baseball:
  Montréal, 27, 114
  Toronto, 27, 67-8
Basilica of Notre-Dame (Montréal), 81
Basilique Notre-Dame (Québec City), 120, 121
Batterie Royale, 122
The Beaches, 69, 70
Beaver Lake (Lac aux Castors), 85, 116
Bed and breakfast:
  Montréal, **101-2**
  Québec City, **125-6**
  Toronto, **55-6**
Beer, 126, 129
Beliveau, Jean, 115
Bennett, Tony, 63
Bernini, Giovanni Lorenzo, 87
Bibliothèque Nationale du Québec, 75
Bicycling:
  Americas Cycling Grand Prix, 28
  in Montréal, 115
  in Toronto, 68
  Le Tour de l'Île de Montréal, 27-8
Bird sanctuaries:
  Bonaventure Island, 133
Black Creek Pioneer Village, 39, **40**
Blue Nights jazz festival, 129
Boat Show (Toronto), 43
Boats and boat trips:
  Gaspé Peninsula, 132

135

Index

Ice Canoe Race, 27
Montréal, 75, 96, 114, 117
rafting, 116
Toronto, 32, 44, 68, 71
Toronto International Boat Show, 27
Bonaventure Island, 133
Bonnard, Pierre, 39
Books:
International Book Fair, 27
Bookstores:
Montréal, 113
Toronto, 67
Botanical Gardens (Montréal), 88, **90**, 94, 116, 117
Blvd. St-Laurent, **86**
Bourassa, Henri, 83
Bourgeau, Victor, 87, 89
Bourgeoys, Marguerite, 83, 89
Bourget, Bishop, 87
Bourich, 85
Bourse (Montréal), 80
Braque, Georges, 39
Breakdowns, car, 26
Breakneck Stairs, 121-2
Breuer, Marcel, 88
Brûlé, Étienne, 29
Buses:
Montréal, 72, 73
Québec City, 119
Toronto, 30

C

Cabaret, Toronto, 63
Cabbagetown, 39, **40**
Cabot, John, 10
Cabs:
Montréal, 72, 73
Québec City, 119
tipping, 27
Toronto, 30
Cafés, Montréal, 103
Cagnon, Clarence, 46
Calèches (horse-drawn carriages), 73, 79, 119
Calendar of events, **27-8**
Campanella, Roy, 114
Campbell House, **40-1**
Canada, **8-9**
Canada Day celebrations, 28
Canada Sports Hall of Fame, **41**, 43, 45
Canada Trust Tower, 35
Canada's Wonderland, 40, **41**, 70
Canadian Baseball Hall of Fame, 47
Canadian Broadcasting Corporation, 14
Canadian Centre for Architecture, **86-7**
Canadian International Air Show, 43

Canadian National Exhibition, 28, 43, 71
Canadian Open golf championship, 28
Canadian Opera Company, 64
Canadian Pacific Railway, 11
Canadiana Collection, **41**
Canals:
Lachine Canal, **91**, 115
St Lambert Lock, **95-6**
Candy, John, 14, 63
Cariban West Indian Festival, 28, 71
Carleton, 134
Carleton, Sir Guy, 79
Carlin, George, 63
Carmichael, Frank, 17
Cars:
accidents, 26
auto-racing, 28, 67, 114
breakdowns, 26
driver's licenses, 21
driving in Montréal, 73
driving regulations, 26
driving to Canada, 22
driving in Toronto, 30
driving in winter, 119
parking, 73, 119
renting, 21, 30, 72, 73, 119
road signs, 119
speed limits, 130
Toronto International Auto Show, 27
Cartier, Jacques, 7, 10, 79, 84, 118, 132
Casa Loma, 19, *19*, 33, **41-2**
Casse-croûte, 103
Casson, A.J., 18
Cathedrals:
Basilique Notre-Dame (Québec City), 120, 121
Cathédrale-Basilique Marie-Reine-du-Monde, 79, **87**, 89
Christ Church Cathedral, 79, **88**
Holy Trinity Anglican Cathedral, 121
see also Churches
Causapscal, 134
Cemeteries:
Notre-Dame-des-Neiges Catholic cemetery, 85
Protestant cemetery (Montréal), 85
Centaur Theatre, 112
Centre d'archives de Montréal, 75
Centre d'histoire de Montréal, 80
Centre Island, 71
Centreville, 50
Châlet de la Montagne, 85
Champlain, Samuel de, 7, 28, 29, 118, 121

Charlier, Henri, 93
Château Dufresne, **87-8**
Château Frontenac, 19-20
Château Ramezay, 18, 82-3, **88**
Chic-Choc Mountains, 131, 134
Children:
Canada's Wonderland, **41**
Centreville, 50
Children's Theatre, 118
Children's Village, 48
in hotels, 51, 97
in Montréal, **117-18**
Parc Angrignon, **93**
La Ronde Amusement Park, 86, 90, **94-5**, 117
in Toronto, **70-1**
China stores:
Montréal, 113
Chinatown (Montréal), **88**
Chinatown (Toronto), 33, 36-7, **42**
Christ Church Cathedral, 79, **88**
Churches:
Basilica of Notre-Dame (Montréal), 81
Église de Notre-Dame-de-Bonsecours, 83, **89**
Église de St-Enfant-Jésus, **89-90**
Église Notre-Dame, 19, **89**
Église Notre-Dame-des-Victoires, 122
Oratoire St-Joseph, **93**
see also Cathedrals
Cigarettes:
duty-free allowances, 22
taxes, 23
Cinemas:
Montréal, 111
Montréal International Festival of New Cinema and Video, 28
Québec International Film Festival, 28
Toronto, 64
World Film Festival, 28
Cinesphere, 48
Circus:
Cirque du Soleil, 118
La Citadelle (Québec City), 18, 120, **122**
City Hall (Montréal) *see* Hôtel de Ville
City Hall (Toronto), 36
City Hall District (Toronto), 33
Classical music:
Montréal, 111
Toronto, 64
Climate, 22-3
Clock Tower (Montréal), 96

136

Index

Clothes:
fashions, 113
Festival of Canadian Fashion, 27
what to wear, 23
CN Tower, 20, 21, 32, 33-4, **42**, 71
Coach travel, 29-30
Colborne Lodge, 45
Communications, 24-5
Constitution, 14
Country music, Toronto, 64
Couvent des Ursulines, 121
Crafts:
Québec Crafts Show, 28
Springtime Craft Show & Sale, 27
Crafts stores:
Montréal, 112
Québec City, 129-30
Toronto, 67
Credit cards, 22
Curling:
International Curling Tournament, 27
in Montréal, 114-15
Currency, 21-2
Currency exchange, 24
Customs and excise, 22
Cycling:
Americas Cycling Grand Prix, 28
in Montréal, 115
in Toronto, 68
Le Tour de l'Île de Montréal, 27-8

D

Dance:
ballet, 17, 64, 111, 112
Dance clubs:
Montréal, 108, 109-10
Toronto, 63
De Gaulle, Charles, 82
Degas, Edgar, 39
Dental emergencies:
Montréal, 74
Québec City, 119
Toronto, 31
Department stores:
Montréal, 113-14
Dickens, Charles, 84
Dinner theaters:
Montréal, 112
Toronto, 63
Disabled travelers, 27
Discos:
Montréal, 109-10
Québec City, 129
Toronto, 63
Documents required, 21
Dorval Airport, 22, 72
Dow Planetarium, **88-9**, 118
Downtown (Montréal), 78
Driver's licenses, 21

Dufresne, Oscar and Marius, 87
Dufy, Raoul, 39
Duty-free allowances, 22

E

Eaton Centre, 33, 36, **43**, 50, 65
Edward VII, King, 37, 79
Église de Notre-Dame-de-Bonsecours, 83, **89**
Église de St-Enfant-Jésus, **89-90**
Église Notre-Dame, 19, **89**
Église Notre-Dame-des-Victoires, 122
Electric current, 25
Emergency information, 26
Montréal, 74
Québec City, 119
Toronto, 31
Ernest Cormier Building, 81
Escalier Frontenac (Escalier Casse-Cou), 121-2
Eskimos see Inuit
L'Estrie, 116
Events, calendar of, **27-8**
Excursions:
Gaspé Peninsula, **130-4**
Exhibition Place (Toronto), **43**
Expo-Québec, 28
Expo world fair (1967), 78, 90, 95

F

Family Compact, 11, 44, 45
Fashion:
Festival of Canadian Fashion, 27
stores, 113
Fax services, 24
Fenian Brotherhood, 43
Ferry, Toronto Islands, 30, 44, 71
Festival of Canadian Fashion, 27
Festival d'été international de Québec, 129
Festival d'hiver de Saint-Émile, 120
Festival of Festivals, 28
Festivals, 27-8
Fête des Neiges, 93
Films see Movies
Financial District (Toronto), 33
Fire services:
Montréal, 26
Québec City, 26, 119
Toronto, 26, 31
Fireworks:
International Festival

of Fireworks, 90
International Fireworks Competition, 27, 95, 117
First Canadian Place, 35-6
Fishing:
Gaspé Peninsula, 132
Montréal, 115
Toronto, 68
Fitness centers:
Toronto, 68
FLQ, 12
Folk music:
Toronto, 64
Food and drink:
beer, 126, 129
Montréal restaurants, 102-8
Québec City restaurants, 126-8
Toronto restaurants, 56-61
wine, 22, 57, 102-3, 126
Football, Toronto, 68-9
Foreign exchange, 24
Fort York, 18, 33, **43**, 45
Fortin, Marc-Aurèle, 81, 92
Fox, Terry, 41
Francis, Sam, 39
French and Indian War, 10
French language, 16-17
Fuller, Buckminster, 90
Furriers, 114

G

Gainsborough, Thomas, 36
Galbraith, John Kenneth, 14
Gardens see Parks and gardens
George R. Gardiner Museum of Ceramic Art, 33, 37, **44**, 49
Gaspé, 132-3
Gaspé Peninsula, 7, 23, **130-4**
Geoffrion, "Boom-Boom," 115
George III, King, 121
Georgian Bay, 7
Golden Square Mile, 78
Golf:
Canadian Open golf championship, 28
Montréal, 115
Toronto, 69
Goulet, Robert, 14
Grande-Vallée, 132
La Grande Crevasse, 134
Les Grands Ballets Canadiens, 17, 111, 118
The Grange, 36, 40, **44**
Great Lakes, 18, 45, 72, 95
Greene, Lorne, 14
Gretsky, Great, 45

137

Index

Group of Seven, **17-18**, 39-40, 46, 91

H
Haida, HMCS, 48
Hang-gliding, 131
Harbor cruises, Toronto, 32
Harbourfront (Toronto), 33, **44**, 66, 71
Harris, Lawren, 17-18, 46
Hébert, Phillippe, 89
Help lines:
 Montréal, 74
 Québec City, 119
 Toronto, 31
High Park, **44-5**, 68, 70, 71
History, **7-13**
Hockey, 14, 28
 Montréal, 115
 Toronto, 69
Hockey Hall of Fame, 43, **45**
Holgate, Edwin, 18
Holidays, public, 24
Holy Trinity Anglican Cathedral, 121
Hôpital général des Soeurs Grises, 81
Horse-drawn carriages (*calèches*), 73, 79, 119
Horse-racing, 28
 Montréal, 116
 Toronto, 69
Hospitals, 31, 74
Hôtel de Ville (Montréal), 19, *20*, 82, 84
Hôtel-de-Ville (Québec City), 121
Hôtel du Parlement, 120, **122**
Hotels:
 Gaspé Peninsula, 131-4
 Montréal, **97-101**
 Québec City, **124-5**
 room tax, 51
 smoking in, 26
 tipping, 27
 Toronto, **51-6**
House of Commons, 13
Howard, John, 45
Hudson Bay, 38
Hudson's Bay Company, 113
Hull, 7
Hull, Bobby, 45
Huron, Lake, 7

I
Ice Canoe Race, 27
Île Ste-Hélène, **90**, 96, 117
Indians *see* Amerindians
Insurance:
 medical, 21
 travel, 21
International Book Fair, 27

International Children's Festival, 71
International Curling Tournament, 27
International Festival of Fireworks, 90
International Fireworks Competition, 27, 95, 117
International Jazz Festival, 110
Inuit (Eskimos), 15, 18, 46, 91, 92, 112, 126
L'Islet-sur-Mer, 130

J
Jackson, Alexander, 17
Japanese Pavilion, 90
Jardin Botanique, **90**, 94, 116, 117
Jardin des Merveilles, 93
Jazz:
 festivals, 28
 Montréal, 110-11
 Québec City, 129
 Toronto, 63-4
Jennings, Peter, 14
John, Elton, 49
Johnston, Franz, 18
Joseph, St, 93
Just for Laughs Festival, 28

K
Kamouraska, 130
Kelly, Ellsworth, 39
Kensington Market, 37, **45**
Kline, Franz, 39
Koffman, Moe, 64

L
La Peltrie, Madame de, 121
La Salle, René-Robert Cavalier de, 10
Lac aux Castors (Beaver Lake), 85, 116
Lachine Canal, **91**, 115
Lachine Rapids, 96
Lafleur, Guy, 115
LaHaie Park, 90
Lambert, Phyllis, 87
Lang, K.D., 14
Language, **16-17**
Laporte, Pierre, 12
Latin Quarter, 97, 108
Laurentian Mountains, 7, 85, 116, 120
Laurier, Sir Wilfrid, 11
Laws and regulations, 25-6
Lester B. Pearson International Airport, 22, 29
Lévesque, René, 79
Libraries:
 Bibliothèque Nationale du Québec, 75

Centre d'archives de Montréal, 75
Metropolitan Toronto Reference Library, 32, 38, **46**
Montréal Central Library, 75
Limousines:
 Montréal, 72
 Toronto, 30
Lismer, Arthur, 18
Lloyd Wright, Frank, 88
Local publications:
 Montréal, 75
 Québec City, 119
 Toronto, 32
Lost travelers cheques, 22, 26
Louis XIV, King, 121, 122

M
McCartney, Paul, 49
MacDonald, James, 17-18
Macdonald, Sir John A., 11
MacDonald, John S., 37
McEwen, Jean, 92
McGill University, 78, 79, 80, 92, 111
Mackenzie, William Lyon, 45
Mackenzie House, **45**
McLaughlin Planetarium, 33, 38, **45-6**, 49, 71
McMichael Canadian Collection, 39, **46**
Maillol, Aristide, 92
"The Main," 86
Maison Calvet, 18, **83**
Maison Chevalier, **123**
Maison des Coopérants, *20*, 21, 79
Maison Papineau, 83
Maisonneuve, Paul de Chomedey, Sieur de, 81, 84, 89
Marathon, Montréal, 28, 116
Marché Bonsecours, 84
Marine Museum of Upper Canada, 33, 43, **45**
Markets:
 Kensington Market, 37, 45
Martin, Abraham, 123
Martin Goodman Trail, 68
Massey, Raymond, 14
Matane, 131
Matapédia, 134
Matisse, Henri, 39
Medical emergencies:
 Montréal, 74
 Québec City, 119
 Toronto, 31
Medical insurance, 21
Medicines, 24
Meech Lake Accord, 12
Mesplet, Fleury, 92

138

Index

Metro (Montréal), 73
  see also Subways
Metro Toronto Zoo, 33, 39, **46-7**, 70
Metropolitan Toronto Convention and Visitors Association, 30, 44
Metropolitan Toronto Reference Library, 32, 38, **46**
Micmac Indians, 134
Mies van der Rohe, Ludwig, 21, 35
Mirabel Airport, 22, 72
Mirvish, Ed, 66
Molson Export Challenge, 28
Molson Grand Prix, 28
Molson Indy auto race, 28, 43, 67
Money, 21-2
Mont-Albert, 133
Mont-Joli, 134
Mont-Royal, 72, 73, 75, 78, 79, **84-5**, 97, 115, 116
Mont-St-Pierre, 131-2
Montcalm, Marquis de, 10, 121, 123
Montgomery's Tavern, **47**
Montréal, 15, **71-118**, 76-7
  addresses and telephone numbers, 73-5
  airports, 22
  architecture, 18-21
  arts, 17
  bed and breakfast, **101-2**
  cafés and snack bars, 103
  for children, **117-18**
  climate, 22-3
  emergency information, 26, 74
  history, 7-10
  hotels, **97-101**
  Metro, 73
  nightlife, **108-12**
  orientation, 75-8
  orientation map, 76-7
  population, 16
  restaurants, 102-8
  shops, 25, **112-14**
  sights and places of interest, **85-96**
  sports, **114-17**
  travel in, 22, 72-3
  traveling to, 22
  walks, **78-85**
Montréal Central Library, 75
Montréal International Festival of New Cinema and Video, 28
Montréal International Jazz Festival, 28
Montréal International Music Festival, 28
Montréal Marathon, 28, 116
Montréal Symphony, 17, 108
Montréal Winter Festival, 27
Moore, Henry, 36, 39, 40, 92
Moranis, Rick, 63
Motor-racing see Auto-racing
Movies and movie theaters, 17
  Montréal, 111
  Montréal International Festival of New Cinema and Video, 28
  Québec International Film Festival, 28
  Toronto, 64
  World Film Festival, 28
Mura, Francesco de, 39
Murray, Anne, 14, 63
Museums:
  Banque de Montréal, 81
  Canadian Centre for Architecture, **86-7**
  Centre d'histoire de Montréal, 80
  David M. Stewart Museum, **92**
  Marine Museum of Upper Canada, 33, 43, **45**
  Musée d'art contemporain, **91**, 94
  Musée de la Chasse et de la Nature, 85
  Musée de la Civilisation, 120, **123**
  Musée des Arts Décoratifs, **87-8**
  Musée des Beaux-Arts, 80, **91-2**
  Musée du Fort, 120, 121
  Musée du Québec, 123
  Musée McCord, 80, **92**
  Musée Marc-Aurèle Fortin, 81, **92**
  Museum of the History of Medicine, **47**
  Redpath Sugar Museum, 44
  Royal Ontario Museum, 33, 37, 38, 41, **48-9**
  Ursuline museum, 121
Music, 17
  classical, 64, 111
  jazz, 63-4, 110-11, 129
  Montréal International Music Festival, 28
  opera, 64, 111
  rock/pop/country/folk, 64, 111

N

National Ballet of Canada, 17, 64
National Film Board, 17
National Home Show, 27
Ned Hanlan, 45
Nelligan, Kate, 14
Nelson's column, 84
New Year's Eve celebration, 28
Newcombe, Don, 114
Niagara Falls, 22, 34, 42
Nielson, Leslie, 14
Nightclubs:
  Montréal, 110
  Québec City, 129
Nightlife:
  Montréal, **108-12**
  Québec City, **129**
  Toronto, **61-4**
Nolan, Kenneth, 39
North York Winter Carnival, 27
Notre-Dame-des-Neiges Catholic cemetery, 85

O

Observatory, Église de Notre-Dame-de-Bonsecours, 89
O'Donnell, James, 89
O'Keefe Centre, 17, 64
Old City Hall (Toronto), 36
Old Fort (Montréal), **92**
Olmsted, Frederick Law, 84
Olympic Park see Parc Olympique
Olympic Stadium, 49, 118
Olympic Village, 94
On-the-spot information, **24-7**
Ontario:
  climate, 22-3
  history, 7-13
  laws and regulations, 25-6
  population, 15
Ontario, Lake, 22, 29, 45, 68, 70
Ontario Legislative Building, 33, 37
Ontario Place, 33, **47-8**, 71
Ontario Science Centre, 33, **48**, 71
Opening hours:
  banks, 24
  Montréal, 112
  shops, 25
  Toronto, 65
Opera:
  Montréal, 111
  Toronto, 64
Oratoire St-Joseph, 85, **93**
Orchestre Metropolitain du Grand Montréal, 111

139

Index

Orchestre Symphonique de Montréal, 111
Orientation maps:
  Toronto, *34-5*
  Montréal, *76-7*, *82-3*
Osgoode Hall, 18, 36
Ottawa, 7
Ottawa River, 130
Outdoors Show (Montréal), 27

P

Palais de Justice (Montréal), 81
Parc Olympique (Olympic Park), 88, 90, **93-4**, 116-17
Paris, Treaty of (1763), 118
Parkin, John C., 39
Parking:
  at hotels, 97
  in Montréal, 73
  in Québec City, 119
Parks:
  Canada's Wonderland, **41**
  Centreville, 50
  High Park, **44-5**, 68, 70, 71
  Île Ste-Hélène, **90**
  Jardin Botanique, **90**, 94, 116, 117
  LaHaie Park, 90
  Metro Toronto Zoo, **46-7**
  Parc Angrignon, **93**, 115, 116, 117
  Parc de l'Artillerie, **123**
  Parc des Champs-de-Bataille, 120, **123**
  Parc de la Gaspésie, 131
  Parc des Gouverneurs, 121
  Parc Jeanne-Mance, 117
  Parc LaFontaine, **93**, 116, 117
  Parc Maisonneuve, 116
  Parc Mont-Royal, 78, **84-5**, 116, 118
  Parc National Forillon, 132
  Parc René-Lévesque, 116
  Queen's Park, 37-8, **48**
  Spadina House, **50**
Parliament, 13
Parti Québécois, 12, 79
Passports, 21
Pavarotti, Luciano, 89
Pearson, Lester, 12
Pei, I.M., 21
Pellatt, Sir Henry, 41-2
Percé, 130, 132, **133-4**
Percé Rock, 133

Pharmacies:
  Montréal, 74
  Québec City, 119
  Toronto, 31
Phillips, Nathan, 36
Piano bars:
  Montréal, 109
Picasso, Pablo, 39, 92
Place des Arts, 17, **94**, 96, 111
Planetariums:
  Dow Planetarium, **88-9**, 118
  McLaughlin Planetarium, 33, 38, **45-6**, 49, 71
Planning:
  before you go, **21-4**
  calendar of events, 27-8
  orientation maps, *8-9*, *34-5*, *76-7*
  walks in Montréal, *78-85*, *82-3*
  walks in Toronto, *33-9*
  when to go, 22-3
Plateau Mont-Royal, 108
Player's International Tennis Championships, 28
Pointe-à-la-Croix, 134
Poison centers, hospitals with, 74
Police:
  Montréal, 26
  Québec City, 26, 119
  Toronto, 26, 31
Politics, **13-15**
Pollack Hall, 111
Poons, Larry, 39
Pop music:
  Montréal, 111
  Toronto, 64
Population, **15-16**
Port de Québec, **123**
Porte St-Louis, 121
Post offices:
  Montréal, 74
  Toronto, 31
Postal services, 24, 25
Poudrière de l'Esplanade, 121
Protestant cemetery (Montréal), 85
Public holidays, 24
Public rest rooms, 25
Public transportation:
  Montréal, 73
  Toronto, 30
Publications, local:
  Montréal, 75
  Québec City, 119
  Toronto, 32
Pubs, Toronto, 62

Q

Quartier Petit-Champlain, 120, 122, 129

Québec:
  architecture, 18
  climate, 22-3
  emergency information, 26, 119
  history, 7-13
  language, 16
  laws and regulations, 25-6
  nationalism, 12, 15
  population, 15-16
Québec City, 7, **118-130**
  addresses and telephone numbers, 119
  architecture, 18-20
  bed and breakfast, **125-6**
  climate, 22-3
  excursions, 130-4
  hotels, **124-5**
  nightlife, **129**
  orientation, 120
  restaurants, **126-8**
  shops, **129-30**
  traveling to, 22, 118-19
Québec City International Theatre Fortnight, 27
Québec City Winter Carnival, 27
Québec Crafts Show, 28
Québec International Film Festival, 28
Québec International Summer Festival, 28
Queen's Park, **48**
Queen's Quay Terminal, 44

R

Racing:
  auto-racing, 28, 67, 114
  horse-racing, 28, 69, 116
Rafting:
  Montréal, 116
Railroads, 22
  Montréal to Québec City, 118
Ramezey, Claude de, 88
Redoute Dauphine, 123
Redpath Sugar Museum, 44
Rembrandt, 36
Renoir, Pierre Auguste, 39
Renting:
  cars, 21, 30, 72, 73, 119
Rest rooms, public, 25
Restaurants:
  Gaspé Peninsula, 131-4
  Montréal, **102-8**
  Québec City, **126-8**
  smoking in, 26
  tipping, 26-7, 57, 103
  Toronto, **56-61**
Restigouche, 134

140

Index

Richard, Maurice "The Rocket," 115
Richler, Mordecai, 86
Rimouski, 130-1
Riopelle, Jean-Paul, 92
River trips:
  Montréal, 75
Rivière-au-Renard, 132
Rivière-du-Loup, 130
Robinson, Jackie, 114
Rock music:
  Montréal, 111
  Toronto, 64
Rodin, Auguste, 39, 92
Rolling Stones, 49
La Ronde Amusement Park, 86, 90, **94-5**, 117
Royal Agricultural Winter Fair, 28, 43
Royal Bank Plaza building, 35
Royal Ontario Museum, 33, 37, 38, 41, **48-9**, 62
Rue Crescent District, 78
Rue Prince Arthur, **95**
Rue St-Denis, **95**
Running:
  Montréal, 116
  Toronto, 69

S

Safety, 25
Sailboarding:
  Toronto, 69
Sailing:
  Toronto, 69
Ste-Anne-des-Monts, 131
St-Denis Latin Quarter, 97, 108
Ste-Flavie, 131
Sainte-Foy, 129
Ste-Foy Airport, 118
Ste-Hélène, 78
St-Jean-Port-Joli, 130
St Lambert Lock, **95-6**
St Lawrence River, 10, 75, 78, 80, 90, 91, 116, 118, 120, 130, 131
St Lawrence Seaway, 91, 95-6, 115
St Lawrence Valley, 18
St-Yvon, 132
Sales taxes, 65, 112
Salle Wilfrid-Pelletier, 94, 111
Santa Claus Parade, 28
Scaasi, Arnold, 14
Science Centre, Ontario, 33, **48**, 71
Scottish World Festival Tattoo, 43
Sculpture, Inuit, 18, 46, 112
Seminaire (Québec City), 120
Senate, 13
Shatner, William, 14

Shops:
  antiques, 66-7, 112-13, 130
  arts and crafts, 67, 112, 129-30
  bookstores, 67, 113
  china and crystal, 113
  department stores, 113-14
  fashions, 113
  furriers, 114
  Montréal, **112-14**
  opening hours, 25, 65, 112
  Québec City, **129-30**
  Toronto, **65-7**
Short, Martin, 63
Sigmund Samuel Building, 37, **41**
Simcoe, John Graves, 11, 29
Skating:
  Montréal, 116
  Toronto, 69
Skiing:
  Montréal, 116
  Toronto, 69-70
SkyDome, 20, 21, 33, **49-50**, 57, 67-8
SkyWalk, 33
Smoking regulations, 25-6
Snack bars:
  Montréal, 103
Snider, Duke, 114
Snowshoeing:
  Montréal, 116
Soccer:
  Montréal, 116
  Toronto, 70
Spadina House, 42, 45, **50**
Speed limits, 26, 130
Sports:
  Montréal, **114-17**
  Toronto, **67-70**
Springtime Craft Show & Sale, 27
David M. Stewart Museum, **92**
Stock Exchanges:
  Montréal, 80
  Toronto, 36, **50**
Stratford Shakespeare Festival Season, 27
Subways:
  Montréal, 73
  Toronto, 30
Summer Zoo, **93**, 117
Sun Life Building, 20, 79
Superior, Lake, 95
Swimming:
  Montréal, 116-17
  Toronto, 70

T

Taillibert, Roger, 94
Taxes:
  alcohol and cigarettes, 23-4

  hotel room tax, 51
  sales tax, 65, 112
Taxis:
  Montréal, 72, 73
  Québec City, 119
  tipping, 27
  Toronto, 30
Telephone services, 24-5
  Montréal, 74
  Toronto, 31
Telex services, 24
Tennis:
  Montréal, 117
  Player's International Tennis Championships, 28
  Toronto, 70
Terrasse Dufferin, 120
Theaters:
  for children, 71, 118
  Children's Theatre, 118
  Montréal, 112
  Place des Arts, 94
  Québec City International Theatre Fortnight, 27
  Stratford Shakespeare Festival Season, 27
  Theatre Maisonneuve, 111
  Theatre Port-Royal, 111
  Toronto, 62
Thicke, Alan, 14
Thomson, Tom, 17-18, 46
Tipping, 26-7
  hotels, 27
  restaurants, 26-7, 57, 103
  taxis, 27
Tobacco:
  duty-free allowances, 22
Toronto, 14, 15, **28-71**, 34-5
  addresses and telephone numbers, 30-1
  airports, 22
  architecture, 18-21
  arts, 17
  bed and breakfast, 55-6
  for children, **70-1**
  climate, 22-3
  emergency information, 26, 31
  history, 7-10, 11, 29
  hotels, **51-6**
  nightlife, **61-4**
  orientation, 32-3
  orientation map, 34-5
  restaurants, **56-61**
  shops, 25, **65-7**
  sights and places of interest, **39-51**
  sports, **67-70**
  subway, 30
  travel in, 29-30

141

Index

traveling to, 22
walks, **33-9**
Toronto Dance Theatre, 17, 64
Toronto-Dominion Centre, 35
Toronto International Auto Show, 27
Toronto International Boat Show, 27
Toronto International Caravan, 28
Toronto Island Airport, 30, 34
Toronto Islands, 44, **50**, 68, 70, 71
Toronto Outdoor Art Exhibition, 28
Toronto Philharmonic, 17
Toronto Stock Exchange, 36, **50**
Toronto Symphony Orchestra, 17, 62, 64
Toronto Transit Commission, 30
Toronto University, 33, 37, 41, 52
Le Tour de l'Île de Montréal, 27-8
Tour operators:
  Montréal, 74-5
  Québec City, 119
  Toronto, 31-2
Tourist information:
  calendar of events, **27-8**
  local publications, 32, 75, 119
  Montréal, 73-4
  on-the-spot, 24-7
  Québec City, 119
  Toronto, 30-1
Trains:
  to Canada, 22
  to Québec City, 118

Travel:
  air, 22, 72, 118
  buses, 30, 73, 119
  cabs, 30, 72, 73, 119
  cars, 22, 30, 73
  coaches, 29-30
  horse-drawn carriages (*calèches*), 73, 79, 119
  insurance, 21
  railroads, 22, 118
  subways, 30, 73
  taxis, 30, 72, 73, 119
Travelers cheques, 21-2
  lost, 22, 26
Trudeau, Pierre, 12, 13

U

Underground City (Montréal), 78, **96**
Underground Toronto, 33, 36, **50-1**
UNESCO, 118
Union Station (Toronto), 33, 34-5
United States of America, 13-15
Université du Québec, 78, 95
Université Laval, 129
University of Toronto, 33, 37, 41, 52
Ursuline museum, 121

V

Van Gogh, Vincent, 36
Vancouver, 14
Vanier Cup, 28
Vauquelin, Jean, 82, 84
Venne, Alphonse, 93
VIA Rail, 22, 118
Viau, Dalbe, 93
Victoria, Queen, 37, 80
Vieux Montréal, **75-8**, 80-4, **82-3**, 108
Vieux-Port (Montréal), **96**
Vieux Port (Québec City), 120, 123
Vieux Québec, **120-2**
Vieux Séminaire des Sulpiciens, 81
Visas, 21

W

Walks:
  in Montréal, **78-85**
  in Toronto, **33-9**
  in Québec City, **120-122**
Weather, 22-3
Wellington, Duke of, 92, 122
Williams, Robin, 63
Wills, Frank, 88
Windsor, 22
Windsurfing:
  Toronto, 69
Wine, 57, 102-3, 126
  duty-free allowances, 22
Winter Carnival, 117
Winter Zoo, **93**, 117
Wolfe, General James, 10, 121, 123
World Film Festival, 28
Wright, Frank Lloyd, 88

Y

York, Duke of, 29
Yorkville, 33, 38, **51**, 62, 66
d'Youville, Mother Marie-Marguerite, 81
d'Youville Stables, 81

Z

Zoos:
  Centre Island, 71
  Centreville, 50
  High Park, 71
  Metro Toronto Zoo, 39, **46-7**, 70
  Summer Zoo, **93**, 117
  Winter Zoo, **93**, 117

STREET NAMES

List of street names

All streets mentioned in the book that fall within the area covered by our maps are listed here. Each street name is followed by a map reference to one or more of the maps that follow this list. Map numbers are printed in **bold** type.

It was not possible to label every street drawn on the maps, although of course all major streets and most smaller ones are named. Those streets that are not named on the maps are still given map references in this list, because this serves as an approximate location that will nearly always be sufficient for you to find your way.

Toronto

A
Aberdeen St., **5**I2
Alexander St., **5**H2
Avenue Rd., **4**G1-2
Avondale Rd., **5**H1

B
Baldwin St., **4**F3-G3
Bathurst St., **3**E1-5
Bay St., **4**G1-**5**H5
Benvenuto Pl., **4**G1
Beverly St., **4**F3
Bleeker St., **5**I2
Bloor St., **4**E1-**5**I1
Bond St., **5**H3-4
Brunswick St., **4**F2

C
Carlton St., **5**H3-I3
Charles St., **4**G1-**5**H1
College St., **4**E2-**5**H2
Cumberland St., **4**G1

D
Davenport Rd., **4**G1
Dundas St., **4**E3-**5**J3

E
Eastern Ave., **5**I4-J4
Edward St., **4**G3
Elizabeth St., **4**G3
Elm St., **4**E1-**5**H3
Esplanade, The, **5**H4-5
Euclid Ave., **3**E1-4
Exhibition Park, **2**C5-D5

F
First Canadian Pl., **4**G4
Fleet St., **3**D5-E5
Front St., **4**E5-**5**I4

G
Garrison Rd., **3**D5-E5
Gerrard St., **4**G3-**5**I3
Gloucester St., **5**H2
Grosvenor St., **4**G2-**5**H2

H
Harbord St., **3**D2-**4**F2
Harbour Sq., **4**G5-**5**H5

J
Jarvis St., **5**H1-5
John St., **4**G4

K
King St., **2**A4-**5**J4

L
Lakeshore Blvd., **2**A4-**5**I5
Lennox St., **3**E1-F1
Lombard St., **5**H4
Lowther Ave., **4**G1

M
MacPherson Ave., **4**F1
Markham St., **3**E1-3

N
Nathan Phillips Square, **4**G4

O
Ontario Pl., **5**I3

P
Parliament St., **5**I1-5
Pearl St., **4**G4
Pears Ave., **4**G1
Peter St., **4**F4
Prince Arthur Ave., **4**G1

Q
Queen St., **2**A4-**3**F4, **4**E4-**5**J4
Queen's Park Crescent, **4**G2
Queen's Quay, **4**F5-**5**I5

R
Richmond St., **4**F4-**5**I4

S
Scollard St., **4**G1
Spadina Ave., **4**F1-5
St. Thomas St., **5**G1
Strachan Ave., **3**D4-5
Sullivan St., **4**F3

U
University Ave., **4**G2-5

W
Wellesley St., **4**G2-**5**I2

Wellington St., **3**D4-F4
Winchester St., **5**I2-J2

Y
Yonge St., **5**H1-5
York St., **4**G4
Yorkville Ave., **4**G1

Montréal

A
Armes, Pl. d', **9**D5
Arts, Place des, **8**E3
Atwater, Rue, **10**H2-**11**J5
Aylmer, Rue, **8**E3-**9**E4

B
Baile, Rue, **10**G3
Berri, Rue, **8**B1-**9**C5
Bishop, Rue, **10**G3-4
Bonaventure, Pl., **11**E-F4
Bonsecours, Rue, **9**C5

C
Calixa-Lavallée, Av., **8**A2-3
Canada, Pl. du, **11**F4
Cathédrale, Rue de la, **11**F4
Clark, Rue, **9**D4
Commune, Rue de la, **9**C5-E6
Côte-des-Neiges, Chemin de la, **10**G1-2
Crescent, Rue, **10**F3-**11**G4

D
Dorchester Sq., **11**F4
Duluth, Rue, **8**B-D2

E
Esplanade, Av. de l', **8**C2

G
Gosford, Rue, **9**D5
Greene, Av., **10**H1-**11**I4
Guy, Rue, **10**G3-**11**G5

J
Jacques-Cartier, Pl., **9**D5

Street names

L
Laval, Rue, **8**C3
Lemoyne, Rue, **9**E5

M
Mackay, Rue, **10**G3
Maisonneuve, Blvd. de, **9**A4-**10**J2
Mansfield, Rue, **11**F4
Montagne, Rue de la, **10**F3-**11**G5

N
Notre-Dame, Rue, **9**A5-**10**J3

O
Ontario, Rue, **9**A4-D4

P
Parc, Av. du, **8**D2-3
Peel, Rue, **10**E2-**11**E6
Phillips, Carré **9**E4
Pins, Av. des, **8**C3-D2
Place d'Armes, Côte de la, **9**D4
Président-Kennedy, Rue, **8**D-E3
Prince-Arthur, Rue, **8**C3

R
Rachel, Rue, **8**B2-D1
Remembrance, Chemin de la, **10**F-G1
René Lévesque, Blvd., **9**A5-**10**J2
Roy, Rue, **8**C3

S
Sherbrooke, Rue, **8**A3-**10**J2
St-Alexis, Rue, **9**E5
St-Denis, Rue, **8**B1-**9**C5
St-Dominique, Rue, **9**E5
St-Francois-Xavier, Rue, **9**E5
St-Hubert, Rue, **8**B1-**9**C5
St-Jacques, Rue, **10**J3-**11**E5
St-Laurent, Blvd., **8**C1-**9**D5
St-Louis, Carré, **8**C3
St-Paul, Rue, **9**D5
St-Pierre, Rue, **9**E6
St-Sulpice, Chemin, **10**H2
Stanley, Rue, **11**F4
Ste-Catherine, Côte, **10**E4-I2
Ste-Catherine, Rue, **8**F3-**9**A6

T
Tupper, Rue, **10**H3

U
Union, Av., **8**E3
University, Rue, **8**E2-**9**F5

V
Victoria, Rue, **8**E3
Victoria Sq., **9**E4
Ville-Marie, Pl., **9**E4-5

Y
Youville, Pl. d', **9**E6

Québec City

A
Armes, Pl. d', **15**C5
Artigny, Rue d', **15**D4
Auteuil, Rue d', **15**C4

B
Berthelot, Rue, **14**D2-E3
Buade, Rue, **15**C4-5

C
Carrières, Rue des, **15**B5
Champlain, Blvd., **14**F3-**15**C5
Chevrotière, Rue de la, **14**D3
Citadelle, Côte de la, **15**D4

D
Dalhousie, Rue, **15**B-C5
Donnacona, Rue, **15**C4
Dufferin, Av., **14**C3
Dufferin, Terrasse, **15**C5

F
Fabrique, Rue de la, **15**B4

G
Grande Allée, **14**F1-D3

J
Jardins, Rue des, **15**B-C4

M
Marché-Champlain, Rue du, **15**C5
Marché-Finlay, Rue du, **15**C5
Montcalm, Pl., **14**D3

P
Petit-Champlain, Rue du, **15**C5

Q
Québec, Pl., **14**D3

R
Remparts, Rue des, **15**B4
Royale, Pl., **15**C5

S
Sault-au-Matelot, Rue, **15**B5
St-André, Rue, **15**B4-5
St-Cyrille, Blvd., **14**C3-E1
St-Jean, Rue, **14**B1-C3
St-Paul, Rue, **14**B3-**15**B5
St-Pierre, Rue, **15**B-C5
Ste-Anne, Rue, **15**C4
Ste-Geneviève, Av., **15**C5-D4
Ste-Ursule, Rue, **15**C4

T
Terrasse Dufferin, Pl., **15**C5

TORONTO, MONTRÉAL & QUÉBEC CITY

2-5	TORONTO
6-7	TORONTO ENVIRONS
8-11	MONTRÉAL
12-13	MONTRÉAL ENVIRONS
14-15	QUÉBEC CITY
16	GASPÉ PENINSULA

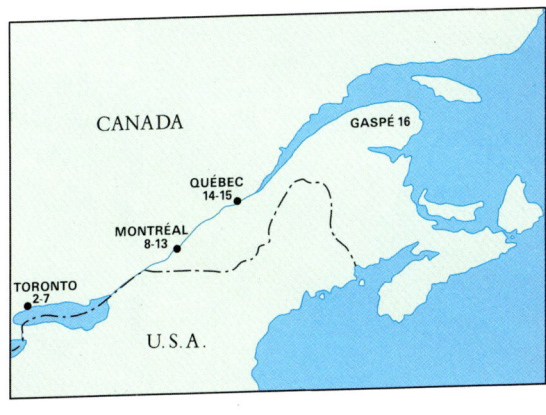

LEGEND

City Maps

- Major Place of Interest
- Other Important Building
- Built-up Area
- Park
- Cemetery
- Named Church, Church
- Synagogue
- Hospital
- Parking Lot
- Information Office
- Post Office
- Police Station
- Subway, Métro
- Adjoining Page No.

Environs and Area Maps

- Place of Interest
- Built-up Area
- National Park / Woods
- Other Land
- Highway (with access point)
- Provincial Highway
- Other Road
- Ferry
- Railroad
- Airport
- Airfield
- International Boundary
- Provincial Boundary
- National Park Boundary

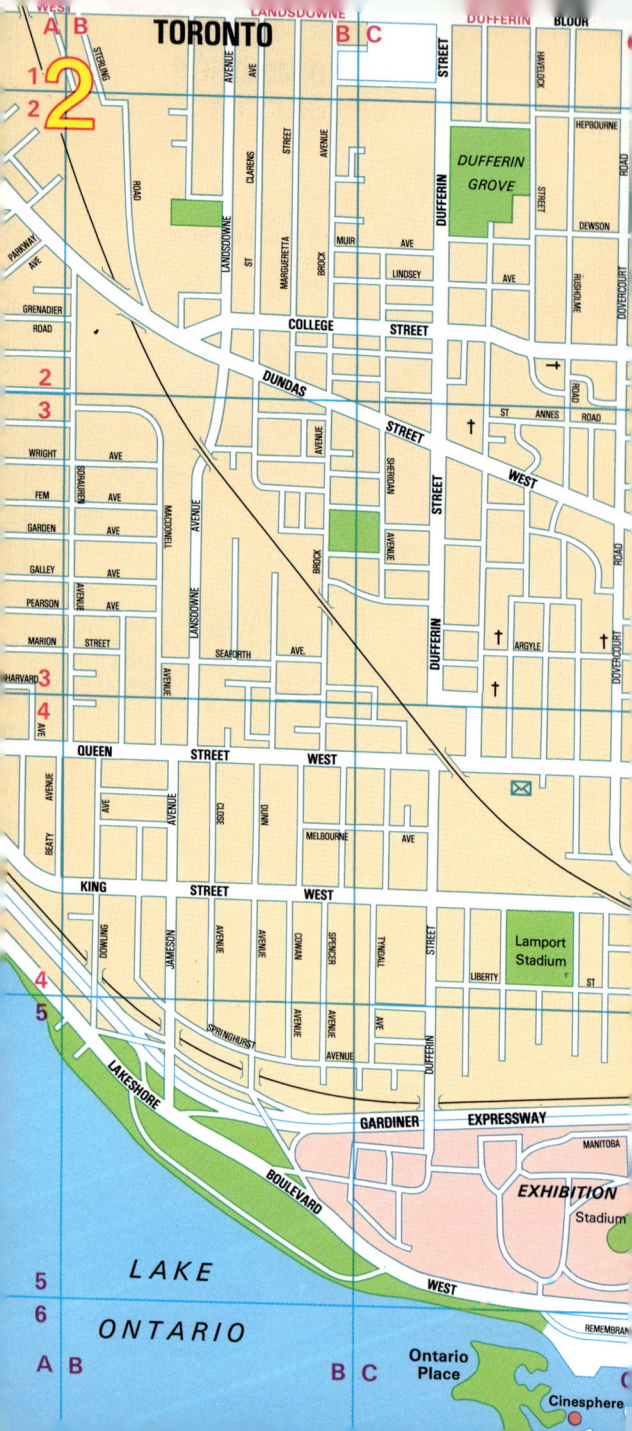

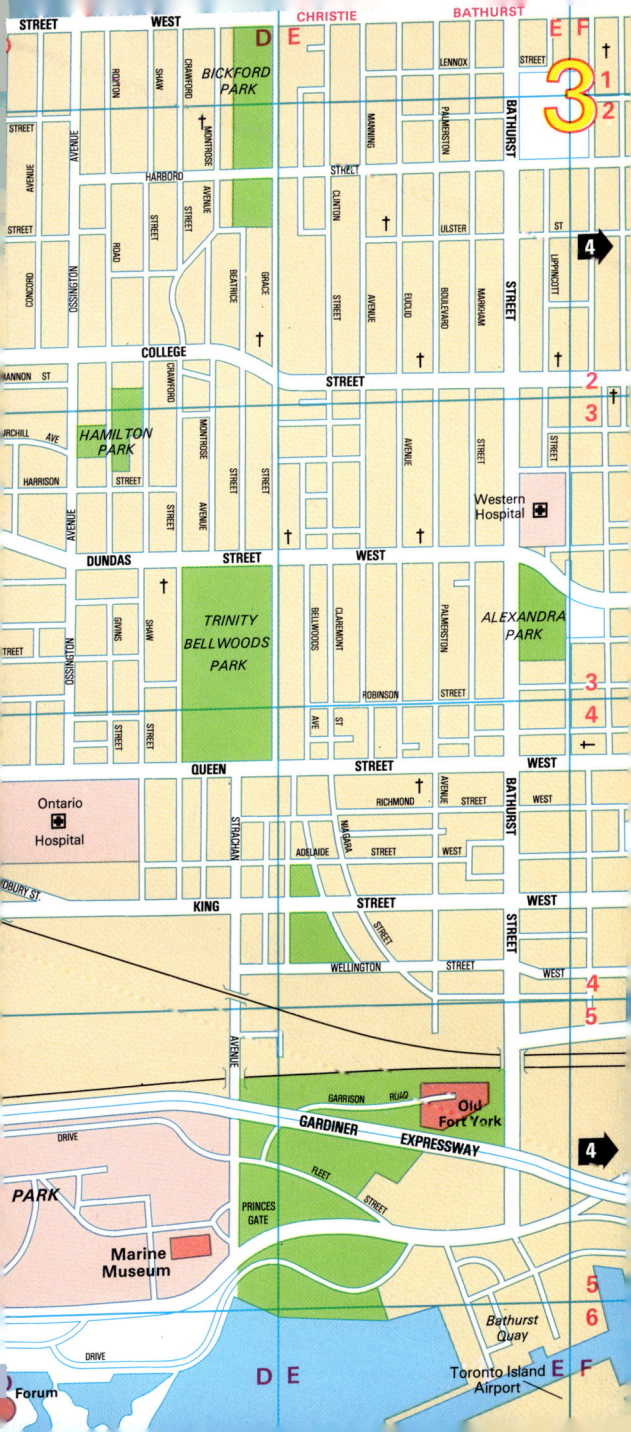

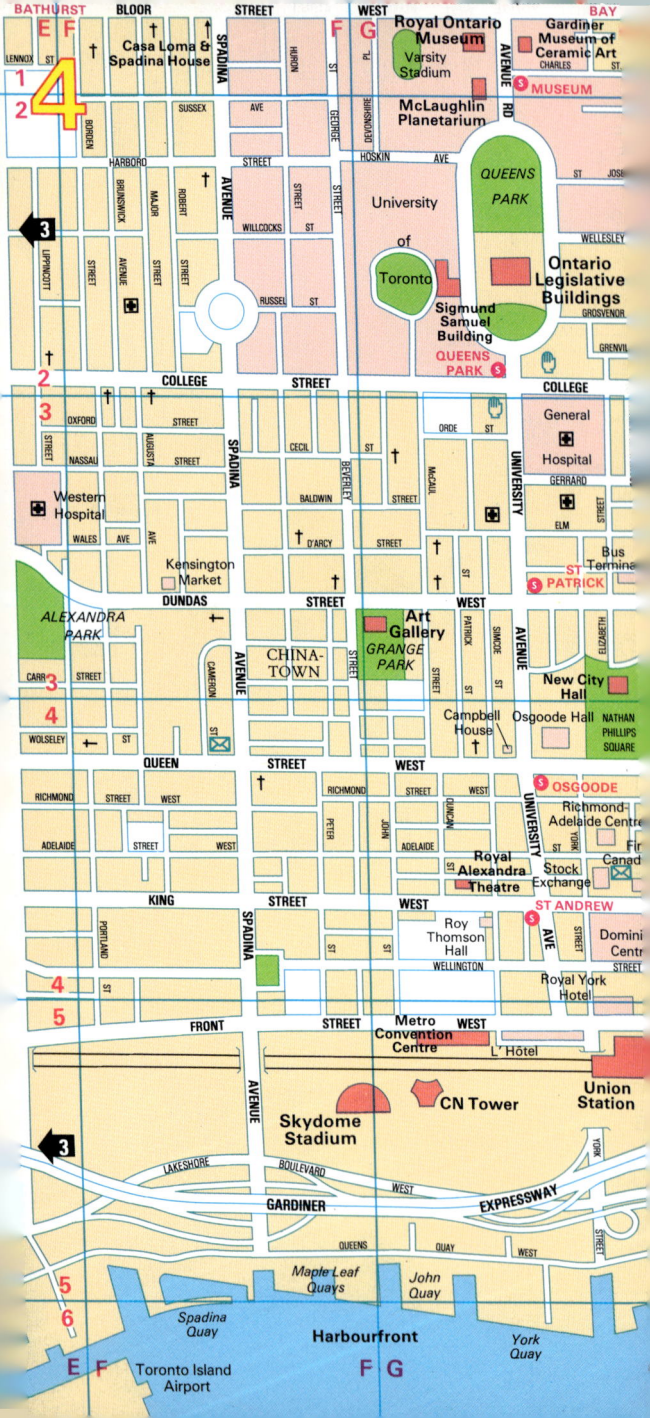

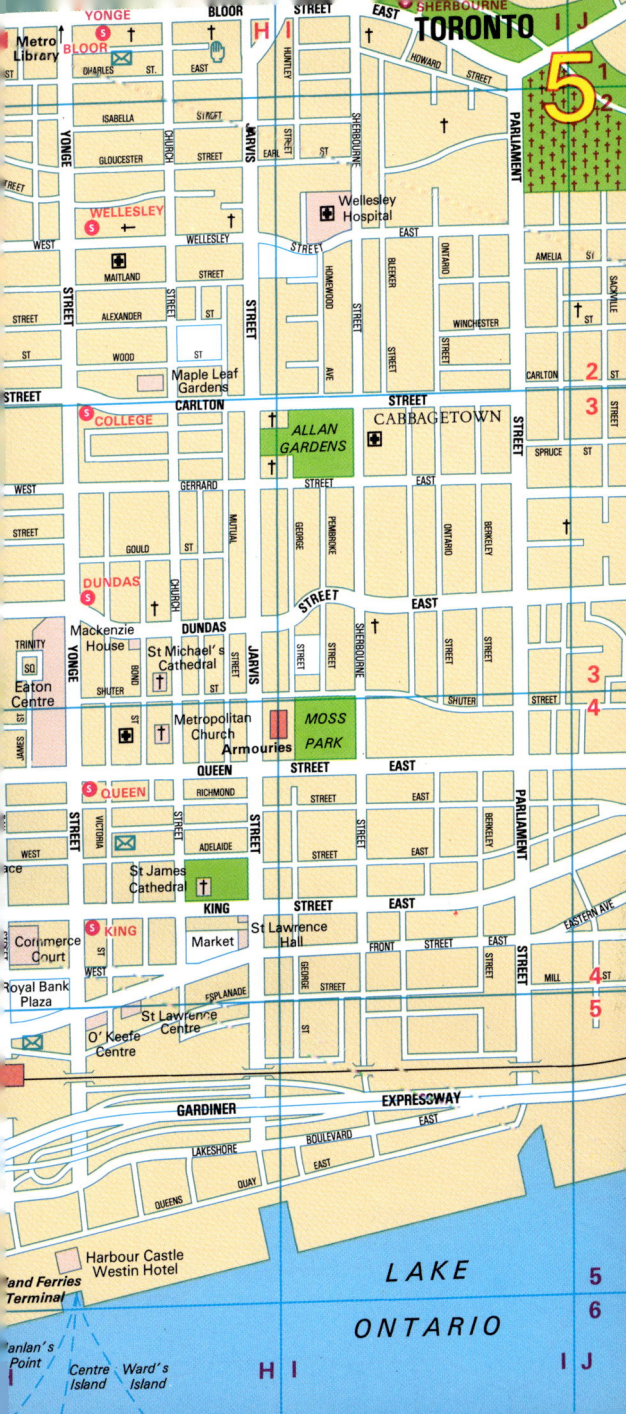

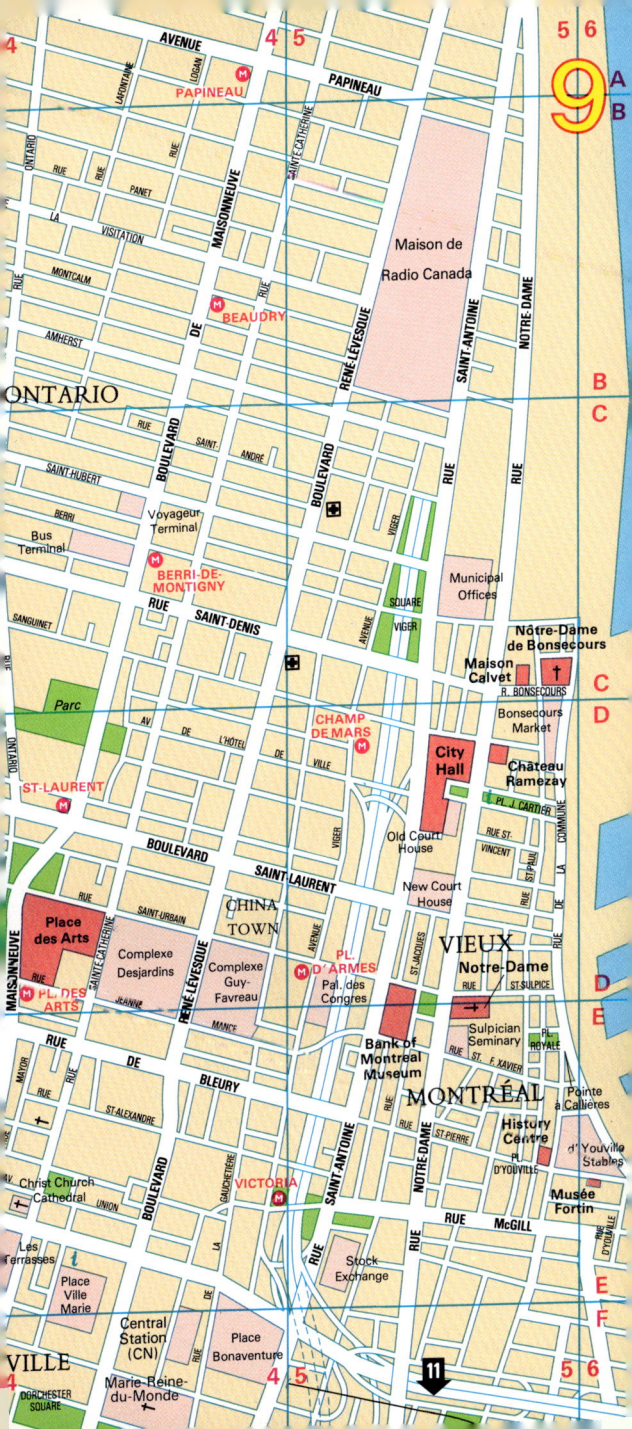

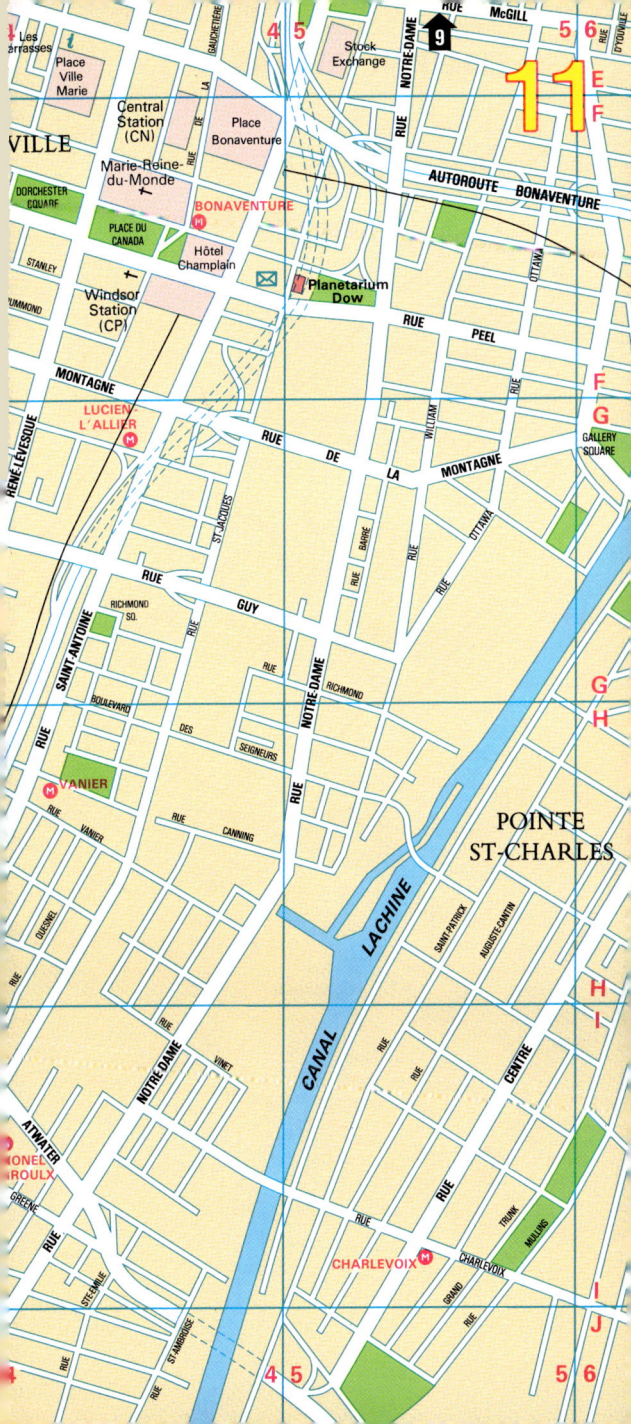